Karen L. Bloomquist,
Craig L. Nessan, Hans G. Ulrich (Eds.)

Radicalizing Reformation

Die Reformation radikalisieren
Radicalizing Reformation

herausgegeben von/edited by

Ulrich Duchrow
(Heidelberg)

Daniel Beros
(Buenos Aires)

Martin Hoffmann
(Nürnberg)

Hans G. Ulrich
(Erlangen)

Band/Volume 6

LIT

Radicalizing Reformation

Perspectives from North America

edited by

Karen L. Bloomquist, Craig L. Nessan
and Hans G. Ulrich

LIT

Bibliographic information published by the Deutsche Nationalbibliothek
The Deutsche Nationalbibliothek lists this publication in the Deutsche Nationalbibliografie; detailed bibliographic data are available on the Internet at http://dnb.d-nb.de.

ISBN 978-3-643-90772-1

A catalogue record for this book is available from the British Library

Klosbachstr. 107
CH-8032 Zürich
Tel. +41 (0) 44-251 75 05 Fax +41 (0) 44-251 75 06
E-Mail: zuerich@lit-verlag.ch http://www.lit-verlag.ch
Distribution:
In the UK: Global Book Marketing, e-mail: mo@centralbooks.com
In North America: International Specialized Book Services, e-mail: orders@isbs.com
In Germany: LIT Verlag Fresnostr. 2, D-48159 Münster
Tel. +49 (0) 2 51-620 32 22, Fax +49 (0) 2 51-922 60 99, e-mail: vertrieb@lit-verlag.de

In Austria: Medienlogistik Pichler-ÖBZ, e-mail: mlo@medien-logistik.at
e-books are available at www.litwebshop.de

CONTENT

Introduction to the Overall Series "Radicalizing Reformation"

How shall we deal with the quincentenary of the Reformation in 2017? There has been much discussion about the character of the "celebrations" in 1817 and 1917. People criticize that in each of these cases the Reformation was manipulated in service of powerful contemporary interests (e.g. Romantic nationalism or German imperialism). However, there is no other way than to start with the burning issues of one's own time. The key challenge is to reflect upon the issues and put our own position clearly on the table.

With this understanding an international group of theologians has come together, asking the question: From which perspective does it make sense to look at the Reformation today? We have chosen a double perspective as the title of our project reveals: "Radicalizing Reformation – Provoked by the Bible and Today's Crises". This means we start from the multiple crises of life today and look at them together with the Reformation, including its impact on history, from the perspective of socio-historical biblical research, i. e. from the material perspective of liberation for life in just relationships.

What does this mean in detail? Looking at the situation in the different regions of the world we clearly see that the life of human beings and the Earth is threatened if the dominant civilization continues as it is. From this follows the

First necessary dimension of today's perspective on the Reformation: What does the Reformation and its historical impact mean in view of the global threat to humanity and the Earth – both positively and negatively? If the cause of this threat has to do with the dominant civilization, what does this mean?

The term "civilization" not only refers to the system of political economy and science, technology and the arts, but also how people live, think and behave. This indicates the all-embracing character of the problem. At the same time we have a terminological dilemma here. The word "civilization" has had bad connotations for oppressed peoples since Hellenism and the Roman

Empire, even more so in the last 500 years of European and later US colonialism, because the term itself has an imperial character. Yet it is difficult to find another term. Probably the only fitting term is "culture" although it has a predominantly positive meaning. Yet it has the capacity of expressing both positive and negative connotations, i.e., it can mean both the dominant culture as the source of the danger, and also relatively independent cultures or counter-cultures. From this follows the

Second necessary dimension: the Reformation must be considered not only in terms of its ecclesial meaning but in its relation to culture as a whole.

In terms of content and character, Europe and North America (the "West") have been the hegemonic powers shaping the dominant culture. However, it has reached the elites in all parts of the earth so there is no way to limit it geographically. This is why we speak of the "global North". The dominant culture is what we call "modernity". With this term we have a direct connection to the age of the Reformation, because it is that period in which modernity began. We live at the end of modernity because it is turning out to be death-bound, indeed, suicidal for humanity and the earth. From this follows the

Third necessary dimension: How does the Reformation relate to modernity at its beginning – positively and negatively? What does this say to us and our churches in the tradition of the Reformation as we experience the end of modernity because it is endangering life on earth?

How can we characterize western modernity? There are two fundamental features: first, the dominant role of money in the form of capital which has to be accumulated at all costs and, second, imperial expansionism. This is not just a structural phenomenon, but it has a subjective side. It is accompanied by mental characteristics, namely rationality in the sense of calculating thinking (masculine means-end rationality). This, on the one hand, is expressed in a certain kind of science, technology and bureaucratic organization of dominion, and on the other hand in egocentric individualism. All these features are again linked to patriarchal structures and conceptions. If all these characteristics are co-responsible for endangering life today and in the future we have to ask how the Reformation and its historical impact relate to them and what this has to say to us. From this follows the

Fourth necessary dimension: How does the tradition of the Reformation relate to imperial capitalism and to the masculine means-end rationality in science, technology and individualistic calculating mentality?

Modernity is not only characterized by the above mentioned features, but also through critical and emancipatory movements. To mention only a few: Rousseau resists the exploitation and rape of nature, Karl Marx the exploitation of working people. He contributes greatly to the emergent labor movement. Movements of women struggle for and achieve more and more rights. This means that modernity is ambivalent. From this follows the

Fifth necessary dimension: How do the Reformation and the churches following from it relate to the emancipatory movements of modernity?

Euro-centrism is part and parcel of European imperialism. Beginning in 1492 when Columbus started Europe's violent aggression against the indigenous people of the Americas, the colonizers also looted the goods of other cultures. Indirectly this starts even earlier when the Renaissance draws upon Greek culture without mentioning that this is unthinkable without the other cultures from Asia. Jews and Muslims were expelled from Spain in 1492, and the contribution of Jewish and Muslim culture to European culture neglected. From this follows the

Sixth necessary dimension: How do the Reformation and the churches following from it relate to the integrity of other cultures and religions? Is our perspective consistently post-colonial?

According to which criteria do we raise these questions? The implicit yardstick of the argument so far is of life in its fullness as a gift. In view of the general danger for life under the dominant circumstances, the most fundamental criterion must be what is life-giving in its fullness, now and for future flourishing (cf. John 10:10). In other words: we judge according to reason that is reproductive rather than the means-end-rationality of modernity. Luther also claims to follow reason, yet linked to the Holy Scriptures. He judges all traditions according to the criteria of reason and scripture (*sola scriptura*). In doing so he gives hermeneutical priority to the historical, literal meaning of the texts. In this respect, socio-historical biblical research has brought a great wealth of insights.

In the 1st of our 94 Theses we put it this way: "From the perspective of the Bible, liberation is the first and foremost act of God. The messianic liberation in the New Testament also is shaped according to the model of the Exodus. In his letter to the Romans the Apostle Paul maintains that Christ brings liberation from the 'terrorizing domination of sin' (Rom 5:12-8:2). By contrast, when justification is not understood according to the pattern of the Exodus but reduced only to individual guilt and forgiveness (as in Augustine and Anselm of Canterbury), it is seriously cut off from the wide social and political richness of the Bible." So if we base our deliberations on Luther's own criterion. The tradition of the Reformation itself has to be judged according to the yardstick of whether it follows the Bible. From this follows the

Seventh necessary dimension: How can we understand and judge the theological positions of the Reformation and the resultant churches on the double criteria as to whether they are both life-enhancing, and according to the Bible, which means in terms of content, do they contribute to liberation for justice?

The reason for this argument is the following: If we take the insights of socio-historical biblical research seriously, we arrive at the canon within the canon, which is God's justice/righteousness liberating Ancient Israel in the first place and then, out of this root, people of all nations towards this justice. The goal is *shalom* – an all-embracing peace in succeeding relationships. Within this historical dynamic God sides compassionately with the victims of injustice and violence, inspiring them with the transformative spirit to become the subjects of building new communities. This is not to be understood as a dogmatic conceptual abstract, but as the context in which we can reread the conflicting texts of the Great Biblical Narrative. In this context the key challenge in view of the life-threatening crisis is to turn around every day (*metanoia*) – in the sense of Jesus call that "God's just world is near – turn around", quoted in the first of Luther's 95 theses. From this follows the

Eighth necessary dimension: Did the Reformation and the churches following from it participate in God's liberating actions towards justice to this day? Can we still today build on this tradition when we have to turn around towards developing a new culture of life in just relationships?

On the basis of these considerations we call our project "Radicalizing Reformation – Provoked by the Bible and Today's Crises". This means: We are not looking at the Reformation for historic reasons, but consciously in the context of the life-threatening crisis of humanity and earth. And we look at the root of the Reformation which itself defines this as being the Holy Scriptures (this is why we say "Radicalizing Reformation" – going back to the root=*radix* in Latin).

On the basis of this approach we made an interesting discovery. The culture of modernity, characterized by capitalism, colonialism and calculating individualism has its pre-history in developments of the Ancient Orient (from China to the Mediterranean) – precisely in that period starting in the 8th century BCE in which most of the biblical texts were written. The philosopher Karl Jaspers called this historical period the Axial Age because it saw the shaping of all world religions and philosophies that have influenced our thinking and feeling until today. What he does not realize, however, is the socio-historical observation that this was precisely the time when the early money economy emerged and linked up with empires. The climax of these early developments is the Hellenistic and Roman Empires – the latter being the context of the Messianic Scriptures of the New Testament. This means that the Bible explicitly confronts the mechanisms of the money economy and its linkage with imperial politics and behavior, booming again in Luther's time with early capitalism and finding its climax today with imperial financial capitalism. So via a context analysis we have a direct hermeneutical connection between the Bible, Reformation and today's crises, which can be elaborated in detail.

This is the objective of the bilingual German and English book series titled "Radicalizing Reformation" starting with five volumes published in the first part of 2015. Our starting point is the general crisis of life today. We look at this crisis and the Reformation, including its impact on modernity, from the perspective of contextual Bible research, i.e. from the perspective of liberation for life in just relationships. According to Luther, all traditions have to be judged on the basis of Scripture. The following publications contain 94 theses which were distilled from the material of the 5 volumes.

Volume 1: Liberation towards Justice

Here we are dealing with the centerpiece of the Reformation: justification – law – gospel. Key is the new interpretation of Paul – against an individualistic understanding, reducing God's justice and liberation to the western Ego, thus preparing the way for calculating capitalism; against the identification of the Torah with the "killing law" instead of with the law of the Roman Empire; against the sharp antithesis of law and gospel leading to the separation of the New and Old Testament, to anti-Judaism and anti-Semitism.

Volume 2: Liberation from Mammon

This issue connects the Bible, Reformation and today's crisis: money in religious, political, economic and mental perspective. In the Old and New Testaments the imperial rule of money is understood as structural sin, making all people into co-perpetrators. God's liberation happens as the formation of Torah led to new messianic communities, which practice solidarity instead of egocentric individualism. This corresponds to Luther's rejection of purchasable salvation and his systemic critique of individualism and early capitalism.

Volume 3: Politics and Economy of Liberation

Luther systemically criticizes early capitalism. He is aware of the religious character of capitalism on the basis of the first commandment. His writings on trade and usury (finance) only marginally affected later Protestantism (e.g. Winstanley in the 17th century) but mainline Lutheranism did not follow this critical line. The potential of Luther's position for the theological critique of neoliberalism and for a political ethics of partisanship and reconciliation were rediscovered only recently.

Volume 4: Liberation from Violence for Living in Peace

The Latin American term, *buen vivir*, serves as a marker for a new, life-affirming culture. This approach can assist us in overcoming several misdirections generated through the Reformation – reclaiming a political interpretation of the Bible, affirmation of the materiality of the natural world as the foundation for faith and ecclesial existence, and overcoming the violent, "religious identity" policy of Luther against peasants, Anabaptists, Muslims, and Jews. This volume calls for a post-colonial reading of Luther and a radical turn toward active non-violent engagement. The authors advocate a "new Reformation" in the trajectory of Bonhoeffer and Soelle.

Volume 5: Church – Liberated for Resistance and Transformation

The cross is a sign of evil, of consolation for all those tortured and suffering, a sign of hope, of liberation. Christ takes on the socio-political, cultural and economic conditions of those who have been deprived of their rights. The church needs to risk its sustainability by being with and for the poor. Whereas in sin we are disconnected, through the Spirit we are re-connected. The Spirit works freely in people and the world, therefore also in other religions besides Christianity. Rather than being only focused on the person or individual, resistance and transformation should have a more communal ecclesial focus.

In short, these are the first attempts to implement the approach "Radicalizing Reformation – Provoked by the Bible and Today's Crises" in the form of specific research. We think that this way of asking questions will prove to be creative so that more publications will follow.

We sincerely thank all institutions who have supported our project financially: World Council of Churches (WCC), Protestant Mission Service in Germany (EMW), Brot für die Welt, Protestant Church in Germany (EKD), the Protestant churches in Baden, Hannover, Mitteldeutschland and Westfalen.

Daniel Beros, Ulrich Duchrow, Martin Hoffmann, Hans G. Ulrich

RADICALIZING REFORMATION – PROVOKED BY THE BIBLE AND TODAY'S CRISES

94 Theses

"You shall proclaim liberation throughout the land" (Lev. 25:10).

Martin Luther began his 95 Theses of 1517 with Jesus' call for repentance as a change of mind and direction: "Return, the just world of God has come near!" Five hundred years later is also a time that brings to mind the biblical "Jubilee Year" (Lev 25), calling for repentance and conversion toward a more just society. For us today, this is not in opposition to the Catholic Church and the many liberation movements rooted there, but in opposition to the realities of empire that rule. As we hear the testimony of the cross (1 Cor 1:18) and the groaning of the abused creation (Rom 8:22) and as we actively hear the cries of those victimized by our world (dis-)order driven by hyper-capitalism – only then can we turn this Reformation commemoration into a liberating jubilee. Christian self-righteousness, supporting the dominating system, is in contradiction to faith-righteousness as proclaimed by the Reformation. This must be lived out through just, all-inclusive solidarity.

We are theologians – predominantly Lutheran but also Reformed, Methodist, Anglican, and Mennonite – from different parts of the world, who are involved in an ongoing project of reconsidering the biblical roots and contemporary challenges facing Reformation theology today. The rampant destruction of human and non-human life in a world ruled by the totalitarian dictatorship of money and greed, market and exploitation requires a radical re-orientation towards the biblical message, which also marked the beginning of the Reformation. The dominant economic system and its imperial structures and policies have put the earth, human communities, and the future of our children up for sale. Our churches, congregations, and individual Christians have often become complacent and complicit with the established status quo and have lost their critical-prophetic power to protest, resist, and change what is occurring. God's justification by grace has been detached from social justice and thus serves as “useless salt” (Mt 5:13). Because the Reformation legacy has gone astray, we must at the same time return to some of Luther’s thought and legacy, as well as standing decidedly against other things he said and did, if this is to become a kairoitic time of transformation today.

The following theses grow out of different traditions and understandings among the reforming movements, as well as from different geographical and political contexts. We have developed these theses from research, published in five volumes. We may not agree on every point, but out of this very diversity and pluriformity, we together call for serious debate on what is asserted here – and we also call for “turning around” and repentance (metanoia). The present moment of crisis that we currently face across the globe on all levels is a time to recognize the predatory and destructive forces inherent in what is dominating our world today, in order to re-orient ourselves in hope towards a new culture of life.

“For liberation the Messiah has liberated us” (Gal 5:1)

1. From the perspective of the Bible, liberation is first and foremost the act of God. The messianic liberation in the New Testament also is shaped according to the model of the Exodus. In his letter to the Romans the Apostle Paul maintains that Christ brings liberation from the “terrorizing domination of sin” in the context of the Roman Empire (Rom 5:12-8:2). By contrast, when justification is not understood according to the pattern of the Exodus but reduced only to individual guilt and forgiveness (as in Augustine and Anselm of Canterbury), it is seriously cut off from the wide social and political richness of the biblical context.
2. Paul analyzes the domination of sin, which, in the Roman Empire of his time, holds all people captive. The central passages about sin (hamartia) have a common denominator: they are to be understood in terms of relationships of domination, only very seldom in categories of individual guilt and sins. When Paul speaks about sin, he is referring especially to its all-embracing terrorizing domination. His overall idea is that sin rules over all human beings as a master over slaves and thus makes them collaborators in the imperial system and laws.
3. Paul speaks about the beginning of an all-encompassing change of rule. He directs his hope towards God's final intervention, which for him has

already begun with Jesus' resurrection. Although Paul has no direct political goals, his faith in Christ's rule and the hope for a final change of rule has deep political implications. He believes that Christ alone is Lord (Kyrios) and that liberation in Christ affects the whole creation, all people, and the whole human being.

4. Faith leads the faithful to live as liberated people, both in their faith community and in their common life with others. This is the beginning of a new life. This claim for liberation from totalitarian reality, such as under the Roman Empire, is more trenchant and empowering for all who live today under the domination of financial and violent markets than are traditional generalizations about sin.

"You cannot serve both God and Mammon" (Mt 6:24)

5. At least two billion people exist in extreme poverty under the present rule of money. The rule of capital is today's expression of Mammon, and thus the central challenge of faith. Today, money is not simply issued by the central banks or cash in your pocket, but commercial banks have the right to create money through unlimited loans that create debt with high interest. Already in the 16th century Luther called Mammon "the most common god on earth" (Large Catechism, Explanation of the First Commandment).

6. This rule of money together with theological opposition to it developed historically with the expansion of an economy based on money and private ownership – from the monetization of the economy in the time of the Prophets; through the early capitalism of Luther's time, based on trade and usury; to modern forms of industrial and financial capitalism. Since the time of the Reformation, the contemporary globalized capitalism of modernity has been manifest in

European exploitation, colonization, and genocide in Africa, Asia, and the Americas.

7. "The land shall not be sold in perpetuity, for the land is mine; with me you are but migrant laborers and tenants" (Lev 25:23). In Scripture, property is intended for the furthering of life for all (use value). By contrast, capitalism makes private property absolute and encloses common land and resources. This continues today in widespread land grabs (for example, in Africa and Latin America), in the privatization of the genetic commons of humanity (through patents), and through the privatization of land, water, air, and so forth.

8. Both ancient and modern individualism begins with the infiltration of money and private property into daily life. For most people in the globalized capitalist world, individualism is self-evident. For Luther, by contrast, there is no such thing as a neutral, observing, and calculating individual. Either people are determined by God – in which case they live compassionately and righteously in relation to others, above all toward those considered the "least" (Mt 5:31ff.) – or they allow themselves to be determined by the power of sin, living distorted, self-centered lives that destroy other creatures.

9. The capitalist economy drives unlimited growth which endangers all life on our planet. Human beings are created by God with the mission "to serve (abad) and keep the garden" (Gen 2:15). Luther begins the 95 Theses by quoting Jesus' call to repentance: "When our Lord and Master Jesus Christ said, 'Repent' (Mt 4:17), he willed the entire life of believers to be one of repentance" (95 Theses, 1). Today this means that, personally and collectively, we seek to break free from the destructive rule of money. By trusting instead in the liberating righteousness of God, we are empowered to live in compassion and solidarity with other humans and the rest of creation.

10. According to Scripture, human beings form one body with many members, who serve one another (1 Cor 12). But according to the logic and practice of advanced capitalism, we are driven by competition. According to Luther, we are created, sustained, and empowered to work with God and others for the sake of justice and peace in the economy, in the political order, and in the church (On the Bondage of the Will). Here Luther follows the Waldensians, Wycliffe, and Hus.

11. Economic individualization is reflected in the religious individualization of salvation. By contrast, both the Bible and Luther speak of free persons in just relationships. From the Middle Ages on, there have been spiritualizing tendencies that are still strong in our churches. Reading and preaching on biblical texts individualistically implicitly or explicitly supports capitalist-based assumptions today.

12. According to Jesus, that person is just who forgives debts for the sake of those indebted, rather than abiding by rules of debt repayment (Mt 6:12). According to Paul the power of sin (as embodied in Roman law, a greed economy, and imperial rule) makes the law into an instrument of death. He proposes building alternative communities of Jews and Greeks who live in solidarity in the spirit of the Messiah who was crucified by the Empire. Those whom Rome had made enemies of each other are reconciled with God and with each other.

13. The Church Fathers interpreted the death of Jesus on the Cross in terms of a ransom theory. Anselm of Canterbury (1033-1109) turns this upside down in his satisfaction theory. According to him the law of debt-repayment stands higher than God. This is why God must sacrifice his son in order to establish a storehouse of merits, which people can draw on in order to pay off their debts. This not only lays the ground for the medieval penitential system, which Luther rejects, but also for capitalism's law of debt repayment.

14. Luther returns to the biblical truth that God forgives with no exceptions, and out of this forgiveness grows the trust that grounds solidarity with the neighbor. Thus, if someone is in need, Christians respond with interest-free lending and giving. It follows that the government should also intervene in the market when public welfare is endangered. Today, however, capitalism makes the market absolute and favors government intervention only for the interest of capital accumulation. Drawing inspiration from Scripture and the Reformation, faith communities must resist!

15. The Spirit of God affirms cultural and linguistic diversity in the story of Pentecost (Acts 2). From the fourth century until the Reformation, the Bible was read only in Latin. Wycliffe and the later Reformers opened up diversity again by allowing people to hear Scripture in their own language. This diversity is once again challenged by the homogenizing force of the global market, which turns all humans into consuming indi-

viduals, agriculture into agribusiness, regional selling of goods into transnational chains, and local and regional products into export-driven monocultures.

16. The Bible establishes a political economy of "enough for all" based on the sharing of what is given for the common good of all (Exodus 16). The reformers were unanimous in believing that the economy should serve the common good and the specific needs of the neighbor. In our time, we are not calling for a return to the historical forms of socialism that have had some effects as destructive as capitalism, but instead call for forms of economic life that build on God's gifts, protect the commons, and produce and distribute goods and services in ways that are both democratic and ecologically sensitive.

17. Scripture affirms that all human beings, female and male, are created in the image of God and thus equal in worth (Gen 1:26-28). In the book of Judges, as well as in Torah texts, this affirmation led to the formation of communities of solidarity. This tradition was taken up in early Christianity (Acts 2 and 4). Voices in the radical Reformation appealed to these texts and sought to establish not only political but also economic democracy.

18. Luther's teaching on justification by grace through faith in Christ alone (Rom 5:1) is a legitimate and liberating interpretation of Scripture within the oppressions of late medieval piety and against emergent money lending-for-interest economy. Forgiveness of sins by grace, deliverance from the power of the devil, and the promise of eternal life in this context meant not only spiritual freedom but freedom for reconciliation with and ethical responsibility to the neighbor (Freedom of a Christian).

19. While for Luther, justification by grace alone expressed this understanding of equality, the Reformation failed to make this concrete socially and economically. In fact, later Lutheranism even turned social and economic inequality into a hierarchical God-given order! This culminated in asserting the autonomy of the market and/or the state, which both Scripture and Luther explicitly critique.

20. According to Scripture, people are justified by grace and not by their performance (Mt 20). The performance myth, according to which people are judged by their merit, or by getting what they deserve, must be set over

against the principle of need, which is the equivalent of the righteousness of faith. The social and ethical consequences that follow from this constitute a critique of today's work world, which is dominated by this performance ideology and the negative effects that result.

21. While Luther's teaching about the two kingdoms has been used to justify political quietism and passive obedience to the state (Rom 13:1), this teaching needs to be reinterpreted as a call to political vigilance and activism by Christians to live out their public responsibility to the neighbor in advocating for peace, justice, and the integrity of the creation.

22. "Do not be conformed to the structures of this world order but be transformed by the renewing of your mind..." (Rom 12:2). Because of their effect on the common people of his day, Luther said a clear "No!" to the structure and practices of the bank and trading companies of his time: "Nothing good can come of them. If the companies are to survive, justice and honesty must perish. If justice and honesty are to survive, the companies must perish" (WA 15, 312). Today the forces of economic growth, monetary expansion, and privatization threaten planetary death. In this regard, tinkering with the social system will not help. A long-term alternative to the neoliberal capitalist system is needed. Many examples show that a new monetary and property order, oriented towards the common good and publicly responsible, is not only necessary but possible.

23. "Blessed are those who hunger and thirst after righteousness, for they shall be satisfied" (Mt 5:6). The new order can take root in any local area. Church communities can participate in decentralized local energy supplies and connect with social movements with slogans such as: "If we leave it to the politicians, it will be too little too late. If we try and do it ourselves, it will be too little. If we work together, however, it may be just enough, just in time" (Transition Town Movement).

"The message of the cross...is the power of God" (1 Cor 1:18)

24. Since the Middle Ages, many churches and theologians have understand Jesus' death as God's "sacrificing his son" in order to save human beings. This interpretation turns God into a sadistic ruler who produces suffering. However, God saves from violence, not through violence.

25. The cross was the Roman Empire's instrument to execute rebels and fugitive slaves. Many innocent people became victims of this public demonstration of power. The picture of the Crucified One with a gas-mask, of a crucified girl or woman, and the painting of a crucified campesino remind us of those many people who in our day continue to be killed by the dominant powers. The crucified Jesus is deeply connected to them.

26. According to biblical tradition, the martyrdom of the just effects forgiveness of the sins for the people (4 Maccabees 17:21) and the innocent death of the servant of God makes the many just (Is 53:11f.), which opens up new meanings of Jesus' death on the cross.

27. The encounter with the risen Christ sheds new light on the cross (Luke 24). God gives life to the dead and calls into existence the things that do not exist (Rom 4:17).

28. In the light of the resurrection, Jesus is written into the lamentations of traumatized people, giving them hope ("My God, why have you forsaken me?" – Ps 22:2; Mk 16:34; "The poor shall eat and be satisfied" – Ps 22:26).

29. Theology of the cross can overcome a previous tainting imagery between the cross and crusade in the colonial time. This refers to a refurbishing of the theology of the cross for the theology of life (resurrection) seen in light of God's solidarity with the minjung, economic justice for all, and integrity of the ecological web of life.

30. So the resurrection proves to be judgment against the powers of violence, the most radical implementation of God's unconditional solidarity with all suffering creatures and an expression of God's faithfulness and justice toward all people and creation.

31. Biblically understood, faith is repentance. Luther declared: "Yet it does not mean solely inner repentance; such inner repentance is worthless unless it produces various outward acts of repentance" (95 Theses, 3). On the one side, we are called to a process of truth and reconciliation about the ethical failings of the Reformation. On the other side, accepting God's justice for us, we allow ourselves to be drawn into this history of liberation by doing justice: "Only the believers obey, and only the obedient believe" (Bonhoeffer).

32. Luther's theology of justification needs to be extended and renewed in different times and places, especially in light of Luther's congenial notion of the Gospel as the living voice of God. The Reformation teaching of justification should break through its encapsulation within Western possessive individualism and political quietism, liberating human beings from all the idolatrous assumptions, upon which we base our lives: the privileges of species, sex, gender, ethnicity, religion, nationality, and class. Justification should be reclaimed as a way of expressing God's deep compassion in the death of Jesus Christ for all, reinforcing our public responsibility for the political realm, economic justice, and recognition of the Other.

"See, everything has become new" (2 Cor 5:17)

33. The Christian gospel is indeed about reconciliation between God and humanity, and about reconciliation between human beings. But if "gospel" does not succeed in reconciling the whole of creation, it is not the gospel (2 Co 5:18).

34. The Reformation's recognition that we are saved through faith by God's grace should also be a recognition that God's gracious presence is in all creation, responding to its cries (Rom 8:18-23).

35. While many gains were achieved in the sixteenth century era when the Reformers criticized the worship of material reality, they went too far when they rejected all notion of the sacramental by stripping away at ma-

terial culture in a surge of iconoclasm. Here they failed to recognize that all of life is divinely infused and that the whole world is a sacramental reality.

36. The Reformation's recognition that by grace we are saved through faith should also affirm that God's gracious presence is in all of creation. God's communion with the world in Jesus Christ means that as followers of Christ we too are called into communion with the world – a this-worldly faith that is made real when we join in God's mission for the renewal of all creation.

37. Mother Earth is being crucified and has to experience resurrection (Rom 8:22). This is very important for our life as human beings, animals, plants, air, water, and earth. We are human beings not because we consume, but because we need to live connected to creation, caring for her and for our life.

38. "The Gospel of all creatures" (Mark 16:15, according to Luther's translation), the good news of God to the entire creation (Psalm 119), is interrupted, if human beings, made in God's image, destroy this order by exercising injustice (Rom 1:18-20).

39. The Gospel challenges us to preserve the creation as God's garden through a righteous personal stance and through new economic, social, and ecological politics for the welfare of the entire creation and all peoples of the world.

40. "Life in fullness" (John 10:10) breaks with previous concepts of economic development: it focuses on our inextricable relation to creation, to which the human community must be oriented. Life in fullness does not aim at "having more," as in accumulation and growth, but in living toward balance in all relationships.

41. All human beings and the whole of nature have a right to and a need for "bread and roses." Human beings and nature have a hunger for bread and beauty. An unfinished task of Reformation theology is to fight for and proclaim the right for life in fullness for the whole creation.

42. The Earth gives life to all creatures (Gen 1:24). What nature brings forth is a gift from God, of which we should take good care as an expression of our gratitude and calling as disciples (Ps 104).

43. Life in fullness does not mean consumerism but being connected to the whole of nature. Human beings and human industry are not the final purpose of creation: God's final act in creation is to bring us to Sabbath rest in worship and in relationships (Gen 2:2).

44. The gospel challenges us to preserve and renew creation as God's garden (Gen 2:15; Isaiah 65:17; 2 Peter 3:13) by adopting a modest personal lifestyle and collaborating with people of different cultures and religions in the world to implement life-affirming economic, social, and environmental policies.

45. The question of creation is closely related to the life of future generations. Theology has consistently been informed by adult personhood and not by childhood. Instead human beings are to be understood as determined by God's story with them. This is particularly true for children and must be taken seriously by theology in view of their endangered future.

46. Children's rights necessitate protecting children against violations, oppression, and exploitation. It is, however, equally important to appreciate children in all their capabilities and weaknesses, in their unique characteristics and their imperfections as with any adult human being. For theology children must be liberated from objectification and become subjects for the sake of their own future.

"Blessed are the peacemakers" (Matthew 5:9)

47. Hear the cries of those who have suffered violence, especially those made victims by followers of the Reformation – such as peasants, Anabaptists (Mennonites), Jews, Muslims! Hear the cries of those suffering violence today – whether through domestic abuse, economic exploitation, violations of human rights, injustice against creation, state imperialism, and ongoing wars!

48. We call for conversion to the praxis of peacemaking (Isaiah 2:2-4). The way of peacemaking, as embodied by Jesus, joins God's nonviolent praxis with the cause of all those who practice nonviolence. Nonviolent praxis is a sign of God's reign of shalom (Isaiah 11:6-9).

Illustration of Jan Luyken in "Märtyrerspiegel": Dirk Willems rescues his persecutor, who had handed him over to the ash heap. (from:http:// de.wikipedia.org/wiki/ Dirk_ Willems)

49. The phenomenon of violence becomes evident wherever there is resistance to the practice of peacemaking, especially in social, political, economic, or state violence where many victims cry out to heaven for God's help.

50. Violence is widespread and present in many forms – structural violence, technological violence, military violence, physical and psychological violence of every kind. The universality of violence becomes evident in the endemic practice of identifying others as "enemies," especially in making others into scapegoats (Acts 7:54-60).

51. Although reasons and analyses of the cause of violence can be given, all violence is in reaction to previous forms of violence.

52. It is not possible to justify or legitimize violence; it is always illegitimate. There is no "measured" violence, no "just" war," no "justifiable" war. Luther, Zwingli and Calvin only tolerated limited violence for minimizing greater violence. However, even this logic is anachronistic in face of modern weapons of mass destruction. Violence can never serve as a means for attaining any goal, for God has reconciled all things to Godself (Colossians 1:19-20).

53. Enforcing the law cannot rest upon violence. Wherever humans suffer violence, they are to be protected by practices of peacemaking. In the time of the Reformation the exercise of violence began exclusively as warfare and police violence on the part of the "authorities," determined exclusively as a protection of the neighbor from violence. This radical

limitation has been largely suppressed. This extremely limited use of violence, where it must be employed, is never to be understood as a matter of course but always as a warning sign of our broken world.

54. Legal systems are established on the basis of violence, a kind of foundational violence. This violence, however, legitimizes no further violence but rather calls for righteous action (Mt 5:38-42). Legal systems must be judged against the yardstick of bringing peace through justice.

55. Practicing peace means living, speaking, and acting without violence. Practicing peace means doing that which promotes peace – doing justice, listening, forgiving, sharing, giving, healing, being merciful, helping – all of these as works of resistance to violence (Mt 5:3-11). All of this is worship (Rom 12:1-2); worship is practicing peace.

56. Practicing peace also entails how one speaks, exercising no rhetorical violence (Mt 5:33-37). The gospel is inherently nonviolent – promising, inviting, witnessing – never forcing.

57. Practicing peace means being dedicated to the common life of all in a political community that is uniquely characterized by peaceful practices. Practicing peace means following the consequences of this conviction, being realistic with regard to one's own responsibility, because only by doing so will peace prevail in the world (Mt 5:43-48).

"Bear one another's burdens, and in this way you will fulfill the Torah of Christ" (Gal 6:2)

58. The Reformation originates with Luther's rediscovery of God's justice as creative and renewing power, as spelled out in the letters of Paul. In his doctrine of justification, Luther interprets this justice as God's merciful care even for the ungodly (sola gratia), and as trust in the faithfulness of God (sola fide) in Christ (solus Christus).

59. For Paul, the justice of God implies the visionary insight, that "in Christ" the polarities and hierarchies of this "present evil world order" (Gal 1:4) have been overcome. "We" are not what segregates us from the "others" but what interconnects us with them. The human divisions of nation, religion, gender, and class, which constitute the "self" as enemy and rival of the "other," are removed in baptism "like old garments." A new praxis

of becoming "one" through mutuality and solidarity creates a new form of being human – and a new world (Gal 6:2.15). "There is no longer Jew or Greek, there is no longer slave or free, there is no longer male and female; for all of you are one in the Messiah Jesus" (Gal 3:28). God's justice, the justification of the human being, and human justice are all inseparably connected.

60. One of the most troublesome and non-Pauline aspects of justification theology (as it was framed by the Reformation and subsequently interpreted by Protestantism) is the concept of "law." Luther regularly juxtaposes "justice/righteousness through the law" with "justice/righteousness through faith" and understands this antithesis as the irreconcilable polarity of Judaism against Christianity.

61. This fateful polarization emerges from Luther's interpretation of Paul's letter to the Galatians. Luther falsely identifies the law that Paul criticizes with the Jewish Torah. The core controversy of Galatians about the non-necessity of the Jewish ritual of circumcision for the Christ believers is thus understood as a rejection of Judaism as such. As recent scholarship has shown, however, the primary target in Paul's struggle with his Galatian opponents was not Jewish Torah, but the law and order of the Roman Empire. It prescribed certain rules of conformity for both Jews and Gentiles. The Pauline community model of solidarity between Jews and Non-Jews "in Christ" clashes in the first place with these imperial settings and social norms, not the least within the framework of Roman emperor religion.

62. The Reformation furthermore identified Judaism with Roman Catholicism, labeling both as "legalistic religions" that achieve "justice/righteousness through works of the law." The polarity of "works versus grace/faith" and "gospel versus law," applied to concrete people, has had a disastrous impact throughout the history of interpretation. It was not only read in an anti-Jewish and anti-Catholic manner but also turned against "enthusiasts", Anabaptists, Muslims, and other "heretics", often with deadly consequences.

63. Up to this day liberation theologies, feminist theologies, and social movements are often accused of "work righteousness" or "legalism" and thus denied legitimacy as expressions of proper faith. Justification theology and this-worldly justice are played off against each other.

64. Against this backdrop, the Protestant tradition at its core is compromised by defining its identity against the "other" – the one who acts, believes, lives, or thinks differently – rather than in line with Paul's radical solidarity with one another across boundaries and segregations. In light of the present world crisis, it is an urgent imperative that Protestant justification theology re-think the justice of God and return to its biblical roots.

65. The negative classification of Judaism and law also has become a major factor in the fundamental downgrading of the whole Old Testament. The trinitarian formula of "Father, Son, and Holy Spirit" as common witness of all Christian churches testifies to the indissoluble bond between the two parts of the scriptural canon. Regaining the unity of both Testaments is an essential task for doing theology in the legacy of the Reformation today.

66. The Messiah Jesus of Nazareth is the invitation to all peoples to participate in the future that has been promised to Israel: a just and equal society inspired by the Torah. The Christian church is not the replacement of Israel. Israel is the root of the church: "You do not support the root, the root supports you" (Rom 11:18).

67. The Messiah Jesus proclaims the kingdom of God, God's just world, coming near (Mt 4:17). In the horizon of this hope, Jesus interprets the Torah of Israel in the context of his time (Mt 5-7). The criteria of his interpretation are the exclusive worship of God and the love of the neighbor, especially to the poor and the disinherited (Mk 12:28-34). The situation of "the least" (Mt 25:31-46) determines how the Torah has to be interpreted. So the Torah, of which not the tiniest commandment is canceled, becomes the orientation for the messianic communities (Mt 5:17-20; 28:19-20; see also Rom 3:31). Jesus' call to his disciples to orient themselves according to his interpretation of the Torah aims at continuously reinterpreting and revitalizing the Torah in the hope of God's coming kingdom.

68. In Paul's letter to the Romans, we hear the cry of people who find themselves caught in the imperial system that makes it impossible to live according to the norms of Torah. Sin is not just an abstract human condition but materializes in concrete social circumstances. For Paul, imperial power structures embody the power of sin that inevitably turns people in-

to transgressors of the life-giving laws of Torah and makes them complicit with the forces of death and self-destruction (Rom 7:24).

69. Paul's justification by grace through faith thus implies a twofold liberation of both human beings and of Torah from the power of sin. The messianic communities establish a space where Jews and non-Jews "in Christ" can fulfill the Torah as law of life through love of one another – even of enemies (Rom 8:2; 12:1-21; 13:8-10).

70. The critical stance against the law in Paul and the Reformation is not directed against the legal order of societies as such (usus civilis legis). Legal rules and law are necessary in order to sustain human societies. The critique is directed exclusively against abusing the law on behalf of the strong against the weak, a practice already critiqued by the Prophets. The law is made for the people, not the people for the law, as both Jesus and the rabbis maintained (Mk 2:27; Babylonian Talmud, Trakt. Eruvin 41b). Human legislation must always be examined critically and continuously adjusted in order to defend justice for the victims instead of "legally" covering up the injustice of the dominant order.

71. Luther's reference to the Ten Commandments simply as "natural law" (Moses as "the Jews' Sachsenspiegel") poses a specific challenge. It eclipses the specificity of Torah as an alternative law that at decisive points moves away from the exploitative legislation of its environment – such as with regard to Sabbath laws, forgiveness of debt, or the prohibition against accumulation through greed (Tenth Commandment). This critical edge vanishes as Torah is simply identified with existing legal codes, like the Roman law, that absolutize private property.

72. Above all, in his Small Catechism Luther dropped the politically concrete preamble of the Decalogue: "I am the Lord your God who brought you out of the land of Egypt, out of the house of slavery" (Ex 20:2; Deut 5:6). Luther also extended the command to honor one's parents to honor authorities as such. These two symptomatic changes of the scriptural base in Luther's most influential catechism are indicative for how Lutheranism became prone to obedience and subservience towards any established order, including severely unjust ones, instead of being faithful to the God of liberation (sola fide) and standing in solidarity with the downtrodden.

73. When the established order lacks righteous action and remains indifferent to the concerns of the common people, especially to the least (Mt 25:31-40), revealing its idolatries and imposing an unacceptable way of life, Christians should not only disobey but also resist such evil authorities.

74. Within imperial structures, the liberating biblical instructions orient us to resist the death-bound logic and laws of violent, enslaving powers. This requires regaining an in-depth appreciation of the liberating traditions of both the Old and New Testaments. As in the time of the Reformation, we need a new "revival" of cutting-edge Bible study in our congregations that engages not only individuals but also the current social and economic problems in critical and liberating ways. For example, forgiveness of debt and God's forgiveness of guilt belong inseparably together biblically (Mt 6:12). Christians today should be empowered to get to know specifically the Old Testament, the Hebrew Bible, as a rich treasure for daily life and ethical judgements.

75. Disciples of Jesus Christ advocate a desire to understand the mystery of God in community with the sacred texts of divine revelation also in other religions and joy in strengthening the dialogue in their common efforts of constructing a better world together with Jews, Muslims, Hindus, Buddhists, and every other religion and culture from Africa, North America, Latin America, the Caribbean, Asia, the Pacific, the Middle East and Europe (Isaiah 49:6). The Gospel contradicts every form of cultural, religious, and military invasion.

76. A postcolonial reading of Reformation theology advances a project of enculturation, in order to underpin inter-religious dialogue as prophetic dialogue, adopting a new departure in the critique of colonization by Reformation theology or misuse of its scholarship in the service of the powerful.

"The Spirit blows where it wills" (John 3:8)

77. In the spirit of the church that emerged out of the Reformation, it is crucial that we listen today to the cries of people around the world, who feel that the church does not see but overlooks and excludes their suffering,

oppression, and cultural realities today (Mt 25:31ff.). Our ignorance and avoidance deepen rather than heal the divisions in church and society.

78. The Reformation movements understood the church not so much as an institution, but as the baptized people of God gathered in local communities. The church as community in the discipleship of Jesus is the holy space in which the universal Word of God is listened to and the sacraments celebrated in many different voices, traditions, and confessions for the sake of the mending of the world (tikkun olam).

79. The priesthood of all believers was a radical cry for democratizing the most powerful institution of that day, the Roman Church. Today it must be translated as a revolutionary call for universal citizenship and equitable distribution of the products of human labor.

80. In the 16th century the church was reformed, but it soon became enmeshed again with structures and practices that are patriarchal, hierarchical, and captive to powerful economic and political interests. Its persecution of Jews, Anabaptists, and Muslims was deplorable! In addition to repenting for such, the Spirit of God impels movement away from such Constantinian expressions of church into more participatory, boundary-crossing embodiments of church that are truly catholic, inclusive of all, and collaborative across boundaries of religion, ethnicity, geography, and self-interest.

81. Discipleship in Christ requires a stance of contemplation, spiritual cleansing, enlightenment, and surrender to the will of God. If we hear the voice of God with the fear of Rahab (Joshua 2) or the fear of Mary and Elisabeth (Luke 1), and allow the flood of God's Spirit into the depths of our being, thereby we undertake the path of discipleship in Christ. The women in the Bible and the women of the Radical Reformation demonstrate for us the way of discipleship, mysticism, witness, and martyrdom.

82. The Spirit of God acts freely, blowing when and where the Spirit so desires, continually renewing the Church. It cannot be a property of anyone, nor kept captive by institutional interests or doctrinal definitions.

83. The Spirit brings about renewal and change both in church and society. In addition to transforming individual persons, the Spirit also enables believers to struggle alongside those of other religions, ideologies, and so-

cial movements, and to endure suffering caused by this commitment to love, solidarity, and justice.

84. When Luther called the cross a mark or sign of the church, he was establishing a criterion: to be the church, the church needs to become vulnerable by being with and for the poor and to risk its social or political status by publicly protesting against unjust structures and policies.

85. Rather than only being focused on individuals, the church must venture a critical communal ecclesial focus for resistance and transformation. Otherwise, injustices continue to have free reign, distorting our most basic relationships to God, ourselves, one another, and the whole of creation. Through practices such as preaching, teaching, celebrating, caring, community-formation, and organizing with others, the church can help counter the sin, bondage, and blindness that enable domination by the many facets of empire to prevail.

86. Through the power of the indwelling and connecting Spirit, those who are most different from one another are transformed into one body or a "new creation" (1 Cor 12:12; 2 Cor 5:17). While fostering renewal and change, the Spirit also draws people together into the unity of the body of Christ, which cannot be used to justify further church divisions. A reforming church must be reconciled with itself and endeavor to overcome divisions between East and West, between Catholics and Protestants, and between the various Reformation churches, in order that all may come to celebrate at the Lord's Table together.

87. A reforming church continually is being transformed by what it receives from other theological traditions and cultures. In emphasizing how the Spirit is linked to the Word, Luther was criticizing anyone claiming to have received special revelations by the Spirit apart from what is revealed in Scripture. This must not be misinterpreted as limiting the Spirit's free work in people, including those of other traditions or religions, as well as in the rest of creation (Rom 8:22-23).

88. Luther's critique of the enthusiasts cannot be transferred to our times as a generalized critique of Pentecostalism. While "theologies of prosperity" must be criticized on the basis of a theology of the cross, we must be attentive to the work of the Spirit within Pentecostal movements for building up community, rescuing people from marginalization, and restoring

the dignity of people who suffer under poverty, disease, addictions, and unemployment.

89. The rediscovery and re-reading of biblical traditions from the perspective of the marginalized on the basis of social analysis, the contextual and intercultural reading of the Bible in many different contexts throughout the world, is an important sign of hope that the liberating hermeneutics of the Reformation traditions are active in many churches today.

90. At the heart of the Reformation was universal access to education, together with a critical re-reading of the Bible in relation to contextual situations of the day. As churches rooted in the Reformation have spread throughout the world, this approach to the Bible often does not prevail. Instead, individualistic spiritualities and religious fundamentalisms, which collude with powerful interests and which perpetuate illusions, are on the increase.

91. Recovering the crucial role of biblical theology and critical theological education (together with education in general) is key to the ongoing reformation and renewal needed within global Christianity in the 21st century.

92. Blessed are those who do not fit into the systems of this world, but who stand in protest of God's continued crucifixion in the schemes of this world (Rom 12: 2) and who cooperate with others in building a new world with justice and peace in human communities!

93. We are in need of a "New Reformation!" Now as then, people can easily be pious. However, they find inadequate forms of expression in the churches, because the churches are alienated from the realities of the actual world in which people live. As with Martin Luther, we need a renewal of language and a return to the liberating message of the Gospel.

94. Bonhoeffer's proposal of a worldly engaged Christianity, which would discover a new language for the old Gospel, must be translated as: "Prayer and action of the righteous among people". All church talk "must be born anew from this prayer and this action" and be taken up in liberation theology's insistence on the inseparableness of orthopraxis and orthodoxy.

"Radicalizing Reformation – Provoked by the Bible and Today's Crises" is not an option but an imperative for church and theology today. Luther himself made Scripture the criterion for all tradition. Contextual interpretations of the Bible have sharpened this hermeneutic critically and prophetically. Living at the onset of modern capitalism, Luther engaged in systemic critique. Living at the end of this murderous and suicidal period of human history, we must listen anew to the sources of our faith and join others in "putting a spoke in the wheel of the car, when the driver is drunk." Let us continue together with others on that pilgrimage of justice and peace!

Halle, 7 August 2014

Prof. Dr. Walter Altmann/Brasilien, Prof. Dr. Charles Amjad-Ali/Pakistan/USA, Dr. Claudete Beise Ulrich/Brasilien/Deutschland, Prof. Dr. Daniel Beros, Argentina, Prof. Dr. Karen Bloomquist/USA, Leonardo Boff, Prof. emer. für Theologie und Ethik/Petrópolis, Rio, Brasilien, Prof. Dr. Klara Butting/Deutschland, Prof. Dr. Paul Chung/Korea/USA, Prof. Dr. Frank Crüsemann/Deutschland, Dr. Marlene Crüsemann/Deutschland, Dr. Silfredo Dalferth/ Prof. Dr. Wanda Deifelt/USA, Dr. Moiseraele Prince Dibeela/ Botswana, Prof. Dr. Martin Dreher/Brasilien, Prof. Dr. Ulrich Duchrow/Deutschland, Prof. Dr. Fernando Enns/Deutschland, Prof. Dr. Antonio González Fernández/Spanien, Prof. Dr. Timothy Gorringe/UK, Prof. Dr. Peter Heltzel/ USA, Prof. Dr. Franz Hinkelammert/Costa Rica, Dr. Martin Hoffmann/Costa Rica, Prof. Dr. Claudia Janssen/Deutschland, Prof. Dr. Carsten Jochum-Bortfeld/ Deutschland, Prof. Dr. Brigitte Kahl/USA, Prof. Dr. Rainer Kessler/Deutschland, Prof. Dr. Karl Koop/ Canada, Prof. Dr. Maake J Masango/Südafrika, Prof. Cynthia D. Moe-Lobeda, Ph.D./USA, Dr. Kenneth Mtata/Zimbabwe, Prof. Dr. Craig L. Nessan/USA, Prof. Dr. Axel Noack/ Deutschland, Prof. Dr. Jaime Prieto/Costa Rica, Dr. Edelbert Richter/Deutschland, Prof. Dr. Santhosh J. Sahayadoss/Indien, Prof Dr. Dr. h.c. Luise Schottroff/Deutschland, Prof. Dr. Sturla Stalsett/Norwegen, Prof. Dr. Marisa Strizzi/Argentinien, Prof. Dr. Samuel Torvend/USA, Prof. Dr. Hans G. Ulrich/Deutschland, Prof. Dr. Karin Ulrich/Deutschland, Lic. Ton Veerkamp/Deutschland, Dr. Dietrich Werner/ Deutschland, Prof. Dr. Vitor Westhelle/ Brasilien, Prof. Dr. Renate Wind/Deutschland, Prof. Dr. Lauri Wirth/Brasilien

UnterstützerInnen/Supporters (Stand 15.2. 2015):

Anna Marie Aagaard, prof. emerita, University of Aarhus/Denmark, Prof. Dr. Evangeline Anderson-Rajkumar/Indien, Pfarrer Norbert Arntz/Deutschland, Prof. Dr. Sigurd Bergmann/Schweden, Prof. Dr. Gregory Baum/Canada, Prof. Dr. Ulrich Becker/ Deutschland; Dr. Dick Boer/Niederlande, Prof. Dr. Allan Boesak/Südafrika/USA, Prof. emer. Dr. Pamela K Brubaker/USA, Prof. Dr. Nancy Cardoso/Brasilien, Bishop Duleep de Chickera, Sri Lanka, Prof. Dr. John B. Cobb, Jr./USA, The Rev. Dr. Norma Cook Everist/USA, The Rev. Dr. Lisa E. Dahill/USA, The Rev. Dr. Susan E. Davies/USA, The Rev. Dr. Moiseraele Prince Dibeela/ Botswana, Dr. Gabriele Dietrich/ Indien, Dr. Beat Dietschy/ Schweiz, Prof. Jacob J. Erikson/USA, Dr. Christopher Ferguson, General Secretary of the World Communion of Reformed Churches/Canada/Germany, The Rev. Dr. Jerry Folk/ USA, Dr. Hartmut Futterlieb/Deutschland, Prof. The Rev. Dr. Arnfríður Guðmundsdóttir, Island, The Rev. Dr. Anna Karin Hammar/Schweden, Prof. Dr. Cees J. Hamelink/Holland, The Rev. Dr. George S Johnson/USA, The Rev. Dr. Kristin Johnston Largen/USA, Jonas Adelin Jørgensen, Generalsekretär, Dänischer Missionsrat, The Rev. Dr Jooseop Keum/Korea/Genf, Dr. René Krüger/Argentinien, Dr. Gerhard Liedke/ Deutschland, Carter Lindberg, Professor Emeritus/USA, Prof. Dr. Dr. Peter Lodberg/Dänemark, The Rev. Dr. David Lull/USA, Man Hei Yip, Ph.D. Candidate/U.S.A./ Hong Kong, The Rev. Dr. Jim Martin-Schramm/USA, Dr. Daniel F. and Dr. Jean B. Martensen/USA, Esther Menn, Ph.D./USA, Dr. Rogate Mshana/ Tanzania, Ched Myers, PhD, Bartimaeus Cooperative Ministries/USA, Prof. Dr. Harry Noormann/Germany, Prof. Dr. Park Seong-Won/Korea, The Rev. Dr. Richard J. Perry, Jr./USA, Prof. Dr. Winston Persuad/U.S.A./Guyana, Dr. Praveen PS. Perumalla/Indien, Pfr. Dr. Vincenzo Petracca/ Deutschland, Prof. Raymond Pickett/USA, The Rev. Dr. Shanta Premawardhana/USA, The Rev. Melinda Quivik, PhD/USA, Prof. J. Paul Rajashekar, U.S.A./Indien, Rev. Christopher Rajkumar/Indien, Prof. Dr. Larry Rasmussen/USA, Prof. Dr. David Rhoads/USA, Prof. Dr. Joerg Rieger/USA, Dr. Martin Robra/Deutschland/Genf, Terra Rowe, Ph.D. Candidate/USA, Prof. Dr. Barbara Rossing/USA, The Rev. Robert Saler, Ph.D./USA, Violaine and Dr. Julio de Santa Ana/Uruguay/Genf, The Rev. Dr. H. Paul Santmire/USA, Prof. Dr. Thomas H. Schattauer/USA, Prof. Dr. Franz Segbers/ Deutschland, Dr. Jirí Silný/ Tschechien, Prof. Dr. Lilia Solano/Kolumbien, Prof. Mary M. Solberg/ USA, Prof. Dr. Kirsi Stjerna/USA, Prof. Dr. Jung Mo Sung/Brasilien, The Rev. Linda Thomas, PhD/USA, Prof. Dr. Detlov Tonsing/Südafrika, Prof. Dr. StylianosTsompanidis/ Griechenland, The Rev. Dr. Alicia Vargas/USA, Prof. Dr. Mammen Varkey/Indien, Prof. Dr. Petros Vassiliadis/Griechenland, Prof. Dr. Vuyani Vellem/Südafrika, Prof. Anna Marie Vigen, Ph.D./ USA, Dr. Klausdieter Wazlawik/Deutschland, Dr. Paul A. Wee/USA, The Rev. Dr. Paul Westermeyer/USA, The Rev. Prof. Philip L. Wickeri, The Rev. Josef Purnama Widyatmadja/Indonesia, Dr. M. E. Greetje Witte-Rang/Holland, The Rev. Nancy Wright/USA.

Website: http://www.radicalizing-reformation.com/index.php/de

PREFACE TO THIS VOLUME

The international project, "Radicalizing Reformation --- Provoked by the Bible and Today's Crises" was begun earlier this decade in anticipation of 2017 (see website: www.radicalizing-reformation.com). This project aims to contribute to an international movement aimed at critical engagement with the legacy of the Reformation in light of the contemporary crises that endanger life in our times. Theses have been issued for debate engaging, criticizing, and reinterpreting the Reformation in relation to global economic injustice, violence and peacemaking, and our endangered environment. Its intent has been to explore the radical roots of what was ignited 500 years ago, in order to bring more attention to the systemic issues that must be addressed today based on both the strengths and the weaknesses of the Reformation legacy.

Various theologians from different regions of the world have met together, developed the contemporary 94 theses presented here, and written articles for a series of five volumes which were published in 2015. Each of these volumes contains articles written in either German or English. But in order to make a selection of key articles available to English-only readers, this sixth volume in the Radicalizing Reformation series has been developed. It brings together chapters from the first five volumes by those currently engaged as theologians in the North American context, together with the 94 theses and general introductory material for this overall project.

Brigitte Kahl examines the established Lutheran interpretation of justification by faith as based on an interpretation of Paul that pits law versus gospel and works versus faith. As law was identified with the Jewish Torah, this antithesis inscribed anti-Judaism into the core of Protestantism. The author shows how the law that Paul contests in Galatians is primarily Roman law, rather than Jewish Torah. Paul's focus on "in Christ" means the radical deconstruction of the imperial law with its hierarchical, competitive order. Based on the principle of *sola scriptura*, this interpretive problem has far-reaching consequences for a re-configuration of justification by faith as a theology of radical transformation, liberation, and reconciliation.

According to Paul S. Chung, Asian irregular theology (represented by second generation *minjung* theology) engages the legacy of Luther (as reinterpreted through Bonhoeffer) from the perspective of the East Asian context in dialogue with Asian religions. This entails a postcolonial reading strategy and theology as a language-event, which is being articulated by the vulnerable, fragile, and victimized—the subaltern-*minjung*. Such a reading of Luther and Bonhoeffer poses a challenge to the Western imposition of its limited theological position, as it reinterprets and contextualizes theological insights from the Lutheran tradition for the multi-religious society of East Asia through appreciation, deconstructive critique, and reconstruction.

Samuel Torvend argues that the table fellowship of Jesus is embedded in the political economy of Roman Palestine. The memory of God as Liberator of the oppressed and Defender of the poor in the context of Passover was the basis for Jesus' own practice of open and liberating table fellowship. Luther wrote that greed is a disobedient and unbelieving scoundrel, a ravenous consumption of what rightly belongs to all. The hungry poor are kept both hungry and poor. While Luther rediscovered the gift character of the Lord's Supper, subsequent reformers reduced the social and economic dimensions, insofar as they concentrated on the forgiveness of sins for individuals. Especially in the face of the disparities in the global economy, we must reclaim the Eucharist's economic, political, and social dimensions.

Cynthia Moe-Lobeda contends that Luther's doctrine of justification originates in resistance against political and cultural views that deprived people of experiencing the gift of God's unconditional love. There is urgent need to retrieve the dangerous project of Luther over against the domesticating tendencies of the dominant mode of interpreting Luther. Traditionally we recall Luther's admonition to obey the authorities but disregard his admonition to disobey them when authorities violate the command of neighbor love. The author develops an understanding of justification that takes seriously this radical inheritance. With Luther we may venture boldly into long-ignored aspects of his claims that disrupt the power alignments and ideological gods of our day.

Craig L. Nessan analyzes Luther's theological writings against the peasants, Anabaptists, and Jews as "religious identity politics." Based on his core theological commitments, Luther's ethics should have taken shape as "neighbor politics," safeguarding the rights of peasants, Anabaptists, and Jews as neighbors in need of protection. This chapter examines these cases in their historical context, including recent reinterpretation of Luther's writings against the Jews. Only by deconstructing religious identity politics can Luther's ethical framework be reconstructed in service of neighbor politics, defending the welfare of the most vulnerable in society regardless of their religious convictions.

Peter Goodwin Heltzel claims that Protestant theology must build a bridge between historical suffering and eschatological hope through a Christ-centered praxis of liberation and reconciliation. Dietrich Bonhoeffer, grounded in Lutheran theology, radicalized the Reformation by interpreting Jesus as a revolutionary, one who lived his life "for others" even unto death. Following Bonhoeffer, we also must view the great events in history "from below," from the perspective of outcast, mistreated, powerless, and oppressed persons, that is, from the perspective of those who suffer. The prophetic vision of Jesus calls us into service of racial and social justice; God's Spirit summons us toward a "new economy." This requires critique of the existing global economic order and imagination about innovative economic alternatives.

Charles Amjad-Ali observes that while the Jewish question in Luther's writings was scrutinized in response to the Holocaust, his attitude towards Islam and Muslims ("the Turks") has been almost entirely ignored. This changed after 9/11, resulting in deep antagonism towards Muslim communities, which are now the most significant minorities in the European context. Given the state of willful neglect or conscious ignorance of Islam in Lutheran scholarship, it is critical to note that Luther mentions the Turks, their religion, and the Prophet Muhammad often in his writings. Even at his most vitriolic, Luther also pays Islam the highest of compliments. Such study of Islam and Muslims is of critical importance, not only in relation to religion but also in relation to peace, just war theories, justice, human rights, and political and economic policies.

While Anabaptists made significant contributions to Christian theology in the Reformation era, Karl Koop argues that they did not develop a theological capacity for thinking positively about the material and natural world. Modern day inheritors of the Reformation do well to retrieve biblical and other pre-modern conceptual frameworks for thinking about the material and natural world, particularly in light of the challenges facing modern civilization—the desecration of land, water, and air, and the consumption of resources. Such retrievals would be in keeping with the spirit of the Reformation itself, which initially called for faithfulness to the Biblical witness, the Christian tradition, and the importance of addressing the pressing issues of the times.

Wanda Deifelt notes that although Martin Luther never developed a political theory, his theology does insist that Christians live in society both publicly and politically. Luther's "two kingdoms theory" has often been misinterpreted to justify passivity and obedience to civil authorities. Christians are called to live not for themselves but in Christ and for their neighbors. Heterotopic citizenship involves political participation and advocacy, based on genuine concern for the wellbeing of others. A Lutheran contribution to citizenship is to reclaim the role of service and calling, informing us about the needs of the neighbor and compelling us to think about our role in the world in light of the gospel. Citizenship is not reduced to individual rights or obligations but is a form of Christian service. By serving the other as neighbor, we are also serving Christ.

Vitor Westhelle claims that for Luther the priesthood of all believers is the reformatory signature. While the implications for ecclesiology are immense and recognized, the political impact has not been appropriated. The church stands squarely in the in-between spaces where life is produced and reproduced, the space of political life, human communication, and policy making. In the "third space" of the church, God works through preaching, consoling, and admonishing. Church happens as God speaks; Luther called it *creatura evangelii*, the creature not of our doing and making, but of God's good word. Moreover, Luther adds another external sign: the cross, as endurance of suffering in the midst of trial. This is the cross we carry between the house and the street, risking exposure by speaking publicly and offering sanctuary as an expression of holy love.

Karen L. Bloomquist proposes that church be seen today as intentionally nurturing resistance practices, that are resonant with the Bible, and familiar in the history and practices of the church. Such practices are both transparent to those who have been formed by the church as well as inviting to those with no interest or involvement in the church. The implications of Luther's theology of the cross needs to be pursued, for the sake of forming an *ekklesia* that becomes transformative, by being subversive of the injustice, empire, and domination of many kinds that hold the world captive today. "Seeing, remembering, and connecting" are key practices through which *ecclesia crucis* for the sake of the world emerges, in ways that collaborate across boundaries of religion, geography and self-interest.

We hope that these challenging contributions will bring in new insights and provoke praxis for confronting pervasive systemic injustices – such as economic inequality, polarization, xenophobia, violence, and destruction of creation – as we move beyond the 500th anniversary of the Reformation in 2017 and continue the radical protest evoked by Luther.

Karen L. Bloomquist

Craig L. Nessan

Easter 2016

A GUIDE FOR DISCUSSION IN YOUR CONTEXT

(includes summaries of the 94 theses)

"You shall proclaim liberation throughout the land" (Lev. 25:10)

Martin Luther began his 95 Theses of 1517 with Jesus' call for repentance as a change of mind and direction: "Return, the just world of God has come near!" Five hundred years later is also a time that brings to mind the biblical "Jubilee Year" (Lev 25), calling for repentance and conversion toward a more just society. For us today, this is not in opposition to the Catholic Church and the many liberation movements rooted there, but in opposition to the realities of empire that rule.

As we hear the testimony of the cross (1 Cor 1:18) and the groaning of the abused creation (Rom 8:22) and as we actively hear the cries of those victimized by our world (dis-)order driven by hyper-capitalism – only then can we turn this Reformation commemoration into a liberating jubilee. Christian self-righteousness, supporting the dominating system, is in contradiction to faith-righteousness as proclaimed by the Reformation. This must be lived out through just, all-inclusive solidarity. The present moment of crisis that we currently face across the globe on all levels is a time to recognize the predatory and destructive forces inherent in what is dominating our world today, in order to reorient ourselves in hope towards a new culture of life.

The rampant destruction of human and non-human life in a world ruled by the totalitarian dictatorship of money and greed, market and exploitation requires a radical re-orientation towards the biblical message, which also marked the beginning of the Reformation. The dominant economic system and its imperial structures and policies have put the earth, human communities, and the future of our children up for sale. Our churches, congregations, and individual Christians have often become complacent and complicit with the established status quo and have lost their critical-prophetic power to protest, resist, and change what is occurring. God's justification by grace has been detached from social justice and thus serves as "useless salt" (Mt 5:13). Because the Reformation legacy has gone astray, we must at the same time return to some of Luther's thought and legacy, as well as standing decidedly against other things he said and did, if this is to become a kairoitic time of transformation today.

"For liberation the Messiah has liberated us" (Gal 5:1) (theses 1-4):

Christ brings liberation from what St. Paul, who lived in the context of the Roman Empire, refers to as the "terrorizing domination of sin." (Rom 5:12-8:2). When justification is not understood according to the pattern of the Exodus but reduced only to individual guilt and forgiveness, it is seriously cut off from the wide social and political richness of the biblical context. This domination of sin holds all people captive as a master over slaves and thus makes them collaborators in the imperial system and laws.

Paul directs his hope towards God's final intervention, which for him has already begun with Jesus' resurrection. Christ alone is Lord (Kyrios). Liberation in Christ affects the whole human being, all people, and the whole creation. Through faith we live a new life as liberated people.

How does this empower us who live under economic and/or political domination today?

"You cannot serve both God and Mammon" (Mt 6:24) (theses 5-23)

The rule of capital is today's expression of Mammon, and thus the central challenge of faith. Already in the 16th century Luther called Mammon "the most common god on earth" (Large Catechism, Explanation of the First Commandment).

This rule of money together with theological opposition to it developed historically with the expansion of an economy based on money and private ownership. Since the time of the Reformation, the contemporary globalized capitalism of modernity has been manifest in European exploitation, colonization, and genocide in Africa, Asia, and the Americas. This continues today in widespread land grabs, in the privatization of the genetic commons of humanity, and through the privatization of land, water, and air.

What are examples of this in your context?

In Scripture, property is intended for furthering life and the common good of all. Human beings are created by God with the mission "to serve and keep the garden" (Gen 2:15). Instead today private property has become absolute and individualism prevails. The capitalist economy drives unlimited growth which endangers all life on our planet. In contrast. the Bible establishes a political economy of "enough for all" based on sharing what is given for the common good of all (Exod 16). In our time, we are not calling for a return to the historical forms of socialism that have had some effects as destructive as capitalism, but instead for forms of economic life that build on God's gifts, protect the commons, and produce and distribute goods and services in ways that are both democratic and ecologically sensitive.

For Luther, either people are determined by God – so that they live compassionately and righteously in relation to others -- or they are determined by the power of sin, living distorted, self-centered, competitive lives that destroy other creatures. By trusting in the liberating righteousness of God, we break free from the destructive role of money and are empowered to live in compassionate solidarity with other humans and the rest of creation. Forgiveness of sins by grace, deliverance from the power of the devil, and the promise of eternal life in this context meant not only spiritual freedom but freedom for reconciliation with and ethical responsibility to the neighbor.

Rather than viewing salvation only in spiritualized or individualist ways, both the Bible and Luther speak of free persons in just relationships. Reading biblical texts individualistically supports capitalist-based assumptions today. According to Jesus, those who are just forgive debts for the sake of those indebted, rather than abiding by rules of debt repayment (Mt 6:12). Paul proposes building alternative communities of Jews and Greeks who live in solidarity in the spirit of the Messiah who was crucified by the Empire.

The majority of Church Fathers interpreted the death of Jesus on the Cross in terms of a ransom theory. The devil, who never forgives debts, demands ransom for the liberation of humankind. Christ exposes this and thus frees us. Anselm of Canterbury (1033-1109) turns this upside down in his satisfaction theory. According to him the law of debt-repayment stands higher than God. This is why God must sacrifice his son in order to establish a storehouse of merits, which people can draw on in order to pay off their debts. This not only lays the ground for the medieval penitential system, which Luther rejects, but also for capitalism's law of debt repayment. Luther returns to the biblical truth that God forgives with no exceptions, and out of this forgiveness grows the trust that grounds solidarity with the neighbor, including interest-free lending or giving and the intervention of the government when public welfare is endangered.

According to Scripture, people are justified by grace and not by their performance. While for Luther, justification by grace alone expressed an understanding of equality, the Reformation failed to make this concrete socially and economically. In fact, later Lutheranism even turned social and economic inequality into a hierarchical God-given order! This culminated in asserting the autonomy of the market and/or the state, which both Scripture and Luther explicitly critique.

How do you especially experience these tensions or conflicts?

Because of their effect on the common people of his day, Luther said a clear "No!" to the structure and practices of the banking and trading companies of his time. Today the forces of economic growth, monetary expansion, and privatization threaten planetary death. In this regard, long-term alternatives to the neoliberal capitalist system are needed and possible. This new order takes root in local communities, in cooperation with others in civil society.

"The message of the cross...is the power of God" (1 Cor 1:18) (theses 24–32)

Since the Middle Ages, many have understand Jesus' death as God "sacrificing his son" in order to save human beings. This interpretation turns God into a sadistic ruler who produces suffering. However, God saves from violence, not through violence. The cross was the Roman Empire's instrument to execute rebels and fugitive slaves. Many innocent people became victims of this public demonstration of power, as illustrated here. The crucified Jesus is deeply connected to them.

Theology of the cross can overcome a previous tainting imagery between the cross and crusade in colonial times the encounter with the risen Christ sheds new light on the cross (Luke 24). In the light of the resurrection, Jesus is written into the lamentations of traumatized people, giving them hope (Ps 22:2; Mk 16:34, Ps 22:26). The resurrection is decisive judgment against the powers of violence, the most radical implementation of God's unconditional solidarity with all suffering creatures and an expression of God's faithfulness and justice toward all people and creation.

The Reformation teaching of justification should break through Western possessive individualism and political quietism, liberating human beings from all the idolatrous assumptions, upon which we base our lives: the privileges of species, sex, gender, ethnicity, religion, nationality, and class. Justification should be reclaimed as a way of expressing God's deep compassion in the death of Jesus Christ for all, reinforcing our public responsibility for the political realm, economic justice, and recognition of the Other.

What implications do these meanings of the cross and resurrection have in your context?

"See, everything has become new" (2 Cor 5:17) (theses 33-46):

The Christian gospel is indeed about reconciliation between God and humanity, and about reconciliation between human beings. But if "gospel" does not succeed in reconciling the whole of creation, it is not the gospel (2 Co 5:18). God's gracious presence is in all creation, responding to its cries (Rom 8:18-23). All of life is divinely infused; the whole world is a sacramental reality. As followers of Christ we too are called into communion with the world – a this-worldly faith that is made real when we join in God's mission for the renewal of all creation.

Mother Earth is being crucified and has to experience resurrection (Rom 8:22). We are human beings not because we consume, but because we need to live connected to and caring for all creation.. "The Gospel of all creatures" (Mark 16:15, according to Luther's translation) is interrupted if human beings destroy or are unjust toward creation. We are to preserve creation as God's garden through a righteous personal stance and through new economic, social, and ecological politics for the welfare of the entire creation and all peoples of the world. This includes how children and their future are seen and treated.

"Life in fullness" (John 10:10) breaks with previous concepts of economic development. It does not aim at "having more," as in accumulation and growth, but in living toward balance in all relationships. An unfinished task of Reformation theology is to fight for and proclaim the right for life in fullness for the whole creation.

How is creation especially being abused in your context? How are you addressing this?

"Blessed are the peacemakers" (Mt 5:9) (theses 47-57):

Hear the cries of those who have suffered violence, especially those made victims by followers of the Reformation – such as peasants, Anabaptists (Mennonites), Jews, Muslims! Hear the cries of those suffering violence today – whether through domestic abuse, economic exploitation, violations of human rights, injustice against creation, state imperialism, and ongoing wars!

All violence is in reaction to previous forms of violence -- – structural violence, technological violence, military violence, physical and psychological violence of every kind. The universality of violence becomes evident in the practice of identifying others as "enemies," making them into scapegoats (Acts 7:54-60).

Violence is always illegitimate; it can never serve as a means for attaining any goal. There is no "measured" violence, no "just" war," no "justifiable" war. Enforcing the law cannot rest upon violence. Legal systems must be judged against the yardstick of bringing peace through justice. Wherever humans suffer violence, they are to be protected by practices of peacemaking.

Practicing peace means living, speaking, and acting without violence, and doing that which promotes peace.

The way of peacemaking, as embodied by Jesus, joins God's nonviolent praxis with the cause of all those who practice nonviolence, which is a sign of God's reign of shalom (Isaiah 11:6-9).

What does this call for in your setting? In relation to others in the world?

"Bear one another's burdens, and in this way you will fulfill the Torah of Christ" (Gal 6:2) (theses 58–76):

The Reformation originates with Luther's rediscovery of God's justice as creative and renewing power. For Paul, the justice of God implies that "in Christ" the polarities and hierarchies of this "present evil world order" (Gal 1:4) have been overcome. "We" are not what segregates us from the "others" but what interconnects us with them. The human divisions of nation, religion, gender, and class, which constitute the "self" as enemy and rival of the "other," are removed in baptism "like old garments." God's justice, the justification of the human being, and human justice are all inseparably connected.

Luther regularly juxtaposes "justice/righteousness through the law" with "justice/righteousness through faith" and on this basis (in Galatians) sees an irreconcilable polarity of Judaism against Christianity. The negative classification of Judaism and law also has become a major factor in the fundamental downgrading of the whole Old Testament. Luther falsely identifies the law that Paul criticizes with the Jewish Torah, rather than with the law and order imposed by the Roman Empire. Paul's community model of solidarity between Jews and non-Jews "in Christ" clashes in the first place with these imperial settings and social norms, and with Roman emperor religion.

Furthermore, Judaism was connected with Roman Catholicism, both being accused of being "legalistic religions" that achieve "justice/righteousness through works of the law." The polarity of "works versus grace/faith" and "gospel versus law" has had disastrous impacts, not only used against Jews and Catholics but also against "enthusiasts," Anabaptists, Muslims, and other "heretics." In our days, liberation theologies, feminist theologies, and social movements are often accused of "work righteousness." Justification theology and this-worldly justice are played off against each other.

The core of the Protestant tradition is compromised by defining its identity against the "other" – who acts, believes, lives, or thinks differently – rather than in line with Paul's radical solidarity with others across boundaries and separations. The Messiah Jesus of Nazareth is the invitation to all peoples to participate in the future that has been promised to Israel: a just and equal society inspired by the Torah. The Christian church is not the replacement of Judaism, which is at the root of the church (Rom 11:18).

In the horizon of hope in the coming of God's just world, the Messiah Jesus interprets the Torah of Israel in the context of his time (Mt 5-7) – worship of God alone and the love of the neighbor, especially those who are poor and disinherited (Mk 12:28-34). The Torah orients the messianic communities (Mt 5:17-20; 28:19-20; see also Rom 3:31). For Paul, imperial power structures embody the power of sin that inevitably turns people into transgressors of the life-giving laws of Torah and makes them complicit with the forces of death and self-destruction (Rom 7:24). Paul's justification by grace through faith thus implies a two-fold liberation of both human beings and of Torah from the power of sin.

How does this challenge common understandings of the Torah and the Old Testament in your context?

Legal rules and law in societies are necessary in order to sustain human societies. But the law must not be misused by the strong against the weak. Human legislation must always be examined critically and continuously adjusted, instead of "legally" covering up the injustice of the dominant order. Torah is an alternative law that moves away from the exploitative legislation of its environment, and must not be identified with "natural law" or existing legal codes.

In his Small Catechism Luther dropped the politically concrete preamble of the Decalogue: "I am the Lord your God who brought you out of the land of Egypt, out of the house of slavery" (Ex 20:2; Deut. 5:6). Luther also extended the command to honor one's parents to honor authorities as such. These are two symptoms of how subsequent Lutheranism became prone to obedience and subservience towards any established order, including when severely unjust, instead of being faithful to the God of liberation (sola fide). When the established order lacks righteous action and remains indifferent to the concerns of the common people, especially to the least (Mt 25:31-40), Christians should not only disobey but also resist the death-bound logic and laws of violent, enslaving powers.

Today, a new "revival" is needed of cutting-edge Bible study in our congregations that engages not only individuals but also the current social and economic problems in critical and liberating ways. We also must engage sacred texts of other traditions, so as to dialogue with and build a better world together with Jews, Muslims, Hindus, Buddhists, and every other religion and culture from Africa, North America, Latin America, the

Caribbean, Asia, the Pacific, the Middle East and Europe. Postcolonial readings of Reformation theology advance enculturation, in order to underpin inter-religious dialogue as prophetic dialogue.

"The Spirit blows where it wills" (John 3:8) (theses 77–94):

The Reformation understood the church not so much as an institution, but as the baptized people of God gathered in local communities -- a holy space in which the universal Word of God is listened to and the sacraments celebrated in many different voices, traditions, and confessions for the sake of the mending of the world (*tikkun olam*). The priesthood of all believers was a radical cry for democratizing the most powerful institution of the 16th century, but the churches of the Reformation soon became enmeshed again with structures and practices that are patriarchal, hierarchical, and captive to powerful economic and political interests.

Today, the Spirit of God impels movement toward more participatory, boundary-crossing embodiments of church that are truly catholic, inclusive of all, and collaborative across boundaries of religion, ethnicity, geography, and self-interest. The Spirit enables believers to struggle alongside those of other religions, ideologies, and social movements, and to endure suffering caused by this commitment to love, solidarity, and justice.

When Luther called the cross a mark or sign of the church, he was establishing a criterion: to be the church, the church needs to become vulnerable by being with and for the poor and to risk its social or political status by publicly protesting against unjust structures and policies. The church must adopt a critical communal focus for resistance and transformation. Otherwise, injustices continue to have free reign, distorting our most basic relationships to God, ourselves, one another, and the whole of creation. While fostering renewal and change, the Spirit also draws people together into the unity of the body of Christ, which cannot be used to justify further church divisions. May all come to celebrate at the Lord's Table together!

A reforming church continually is being transformed by what it receives from other theological traditions and cultures. In emphasizing how the Spirit is linked to the Word, Luther was criticizing anyone claiming to have received special revelations by the Spirit, but this must not be misinterpreted as limiting the Spirit's free work in people, including those of other traditions or religions, as well as in the rest of creation (Rom 8:22-23). His critiques of enthusiasts must not be transferred to our times as a generalized critique of all Pentecostalism today.

The rediscovery and critical re-reading of biblical traditions from the perspective of the marginalized is an important sign of hope that the liberating hermeneutics of the Reformation traditions are active in many churches today. In many places instead, individualistic spiritualities and religious fundamentalisms, which collude with powerful interests and perpetuate illusions, are on the increase. Recovering the crucial role of biblical theology and critical theological education (together with education in general) is key to the ongoing reformation and renewal needed within global Christianity in the 21st century.

Blessed are those who do not fit into the systems of this world, but who stand in protest of God's continued crucifixion in the schemes of this world (Rom 12: 2) and who cooperate with others in building a new world with justice and peace in human communities! As with Martin Luther, we need a renewal of language and a return to the liberating message of the Gospel, lest churches be alienated from the realities of the actual world in which people live. We need a "New Reformation!"

How will you pursue this?

Paul and the Law in Galatians: Roman Nomos or Jewish Torah?

Brigitte Kahl

1. Justification Theology and "Sola Scriptura" – statement of a problem

Written in the middle of the first century CE and antedating the letter to the Romans, the Epistle to the Galatians represents the "magna charta" of justification theology in its shortest and sharpest version. No other letter of Paul is so belligerent, categorical and uncompromising in wrestling with what Paul sees as the truth and perseverance of the gospel as such (Gal 2:5.14). Nowhere else are Pauline congregations exposed to as a harsh criticism. This includes a double curse of anathema that is hurled right at the beginning (Gal 1:9-9) against Paul's opponents and their "other gospel." As the first church historian (Gal 1-2), tracing the early developments of the Jesus movement from 33-50 CE, Paul indicates that this was a period of continual deep-reaching clashes regarding the focal issue of faith.

One and a half millennia later, in his momentous battle with the medieval church, Martin Luther could see himself mirrored and affirmed in this Pauline conflict setting. With its unbending truth claim and as biblical paradigm of protest, the letter to the Galatians has become the theological witness, authoritative endorsement and prophetic inspiration of the Reformation. Martin Luther declared it "his letter" to which he had entrusted himself as his "Katie von Bora."[1] Melanchthon saw it as "Theseus's thread in the labyrinth of New Testament exegesis."[2]

1 "...mein epistelcha, der ich mir vertraut habe," WA,TR 1,146. (The German term "vertraut" has the double meaning of "trust" and "marriage.")

2 WA 2,437.

Martin Luther exegeted Galatians two times in lectures (1516/17 and 1531) that were published as commentaries in 1519/23 and 1535.[3] This coincides with the beginning and the crucial years of the Reformation. The problem we are focused on here is not so much Luther's interpretation of Galatians, however, rather the subsequent relationship that evolved between scripture and tradition in Protestantism.[4] If during the Reformation Galatians became a "material force" that took hold of the masses and changed a society, what does this mean for the prevalent readings of Galatians in contemporary Lutheranism and beyond? Protestant and specifically Lutheran interpretations today have become widely synonymous with a "conservative Paul." Justification theology is claimed as the "mighty fortress" of an embattled faith that has been deserted elsewhere. Yet it fails to develop the spiritual power and to grasp the congregations as it did during the Reformation, nor is it anywhere close to becoming an inspirational or material force outside of organized churches.[5] In this way justification theology today appears as somewhat "un-Lutheran," no matter how firmly it sticks to the letter of Lutheran doctrine.

Of course, appealing to "the masses" is not a criterion of truth. Nonetheless, five hundred years after Luther might be time for Lutheran tradition to be tested anew against its own truth criterion of "scripture alone," most nota-

3 WA 2,436-618; WA 40,1-2,184.

4 For Luther, the foundational Protestant antithesis of scripture versus tradition did not mean complete departure from all tradition, e.g. early church credal statements that Luther took for granted, rather the necessity to submit all human tradition to the normative control and critique of "scripture alone" (*sola scriptura*) as the supreme authority and word. This critique of "tradition" applied particularly to the institutional and interpretation authority of the papal church; cf. Hans- Martin Barth, *Die Theologie Martin Luthers . Eine kritische Würdigung*, Gütersloh 2009, 142-43.

5 On the other hand, there are some most stimulating debates about Paul (most notably the letter to the Romans) today that are happening entirely outside of churches and theology among the philosophers; cf. Giorgio Agamben, *The Time that Remains. A Commentary on the Letter to the Romans*, Stanford 2005; Jacob Taubes, *The Political Theology of Paul. Cultural Memory in the Present*, Stanford 2004; Alain Badiou, *Saint Paul: The Foundation of Universalism*, Stanford 2003.

bly Pauline scripture.[6] This implies not only listening to the outcry and moaning of common people who are suffering around the globe[7] but also to the groaning of the oppressed creation and all of its non-human components (Rom 8:22-23). However, some of the most ground-breaking impulses for Pauline interpretation emerging from New Testament Studies over the past fifty years so far have not reached the congregational level or even academic theological discourse. While "justification by grace through faith" is widely and productively re-examined from global, liberationist, feminist, womanist, mujerista and queer perspectives, or the relationship of faith and love in Luther's theology by the Finnish Mannermaa-School, all these innovative approaches usually sidestep the New Testament (con-) text.[8] It seems that the synthesis of biblical and systematic-theological work that once was foundational for the Reformation, today has been widely replaced by mono-disciplinary provincialism. A conversation between scriptural and theological disciplines is urgently needed as a reformatory bridge-building between "church and world," academia and pews.

6 As Luther explains in his introduction to the letter of James, the criterion of scriptural critique is Christ alone ("*was Christum treibet*"). This criterion is not only applied to tradition but also to scripture itself, which is the reason why Luther refuses to recognize James as "apostolic" (cf. WA, DB 7,385). If Luther vehemently insists that even Peter and Paul (apart from James) have to submit to this scripture-based critique of "Christ alone," then this undoubtedly also applies to the Protestant tradition post-Luther.

7 cf. Luther's claim that a translator and interpreter of the Bible had to listen carefully to the language of the common people ("*dem Volk aufs Maul schauen*") ; WA 30,2,637.

8 For an introduction to "new" readings of Luther see e.g. Walter Altmann, *Luther and Liberation, A Latin American Perspective*, Minneapolis 1992; Carl E. Braaten, *Union with Christ. The New Finnish Interpretation of Luther*, Grand Rapids 1998; Paul S. Chung, Ulrich Duchrow, Craig L. Nessan, *Liberating Lutheran Theology. Freedom for Justice and Solidarity with Others in a Global Context*, Minneapolis/Geneva 2011; Sun-young Kim, *Luther on Faith and Love: Christ and the Law in the 1535 Galatians Commentary*, Minneapolis 2014; Tuomo Mannermaa, *Two Kinds of Love. Martin Luther's Religious World* (transl./ ed. Kirsi I. Stjerna), Minneapolis 2010; Mary J. Streufert (ed.), *Transformative Lutheran Theologies. Feminist, Womanist, and Mujerista Perspectives*, Minneapolis 2010.

Since the end of the 1960s the traditional perception of Paul has been profoundly challenged by post-Holocaust, feminist, liberationist, empire-critical, post-colonial and secular philosophical approaches. For example, Krister Stendahl, E.P. Sanders, James Dunn, Dieter Georgi, Jacob Taubes, Elsa Tamez, Richard Horsley, Neil Elliott, Luise Schottroff, Franz Hinkelammert and many others, although with different readings and presuppositions, together mark a fundamental paradigm shift in Pauline interpretation. A few examples highlight the nature of this:

- Paul as the Christian is morphed into Paul the Jew.[9]

-Paul as the spokesperson of misogyny and homophobia (e.g. 1 Cor 14:34; Rom 1:26-27) reveals an unexpected penchant for emancipatory, gender-bending and even trans-identitarian moves (Gal 3:28;4:19).[10]

-The Pauline terms of "faith and grace" and "works and law," previously understood in exclusively religious and individualistic ways, get socio-economic-political grounding when historically contextualized within the Roman empire. Anti-Judaism as the all-pervasive feature of established Pauline interpretation gives way to anti-imperial readings.[11]

[9] For the "New Perspective" see e.g. James D.G. Dunn, *The New Perspective on Paul*. Collected Essays, WUNT 185, Tűbingen 2005; N.T. Wright, *Paul: In Fresh Perspective*, Minneapolis 2005; for Jewish re-readings of Paul in particular see e.g. Daniel Boyarin, *A Radical Jew. Paul and the Politics of Identity*, Berkeley 1994; Mark Nanos, *The Irony of Galatians. Paul's Letter in First-Century Context*, Minneapolis 2002; Pamela Eisenbaum, *Paul was not a Christian. The Original Message of a Misunderstood Apostle*, New York 2009.

[10] For feminist readings see e.g. Kathy Ehrensperger, That we May be Mutually Encouraged. Feminism and the New Perspective in Pauline Studies, New York 2004; Claudia Janssen, Luise Schottroff, Beate Wehn (Hg.), Paulus. Umstrittene Traditionen – Lebendige Theologie. Eine feministische Lektűre, Gűtersloh 2001; Brigitte Kahl, "Gender Trouble in Galatia? Paul and the Rethinking of Difference." In: Is there a Future for Feminist Theology? (ed. Deborah F. Sawyer and Diane M.Collier, 57-73), Sheffield 1999; id., "No longer Male: Masculinity Struggles behind Gal 3:28?" JSNT 70 (2000), 37-49; Davina Lopez, Apostle to the Conquered. Reimagining Paul's Mission, Minneapolis 2008.

[11] For a basic introduction to empire-critical approaches to Paul see Richard A. Horsley (ed.), Paul and Empire. Religion and Power in Roman Imperial Society, Harrisburg

-Paul, the allegedly conformist and conservative theologian of unconditional state obedience (Rom 13), actually had to renegotiate his position between the polar opposites of radical dissidence and accommodation.[12]

-The Paul of Galatians, previously the uncontested founder of Christian world mission and of Christianity as a pro-Roman, anti-Jewish universal religion, now is seen as providing the basis for a non-conformist Jewish-messianic alliance of nations "from below," for a new type of global horizontal solidarity that challenges the boundary markers and hierarchies of empire;[13]

- "Green" readings of Paul have emerged.[14]

Most of these new approaches, however, tend to bypass the doctrine of justification, perhaps because it has been seen as part of the problem rather than a potential solution. Already Albert Schweitzer as one of the most interesting Pauline interpreters of the 20th century had profoundly distrusted justification theology because of its purported irrelevance for ethical questions, declaring it as a mere "subsidiary crater" of Pauline theology.[15] Considering the history of interpretation that consistently has pitted "faith" against "works," this suspicion is plausible. Nonetheless, from a scriptural perspective, the de-

1997; Id., (ed.), Paul and Politics. Ekklesia, Israel, Imperium, Interpretation. Essays in Honor of Krister Stendahl, Harrisburg 2000; Neil Elliott, Liberating Paul. The Justice of God and the Politics of the Apostle, Maryknoll 1994; Dieter Georgi, Remembering the Poor: The History of Paul's Collection for Jerusalem, Nashville 1992; for a broad collection of post-colonial approaches see Christopher Stanley (ed.), The Colonized Apostle. Paul through Postcolonial Eyes. Minneapolis 2011. For a post-colonial reading of Galatians from an African perspective see Aliou C. Niang, Faith and Freedom in Galatia and Senegal. The Apostle Paul, Colonists and Sending Gods, Leiden 2009.

12 A first major and ground-breaking empire-critical commentary on Romans appeared in the prestigious Hermeneia-Series: Robert Jewett, *Romans. A Commentary*, Minneapolis 2007.

13 Brigitte Kahl, Galatians Re-Imagined: Reading with the Eyes of the Vanquished, Paul in Critical Contexts, Minneapolis 2010.

14 David G. Horrell, Cheryl Hunt, Christopher Southgate (Hg.), *Greening Paul: Rereading the Apostle in a Time of Ecological Crisis*, Waco 2010.

15 Albert Schweitzer, *The Mysticism of Paul the Apostle*, London 1931, 225.

ethicized , individualized and de-politicized understanding of justification in Paul needs to be fundamentally questioned – a task the Latin-American New Testament scholar and liberation theologian Elsa Tamez took on in her pioneering study of Romans.[16]

Thus, the lead question here can be framed: In light of the present ecological and economic survival crisis of humanity, is there a way to retrieve Paul's justification theology from within its own historical and scriptural context as a theology of radical transformation? Can it again, as in the time of Reformation, challenge the power of the established order, and announce that "another world is possible?"

This takes us back to Galatians. At the core of this letter is the clash between the two mutually exclusive demands of "foreskin versus circumcision." Luther has seamlessly translated this conflict into his own combat scenario of "Wittenberg versus Rome." In developing his justification theology from this "double context," he blended the first century setting of Galatia with his own sixteenth century framework. If we follow this analogy, what would be the biblically and historically adequate parallel of the Galatian circumcision controversy with today's conflicts and challenges? Justification by faith and grace as the "article with which the church stands and falls" (*articulus stantis aut cadentis ecclesiae)*[17] today "stands and falls" with this very concrete scriptural question. This requires us, five hundred years after Luther, to venture anew into an exegetical exploration of his most favorite letter.[18]

[16] Elsa Tamez, *The Amnesty of Grace*, Nashville 1993; for a reading of Galatians from the perspective of liberation theology see also Néstor Oscar Míguez, "Galatians", in *Global Bible Commentary*, edited by Daniel Patte, Nashville 2004, 463-472.

[17] WA 40/3, 352,3.

[18] For a condensed introduction into the exegesis and history of interpretation of Galatians, as well as a broad range of potential re-interpretations of Galatian justification theology in contemporary conflicts (HIV/Aids, political reconciliation and conflict-resolution, inter-religious dialogue, economic justice, queer readings, disability, ecology) see Brigitte Kahl, "Galatians", in *The New Testament: Fortress Commentary on the Bible*, edited by Margaret Aymer, Cynthia Briggs Kittredge, David A. Sánchez, Minneapolis 2014, 503-525.

2. Law versus Gospel: Luther's reading of Paul

> We ourselves are Jews by birth and not Gentile sinners; yet we know that a person is justified not by the works of the law but through faith in Jesus Christ. And we have come to believe in Christ Jesus, so that we might be justified by faith in Christ, and not by doing the works of the law, because no one will be justified by the works of the law. (Gal 2:15-16)

Works of the Law versus Faith in Jesus Christ: No less than three times this polarity is highlighted within one single verse in Gal 2:16. Such an emphasis and unconditional either-or stands out in the text. Galatians 2:15-21 and Romans 3:21-31 are the two classic Pauline statements on justification theology. From Paul, Martin Luther took over the strict polemical bi-polarity of this phrase; both the strength and the *crux* of Reformation theology are condensed into a nutshell. The "faith alone" ("sola fide") for Luther is so focal that it cannot coexist with anything opposite and different. This is why he added this "alone" in his German translation of Romans 3:28, although it is not contained in the Greek text. Gospel stands in irreconcilable opposition to law, or faith (or grace) "alone" against works, and faith justification against work righteousness.[19]

Luther is an excellent exegete and this heightened antithesis of gospel versus law (which became the signature formula of the Reformation) indeed renders the letter and spirit of the Galatian controversy with textual and hermeneutical precision. But what is at stake here for Paul in his original encounter with the Galatians? Historically speaking, in Galatians 2:16 the theological polarity of faith righteousness versus law righteousness is located within the framework of a twofold dispute. On the one hand, Paul reported on what had been a violent clash regarding the practice of Jewish-Gentile table community in Antioch, where he had a particularly heated collision

[19] In his "Sendbrief vom Dolmetschen" (Open Letter on Translating) of 1530 Luther rejected the notion that the addition of *sola/allein* in his German translation of Rom 3:28 (…dass der Mensch gerecht wird ohne des Gesetzes Werke, *allein* durch den Glauben/through faith *alone*) is not "scriptural" with humor and stinging irony, as well as with brilliance in terms of translation science. (WA 30, 2, 632-646).

with Peter (Gal 2:11-14). On the other hand, and within the overall context of the Galatian letter, the key topic is the demand to have non-Jewish/Gentile men in the Galatian communities circumcised so that they might gain full status as Jews and proselytes. (Gal 2:3-5; 5:3; 6:12) This is the reason why Paul writes to the Galatians.

Although these two controversies about table community and circumcision might appear very different, for Paul they are theologically connected through the same threat they pose to the "truth of the gospel"– faith in Christ and justification through grace – the core theme of the letter.[20] In particular the concept of "grace" is for Paul so important that he adds it throughout his letters in the greeting formula: *Grace to you and peace*... (e.g. Gal 1:3). This modifies both the customary ancient letter-head and the traditional Jewish peace-greeting. It is *grace* that is in danger of being erased by a righteousness based on law and works (Gal 2:16.21), both in Antioch and Galatia. Paul sees this as annulling the life-giving power of the cross, as rejecting the liberating love and Self-giving of the Messiah/Christ "for us" (Gal 2:20-21; 1:4). It means non-acceptance of God's grace and empties the messianic

[20] The terms gospel and gospel-proclamation (*euangelion/euangelizomai*) appear no less than 13 times in Gal 1:6-2:14, which makes for the highest density of this terminology in the entire New Testament. The two chapters Gal 1-2 contain a summary statement as to what "gospel" means for Paul – and what it doesn't mean. Starting with a strong rejection of the "other gospel (of circumcision) that is not another one" (Gal 1:6-9), Paul moves to the apocalyptic call at Damascus to proclaim the gospel of the Messiah/Christ among non-Jews/Gentiles (Gal 1:11.16.23). This results in *two* differing gospels – the Pauline "gospel of foreskin" and the Petrine "gospel of circumcision" (Gal 2:7) that at first clash and then reconcile at Jerusalem (2:4-5.9-10). In this reconciliation ("right hand of fellowship," Gal 2:9) *both* gospels despite their difference are recognized as co-existent and equally legitimate proclamation of the *one* gospel of Christ. This coexistence and community-in-difference Paul sees breaking apart in Antioch when the established table community between circumcised and uncircumcised is revoked (Gal 2:11-14); he thus accuses Peter and his followers of betraying the "truth of the gospel." (Gal 2:14) This "truth of the gospel" then is the topic of the immediately following statement on justification by faith rather than by works of the law. (Gal 2:15-21) It is further elaborated in chapters 3-6. For the overall argument see Kahl, "Galatians," 503-525.

Christ-faith of its most crucial content, namely a new existence of no longer living as/for myself. (Gal 2:20)

This short summary of Gal 2:15-21 contains the entire theological "grammar" that structures justification theology for Paul as well as for Martin Luther. It is condensed in two strictly antithetical strings of terms that mutually interpret each other:

(I) Circumcision=Law=(Law-)Works=Justification/Righteousness through Works

versus

(II) Foreskin=Gospel/Christ=Grace/Faith=Justification/ Righteousness through Faith.

The problem of justification theology is not in this antithesis as such. Rather this begins when it is applied contextually to specific groups of people. This is as much an exegetical as it is a theological and ethical problem. It starts already in the New Testament. Circumcision was so obviously a marker of Judaism, that the "law" attached to it almost inevitably was identified as Jewish Torah. Thus the "opponents" of Paul, although incognito in the letter itself, automatically were defined as Jewish or Jewish-Christian, merely because of this circumcision requirement. Conversely, "gospel" and non-circumcision/foreskin were labeled as "Christian." Thus the antithesis of Christianity versus Judaism was firmly anchored at the core of justification theology.[21]

(I) Circumcision=Law=(Law-)Works=Justification/Righteousness through Works= JUDAISM

versus

(II) Foreskin=Gospel/Christ=Grace/Faith=Justification/Righteousness through Faith= CHRISTIANITY.

This structured within justification by faith an enemy construct that in its anti-Judaistic oppositonal pattern persisted throughout the centuries and

[21] For the overall problem see e.g. Peter von der Osten-Sacken, *Martin Luther und die Juden. Neu untersucht anhand von Anton Margarithas* "Der gantz Jüdisch glaub" (1530/31), Stuttgart 2002.

eventually became one of the sources of the *Shoah.* At the same time, this enemy construct developed a surprising and often spooky adaptability to changing historical configurations. As Luther himself exemplifies, "Judaism" (as the supposedly anti-Pauline position rejected in Galatians) could be transferred with stunning swiftness to Catholics, Anabaptists, "enthusiasts," Turks and Muslims – all of them in different but similar ways guilty of "work righteousness." In the introduction to his Commentary on Galatians (1535), Luther asserts that all who don't submit to the doctrine of justification are "fanatical spirits" and "Jews or Turks or papists or sectarians." Even if their names and concrete works were different, in terms of content they were all the same: attached to "works" (*opera*) and as such not Christians but "Work-lers" (*operarii*), no matter whether they were called Jews, Muslims (Mahometistae/Mohammedans), Papists, or Sectarians.[22]

(I) Circumcision=Law=(Law-)Works=Justification/Righteousness through Works= JUDAISM=CATHOLICISM=ENTHUSIASTS=TURKS=MUS LIMS

versus

(II) Foreskin=Gospel/Christ=Grace/Faith=Justification/Righteousne ss through Faith= (PROTESTANT/PROPER) CHRISTIANITY.

This was the moment when "works" became "weaponized" as a tool to be turned against "opponents" of different shades in the multiple skirmishes of Lutheranism with "work righteous" Others. Yet even when understood as the religious, or simply human effort to "earn" justification and redemption through one's own efforts, thus by-passing God's grace, the prototype of such "work-righteousness" nonetheless always remained "Jewish." Judaism was characterized as the false "working out" of one's redemption through detailed observation of individual laws and rituals.

With the emergence of feminist and liberation theologies after the Second Vatican Council and following the visionary social eruptions of the 1960s, it was specifically the theory and praxis of concrete social transformation that

[22] Et quia ea faciunt, non Christiani sed operarii sunt et manent, sive vocentur Iudaei, Mahometistae, Papistae, Sectarii. WA 40,1,49.

became targeted as "sinful self-reliance" and "self-justification through human works," a pattern that goes back to the time of the Reformation and Luther's harsh judgment against the "robbing and murderous hordes of the peasants."[23] In a similar way, the alarming present-day resurgence of anti-Islamism in Europe and the US reaches back in one of its genealogical roots to Luther's stern rejection of the "Mohammedans," which he firmly tied to justification theology.[24]

Thus, today three heavy liabilities need to be addressed by a Reformation-oriented re-reading of Lutheran justification theology rooted in Paul:

-its anti-Judaism and anti-Islamism as rejecting the religious and cultural Other;

-its inherently problematic divisions that strictly separate justification from justice and alienate faith from "works" as a political ethics, from the biblical perspective of the Exodus and social transformation towards equality;

-its construct of a Christian-Protestant Self that draws its "justification" not just from God's grace but also from its superiority and Self-distancing *vis-à-vis* an inferior ("works-righteous") Other.

This brings us back to historical-textual questions of scriptural exegesis. In his circumcision dispute with the Galatians, is Paul really taking on the works of Jewish Torah, and later, works of justice when he fiercely attacks "work righteousness" (Gal 2:16)? Does the "alone" of faith mean an exclusively individual and internal encounter between God and a single human being? Is the I/Ego that is constituted by a hierarchical opposition to its Other

[23] Cf. Christine Schaumberger/Luise Schottroff, *Schuld und Macht. Studien zu einer feministischen Befreiungstheologie*, Műnchen 1988, 17-29.

[24] Luther's anti-Muslim stance was linked to his experience of an acute threat to the "Christian occident" caused by the Turkish invasion of Europe. The appearance of the Osmanic forces in front of Vienna in 1529 created shock waves comparable to the attack at the World Trade Center in New York in 2001; cf. Hans-Martin Barth, *Martin Luther,* 64. Regarding Luther's categorization of Islam as "work-righteous" and the connection he made between Islam and Satan see ibid., 71-72. Cf. also Johannes Ehmann, *Luther, Tűrken und Islam, Quellen und Forschungen zur Reformationsgeschichte* Bd.80, Göttingen 2008.

really the messianic Self that emerges at Damascus? Or is there a way to read Paul's letter to the Galatians differently?

3. Krister Stendahl and the unfinished exegetical Reformation

The actual point of departure for the emergence of "new" readings of Paul was a pioneering publication that reached across different continents, disciplines, and religions. In two essays, one of them going back to a presentation at the American Psychological Association in 1961, the Swedish scholar Krister Stendahl, who was teaching New Testament at Harvard and later became the Lutheran bishop of Stockholm, challenged the established Protestant interpretation of Paul in three main points, all of them of focal relevance for the theology of justification:[25]

-The Paul of the New Testament was a Jew and stayed a Jew. "Damascus" was not the *conversion* of the Jewish Paul (or Saul) to the Christian Paul, but his prophetic *call* as Christ's ambassador among the non-Jewish/Gentile nations.

-Paul's context is not (yet) the conflict and coexistence of Jews and Christians but of Jews and Gentiles.

-Justification by faith is not a "doctrine of combat" in the crusade of "Christians against Jews" but a theology of reconciliation and peacemaking between "Jews and Gentiles."

Stendahl derived his ground-breaking insights (which fifty years later still are rather alien to the broader Christian community) mainly from the letters to the Romans and Galatians, specifically Galatians 2:15-21. What does the opposition between faith and works, grace and law that Paul so sharply emphasizes in this passage mean for him? Already the opening statement in 2:15 is pointing to an inconsistency in the traditional interpretation of Paul's justification belief: *We ourselves are Jews by birth and not Gentile sinners...* Paul here highlights the shared Jewish genealogical and theological root paradigm. At Antioch, Paul and Peter as well as other members of the Jewish

[25] Krister Stendahl, *Paul among Jews and Gentiles, and Other Essays*, Philadelphia 1976

Christ-community "used to eat with the Gentiles" (Gal 2:12), but then they separated themselves and abandoned the table community.[26] All of them, including Paul, had in common their Jewishness "by birth," and saw themselves as separate from "Gentile sinners." Paul never revoked his being a Jew.

The following argument in 2:16ff does not use justification theology to argue that being a Jew is now superseded by the gospel of grace. Jewishness is not terminated through a new identity as "Christians." The "works" of Jewish food and purity laws, or the "work-righteousness" of being circumcised are not made irrelevant. Strange as it may sound to us today, for Paul, there were yet no "Christians."

This has fundamental implications for the hermeneutics of Pauline justification theology. If Paul is commonly seen as the "father of Christianity" in opposition to "Judaism," could it be that he simply "forgot" to name the religion he founded? This is what the Christian history of interpretation generally has assumed when it took the liberty to declare that Paul certainly must have "meant" what he never said. Thus, the missing Christians were copiously transplanted into Paul's language of Christ-believing Jews and Gentiles, mostly by way of commentary that "translated" them as Gentile *Christians* or Jewish *Christians.*[27]

[26] The community-aspect of this table fellowship is particularly emphasized through two prepositions that both signal co-eating: *meta* tōn ethnōn *syn*ēsthien – *together with* the Gentiles he *co*-ate (= Peter). This highlights the severity of the subsequent separation: *hypestellen* und *afōrizen* - he (Peter) withdrew and dissociated himself. Even worse, also the "other Jews" and even Paul's companion Barnabas join in this break-up (Gal 2:12; cf. 2:10).

[27] Hans Dieter Betz stands for the majority of commentators when he sees the withdrawal of the Jewish *Christians* from the table shared with the Gentile *Christians* as reverting "their emancipation from Judaism." Peter "destroys the integrity of the Gentile Christians as believers in Christ. Instead of welcoming them as converts to Christianity, he wants to make them into converts of Judaism. This contradicts the principles of the doctrine of justification by faith…." (Hans-Dieter Betz, Galatians. A Commentary on Paul's Letter to the Churches in Galatia. Hermeneia, Philadelphia 1979, 112).

Did this "free" translation make Pauline scripture comprehensible – or rather illegible? Why does Paul himself nowhere think of labeling the messianic Christ-communities as *Christianoi*/Christians and juxtaposing them to the *Ioudaioi*/Jews, for example, as Hans-Dieter Betz constantly does in his classic commentary on Galatians?[28] Yet it is only in Acts, at least three decades after Paul, that this term is introduced.[29] Paul himself was very capable of coining new words when he needed them, as for example the highly unconventional term "gospel of the foreskin" in Gal 2:7 demonstrates. We have to assume that he could have said "Christians" if he had meant "Christians." But what if this is exactly what he did *not* mean to establish, although it is perpetually attached to his person: a separate Christian identity within a framework of mutually exclusive identity constructs of Christian versus Jewish or Christian versus Gentile/pagan/any other religion?

Despite its sharp polemics, the whole of Galatians is about integration and the removal of separation walls. "Damascus" (Gal 1:15-16) means the "turning around" of the Jew Paul into an apostle of the Jewish Messiah among the Gentiles. He is turned toward those outside and inside Judaism (including the Jesus followers) that as a "holy warrior" he had pursued and mercilessly tried to eradicate because he saw them as "sinners" and a threat to Jewish integrity (cf. Gal 1:13-14). Paul's "mission" among the Gentiles is a movement of grand peace-making, not the birth of a new (Christian) definition of Self in contradistinction to a Jewish or another Other.

At the Jerusalem meeting the decisive act is an unusual ritual of reconciliation: the "handshake of community" between the "gospel of the foreskin" and the "gospel of circumcision" (Gal 2:7.9). The uncircumcised Greek Titus who accompanies the circumcised Jews, Paul and Barnabas, does not have to be circumcised in order to be fully part of the community (Gal 2:3).Yet the collection as a practical gesture of economic solidarity of the Gentiles with the "poor" of Jerusalem is indispensable (Gal 2:10). Finally, after the debacle of the Antioch break-up of table community, throughout Galatians unity and

[28] Cf. note 27 above.

[29] The term *Christianoi* for the first time turns up in Acts 11:25;26:18 and 1 Peter 4:16, altogether no more than three times in the entire New Testament and only several decades after Paul.

community between the "ones" and the "others" is the focal topic of its theology and practice. The climactic statement of this Oneness is Gal 3:28. Paul leads a biblical-messianic re-reading of the Abraham narrative in Genesis to the grand conclusion:

There is no longer Jew or Greek, there is no longer slave or free, there is no longer male and female; for you are all one in Christ/Messiah Jesus.

Rather than racially, culturally, religiously opposite through the customary boundary marker of circumcision, both groups, like Paul the circumcised Jew and the uncircumcised Titus (Gal 2:3), now become "all one in Christ".[30] The text does *not* say that with this the *difference* between the two is erased. If that was the case, then the Greek Titus could have got himself circumcised and the Galatians could do the same. Rather, the decisive point is not to establish *sameness* but to establish that difference is no longer an obstacle to community and becoming-one-in-Christ.[31] Gal 3:18 does *not* state: "There is no longer Jew or Greek,… for you are all *Christians.*" It states that "you are all one *in Christ*." It is Christ who establishes a trans-identity cohesion between the Self and the Other. It is their shared "in-Christness" that becomes the basis for the unity of those who by birth are different from and hostile to each other, not a unified identity as "Christians." Neither uniformly circumcised nor uniformly uncircumcised becomes the "Christian" norm.

It might seem that there is no significant difference between "being Christian" and "being in Christ." However, the entire incompatibility between gospel and law, old world order and new creation is at stake here, and thus in Paul's justification theology as a whole. For Paul the decisive point is not that Jews and Gentiles become *Christians*, thus taking on a unified and uniform identity in contrast to other identities. Rather what Paul envisions is that *in Christ* Jews and Gentiles can learn to live together by practicing a new type of solidarity, because Christ as the *Other* for the Jew lives "in" the Gen-

[30] For circumcision as a commonly legible marker of Jewish Otherness from the perspective of non-Jews see Tacitus, Hist 5.5; Louis H. Feldmann, *Jews and Gentile in the Ancient World: Attitudes and Interactions from Alexander to Justinian*, Princeton 1993, 153-158.

[31] Cf. Jae-Won Lee, Paul and the Politics of Difference. A Contextual Study of Jewish-Gentile Difference in Galatians and Romans, Eugene, OR, 2014.

tile and for the Gentile "in" the Jew. He thus lives in both of them (Gal 2:20) as they both live "in him." (Gal 3:28)[32] It is precisely the relationship between I and You, Self and Other, we and the alien that is radically transformed by the Christ event. This is the reason why Paul develops his justification theology in Gal 2:15-21, *not* in order to stop the relapse of Christians into Judaism, but to stop the relapse into the old dichotomies of Jews versus Gentiles.[33] These re-emerge both at the "Antiochene incident" when Jews break away from Gentiles (Gal 2:11-14) and in the circumcision demands in Galatia: The dismantled equation of Jewish=circumcised=righteous/justified (cf. Gal 2:15) again is built up into an impenetrable separation wall towards Gentile = uncircumcised = sinful/impure (Gal 2:18).

This means that the antithetical polarity of foreskin versus circumcision, law and gospel is completely re-defined in its genuinely Pauline meaning:

(I) Circumcision=Law=(Law-)Works=Justification/Righteousness through Works= ONE/SELF-AGAINST-OTHER, e.g. JUDAISM AGAINST GENTILES

versus

(II) Foreskin=Gospel/Christ=Grace/Faith=Justification/Righteousne ss through Faith= ONE-AN(D)-OTHERNESS OF JEWS AND GENTILES, SELF AND OTHER

No one understood this community-oriented practical core concern of Galatians with greater clarity than Krister Stendahl, when he rediscovered Pauline justification theology as a Jewish-Gentile theology of emancipation.[34]

32 The presence of Christ in faith (*in ipsa fide Christus adest*) and the participation of the believers in Christ is a basic assumption in Luther's interpretation of Galatians (especially Gal 2:15-21) from 1535; cf. e.g. WA 40,1,228-229. This is the decisive point of departure for Tuomo Mannermaa's re-reading of Lutheran justification doctrine as based on the inseparable connection of faith and love.

33 Cf. Brigitte Kahl, "Peter's Antiochene Apostasy: Re-Judaizing of Imperial Conformism?" in *FORUM*, Third Series. Spring 2014, 27-38.

34 According to Stendahl, justification theology was "hammered out by Paul for the very specific and limited purpose of defending the rights of the Gentile converts to be full and genuine heirs to the promises of God to Israel." (Stendahl, *Paul among Jews and*

The full implications of this "Stendahl-revolution" for Christian and Protestant identity constructs, however, still need to be drawn out.[35] In a similar way, Paul's concept of "work-righteousness" or "justification through works" requires a re-conceptualization with regards to "works of justice." For "works of justice" are indispensable when mutually hostile and alienated groups like "Jews and Gentiles," "Greek and Barbarians" at the time of Paul or "Christians and Muslims," "citizens and immigrants," "documented and undocumented" in our present world are entering into processes of community-building. For Paul, at no point along this path can faith and works be perceived in terms of a human-God relationship that is not at the same time also a human-human relationship. Paul is deconstructing himself and his fellow-Jews not *as Jews* but as the ordinary mode of being human that was common among Jews and non-Jews in his time, as it is among Christians and non-Christians in our time: constructing the Self as "being right" over and against an inferior, unrighteous Other – the sinner, the barbarian, the un/other-civilized, the savage, the *Untermensch* in all their countless variations. At the cross of Christ God has identified God-Self precisely with/as this Other. Thereby the dichotomies and hierarchies between Self and Other are abolished and people are equalized "in Christ" (Gal 3:28).

Paul experiences this messianic transformation as co-crucifixion of his old Self – of the Ego that is established by endless competition for status and

Gentiles, 2) Stendahl deplores that this concrete embeddedness of justification into the conviviality of Jews and Gentiles was completely erased in the history of interpretation, which led to a highly problematic spiritualization and de-contextualization of Pauline theology. Especially following Augustine, justification theology "no longer 'justified' the status of Gentile Christians as honorary Jews, but became the timeless answer to the plights and pains of the introspective conscience of the West." (ibid., 5) It required individual soul-searching and occidental navel-gazing which Stendahl criticizes in his essay "The Apostle Paul and the Introspective Conscience of the West." (in ibid., 78-96)

35 Stendahl himself continues to use the term "Christian," even after he has shown its anachronistic character within the context of Paul. As the antithetical structure of our language inevitably defines "Christian" as "non/anti-Jewish," the un-Pauline character of this terminology needs to be made conscious, e.g. by using an alternative term like "messianic" (derived from the Hebrew term for Messiah= Christ) instead of "Christian."

standing – and as resurrection into a new mode of being human, where the Other becomes part of the Self: *I have been co-crucified (*synestaurōmai*) with Christ. But I am living, no longer as I (*hōs egō*), but it is Christ who lives in me.* (Gal 2:19-20; transl. BK) At the absolute breaking-point of this Christ encounter, however, after livelong boasting of his righteousness in contrast to Gentile sinfulness (Gal 1:13-14),[36] Paul comes to see himself, and to be seen by others, as simply a sinner like the Gentiles (Gal 2:15.17). What he never was, never wanted to be, and where "by birth" he didn't belong – there precisely he has been catapulted through Christ and the process of justification. Galatians 2:15 and 2:17 convey some of his incredulity and bewilderment at this reversal of roles: *We ourselves are Jews by birth and not Gentile sinners. (...)But if, in our effort to be justified in Christ, we ourselves have been found to be sinners, is Christ then a servant of sin?* (Gal 2:15.17)

In this situation of Self-loss and complete identity-crisis nothing would make more sense than to re-build the old separation walls and to recede into the shelter of friend-foe definitions where "our own" and "the others" are separated by clear-cut and well-known demarcation lines (Gal 2:18). This is what happened at Antioch. But this is exactly what *in Christ* has made visible as the actual sin: the sin of Self-superiority vis-à-vis the Other and God.

4. Paul critiques Law from the perspective of "being-in-Christ"

In Galatians, "works of the law" are opposed to faith not only because they create a false confidence that human beings could make themselves righteous before God through their own doing. The problem with such works in a *negative* sense, such as circumcision in Galatia or a return to strict food laws in Antioch, is the Self-superiority as Self-distancing from the Other/neighbor to which they lead. For Paul "works of the law" imply a human practice of separation, fixation, and elimination that in the name of God and God-given norms leaves the neighbor behind. In cutting oneself off from the neighbor,

[36] For the pre-Damascus Paul this implied, as an in-group variation, also Jewish laxity and deviance in observing the law, which he detected in most of his "peers among my nation," including the messianic community that he calls the *ekklēsia* of God (Gal 1:13-14).

one is cut off from God as well, even if one can "righteously" quote the law. In its attempts to fend off sin the law can promote this division of humanity into righteous ones/us and sinners/Others. Thus the core sin is of lovelessness towards the Other/neighbor who is intended to be protected by the law. This is the inherent ambivalence of the law with which Paul continually wrestles. The law has the power to condemn the transgressor to death yet although it is meant to sustain life (Gal 3:19-21), it cannot make alive again.

If Self-obsession and Self-righteousness vertically disturbs the relationship with God, horizontally it negatively affects the relationship with the Other. These work synergistically in turning another human being into a "thing," or a no-thing, and ultimately a potential object of annihilation (cf. 1 Cor 1:26-28). "Boasting" thus is an essential feature of "work righteousness" (Rom 3:27) and a main antithesis of "faith righteousness." As Robert Jewett has shown, works in the negative sense are always embedded in a competitive relationship with the Other, aiming to enhance one's own status, prestige or privilege, at the expense of or by downgrading an Other. This means that "work righteousness" and "works of righteousness" refer to fundamentally opposite types of works. Through Christ the point of view shifts from the perspective of the "winners"/Self to the "losers"/Other. Robert Jewett captures this logic in his analysis of Romans 3:21-26: "God's righteousness is manifested in Christ in such a way that it shatters ordinary definitions of righteousness as conformity to a particular culture's norms. In Christ divine righteousness acts to counter the arrogance of the dominant groups and the shame of the subordinates."[37]

[37] Robert Jewett, *Romans*, 275. The exclusionary aspect of (Jewish) Law with regard to the Gentiles is the focal point where the "New Perspective" (James Dunn and others) locates the law criticism of Paul. This primarily religious aspect is modified and expanded by Jewett and other empire-critical/liberationist interpreters to include the social, political and economic logic of exclusion inherent to the established law in general, specifically in its Roman and imperial versions. Already Elsa Tamez, in dialogue with Franz Hinkelammert's law-critique, had re-read Paul's wrestling with justification in a liberationist key from the perspective of the "excluded"- i.e. the impoverished and marginalized masses in Latin America. The original title of her seminal interpretation of Romans (1991) in Portuguese was "La Justificación por la Fé desde los Excluidos." (cf. note 16 above). From a similar point of departure Andrea

Going one step further, this means that the theological-ethical center and the community-related point of reference in Paul's letter to the Galatians is not the antithesis of Jews and Christians, nor any of the enemy constructs subsequently derived from it. Rather, following Louis Martyn's groundbreaking work on the "Apocalyptic Antinomies," at the center is Paul's visionary/apocalyptic insight that "in Christ" the dichotomies of the "present evil age/world order" (Gal 1:4) have been de-polarized, and with it all structures that establish the identity and social location of Self and Other in hierarchical, exclusionary relationships of superiority and inferiority.[38]

From a different perspective yet with similar implications, Dieter Georgi concludes that Paul's justification theology contains a significant potential of "pragmatic utopia." Financial and economic counter-models emerged, for example, in collecting for the "poor in Jerusalem." For Georgi this brought Paul in close proximity to the "enthusiasts" of the Reformation who were so furiously contested by Luther – in the name of Paul's law-criticism.

> It has been a fatal side of much of Protestant exegesis that the rational as well as utopian elements of Paul's understanding of justification have been weakened or even covered up. As Paul transforms his understanding of justification into a praxis and theory of the collection, the climate of a pragmatic utopia becomes apparent. In the terminology of the established Reformation theology, Paul's reflections on the collection and on money, if brought out in their full historical meaning, qualify for the

Bieler and Hans-Martin Gutmann have more recently explored the "justification of the expendables" within the context of the First World (Andrea Bieler and Hans-Martin Gutmann, *Embodying Grace. Proclaiming Justification in the Real World*, Minneapolis 2010). These are important hermeneutical re-orientations towards a re-alignment of Justification and Justice.

38 Louis Martyn, "Apocalyptic Antinomies in Paul's Letter to the Galatians," NTS 31(1985), 410-24. For Martyn, Paul's law-criticism is aiming at a de-dichotomization of the prevalent binaries which form the basic building blocks of the dominant and cosmic order, i.e. the *stoicheia tou kosmou* (Gal 4:3.9). The Galatians want to resubmit themselves to the enslaving power of these hierarchical oppositional systems. (Gal 4:9) – cf. Louis Martyn, *Galatians. A New Translation with Introduction and Commentary* (Anchor Bible Commentary), New York 1997, 405-6, 560, 571; Kahl, *Galatians Re-Imagined,* 15-25.

verdict of 'enthusiasm' as it was leveled against revolting peasants, anabaptists, and spiritualists.[39]

In the new messianic practice of solidarity and reconciliation that Paul envisions, unity is established as One-an(d)-Otherness between friend and enemy, us and them, Self and Other.[40] In this messianic community circumcised and uncircumcised stay different but still can live together as "one in Christ," transforming their differences from antagonism to solidarity. For Paul, this is the beginning of the new creation (Gal 6:15). Love fulfills the Torah and keeps it valid (5:14-14); love is the decisive "work of faith" (Gal 5:6)[41] that is practiced when the One bears the burden of an Other and thus "fulfills the law of Christ" (Gal 6:2).

Nevertheless, an antagonism remains. This reflects the "already" and "not yet" in the relationship of old and new creation, flesh and spirit. As the law and its works, the principle and practice that attempts to live without, against or at the expense of others, are still predominant and massively present now, Paul attacks it passionately. It is this principle of One-against-Other that he sees active through his "opponents" in Galatia and that he anathematizes at the beginning of his letter (Gal 1:8.9) With their insistence that integration as Abraham's children is only possible through circumcision, these proponents of the status quo re-establish the fundamental division of humanity as circumcised and uncircumcised, Jews and Gentiles, and the exclusive adherence to God as privileging one group alone. But God is not "the God of the Jews alone" (Rom 3:29). At the cross, the God of Israel has been re-identified as

39 Dieter Georgi, "Is there Justification in Money? A Historical and Theological Meditation on the Financial Aspects of Justification in Christ," in Id., *The City in the Valley: Biblical Interpretation and Urban Theology*, Atlanta 2005, 302.

40 "One-an(d)Otherness" is a term I use to render the double meaning of mutuality *and* difference between One/Self and Other that is at the core of Paul's new community construct; e.g., it is expressed in the Greek term *allēlōn* that is used in Gal 5-6 no less than seven times. Translations usually render it as "one another;" literally it means "other-other" (from *allos-allos*) and for Paul implies the Other as the decisive criterion of Self, as well as a community-dynamics of Self-Othering.

41 Faith *working* through love: *energoumenē*, from *ergon* =work (Gal 5:6)

God with and for the Others, making the people of God the space that is open to these Others (i.e., the Gentiles) as well.

The implications of this "trans-identity" re-definition of Jewishness at the time of Paul as messianic One-an(d)-Otherness perhaps can be best understood when they are applied to present-day Christianity. If "being in Christ" according to the baptismal formula of Gal 3:28 is the opposite of a "Christian" identity that is defined as non-Jewish, non-Muslim, non-pagan, then it could mean an identity as *not* non-Jewish, *not* non-Muslim, *not* non-pagan. Quoting the mystic Nikolaus Cusanus and his *De non Aliud* (about the non-Other), the Italian philosopher Giorgio Agamben has emphasized the foundational importance of this double negation for Paul's law criticism.[42] Thus for Paul, being "in Christ" is the opposite of a "Christian" non/anti-identity; instead, it implies, within a basically Jewish configuration, a fundamentally new type of community that holds non-binary mixed identities together. Within this community, believers are no longer identified through who they are *not* (and who thereby are excluded and negated as no-thing and no-body) but through messianic solidarity between "us" and "those there," transcending all hierarchical demarcation lines of race, class, gender and religion.

5. "Works of the Law" within the context of the Roman Empire

5.1 Galatia and the Galatians

Ultimately, none of the issues outlined so far can become fully transparent unless it is understood in a historical-critical manner against the backdrop of the "real world" where Paul and his Jewish or Galatian addressees lived. This is one of the most severe lacunae in Luther's scriptural interpretation, imposed by the epistemological limitations of his time. While the Reformation effortlessly equated the Jerusalem of Galatians with the papal Rome of the 16th century, it barely gave any thought to the historical position of Rome, Jerusalem or Galatia in the first century CE. Yet Rome at the time of Paul was the global colonial superpower that ruled over both Jerusalem/Judea and Galatia.

[42] Giorgio Agamben, *The Time that Remains*, 49-52.

For a long time, the literature on Galatians has profusely discussed the question of whether Paul's Galatians lived in the North or to the South of the (Roman) province of Galatia; the "South-Galatian" hypothesis in the history of interpretation went down as the "provincial hypothesis." What stayed completely out of this were the political, social and ideological realities that shaped Galatia as a multi-ethnic Celtic province in the Roman East, founded in 25 BCE by Emperor Augustus. The effects of this myopic view are particularly troublesome because the term *Nomos*/Law at the center of the Galatian controversy is at least as much a Roman term as it is a Jewish one; in the conflict-laden triangular relationship of Jews-Galatians-Romans at Paul's time it clearly connoted Roman hegemony.[43]

The Galatians had arrived in Asia Minor in 279 BCE. They were part of the centuries-long overall Celtic migration that took its eastward moving branch from the center of Europe (Gaul) through the Balkans and Greece. From there three Galatian tribes moved over to what today is Turkey, where they settled around Ancyra (Ankara). Galatians or Gauls (the two widely synonymous terms for Celts in antiquity render the Greek *Galatai* and the Latin *Galli*) were seen as quintessential barbarians by both Greeks and Romans. In countless minor and two large-scale attacks – the conquest of Rome in 387 BCE and the assault at Delphi in 279 BCE – they had again and again turned against the shrines and outposts of civilization, *terror et tumultus* in their wake.[44] Only Rome was eventually able to "pacify" them, which included a brutal Roman massacre in 189 BCE of 40 000 unprepared Galatians in Asia Minor, and the famous "Gallic War" of Julius Caesar in the West (58-52

43 The Greek term *nomos* that Paul uses all throughout his letters can mean both Torah as specifically Jewish law and "law" in general, including cosmic, natural, Roman or any other particular law. Already Jacob Taubes pointed out that it may be very difficult to specify what kind of law is actually meant in a given context, as the law-terminology often was used in a deliberately blurry way, but ultimately serves as a "compromise formula for the Imperium Romanum." (Taubes, *The Political Theology of Paul*, 23); see also Kahl, *Galatians Re-Imagined,* 5-11, 42- 75.

44 It is noteworthy that ancient authors frequently use the term "terror" in connection with Gauls/Galatians; see e.g. Livy 38.16-17; also Bernhard Kramer, *Das Bild der Kelten bis in augusteische Zeit: Studien zur Instrumentalisierung eines Feindbildes bei griechischen und römischen Autoren*, Suttgart 1994, 64-65.

BCE). The Celtic victory by the Romans was celebrated as "salvation of civilization" (*sōtēria*) and became an important ideological legitimation for Roman world rule. In the arts this triumph was enthusiastically "pictured" through a broad stream of sculptures featuring dying or dead Gauls/Galatians (most notably the Ludovisi *Dying Trumpeter* and *Suicidal Galatians)* who until today are represented in the famous museums of Europe and the US. The most prominent location that has monumentalized the direct ancestors of Paul's Galatians in the moment of their defeat is the Pergamon Altar at Berlin. It shows the Celts of Asia Minor as lawless mythological "giants" who have to succumb to the superior law and power of the Olympic Gods.[45]

This overall historical and ideological context is relevant for understanding the Pauline doctrine of justification in its own terms. The most conspicuous feature of the Celtic Galatians/Gauls from the perspective of the Hellenistic-Roman civilization was their "lawlessness" that stood against the dominant order and its value systems. The colonization, acculturation and co-optation of these "arch-barbarians" by Rome – a process that was rather successful in Asia Minor, especially with regard to the Galatian aristocracy – was their gradual subordination to the "law," which meant their "justification" as no-longer-barbarians. In the course of becoming "lawful" they not only consented to the Roman order *per se* but also to the Law and Right of the conqueror, which included the righteousness of their own subjugation. This specific Roman semiotics of the law-related terminology in Galatians is an integral part of a historically accountable interpretation of Paul's justification theology.[46]

45 For the history of the Galatians in Asia minor see chiefly Stephen Mitchell, Anatolia: Land, Men, and Gods in Asia Minor, Oxford 1993; Karl Strobel, Die Galater. Geschichte und Eigenart der keltischen Staatenbildung auf dem Boden des Hellenistischen Kleinasien, Berlin 1996; for the connection between this Galatian history, its artistic/architectural representations (like the "Dying Galatians" and the Pergamon-Altar) and Roman ideology versus Pauline theology see Kahl, Galatians Re-imagined.

46 For the overall notion of imperial Law, Galatian barbarianism and its gradual integration into the Roman order between 189 BCE and 50 CE, see Kahl, *Galatians Re-Imagined*, 1-11, 31-75, 169-207.

5.2 Roman Nomos or Jewish Torah

Within this overall Roman semiotics, Jewish Torah needs to be considered as the second layer of meaning-making in Paul's law/justification discourse. Jewish Law from a Greco-Roman perspective is distinctly different from barbarian lawlessness, and valued because of its antiquity. Nonetheless, Torah also was a permanent or at least potential point of friction with the established law systems of the foreign overlords that ruled Palestine, as well as within the *polis* structure in the East. Torah-observance implied exemption rules for Jews and thus at least a partial refusal to submit to the power of the normative order. At the core of the conflict was the strict monotheism of the First Commandment and the refusal of images that went with it. (Ex 20:1-5) Both led to collisions with the political religion inherent in Hellenistic and Roman power apparatuses, such as in the Maccabean Revolt in the middle of the second century BCE or the Caligula crisis at the time of Paul, when the emperor wanted to place his statue into the Jerusalem temple. Even though Rome granted Judaism a special status, not only with regard to food laws, the Sabbath, and the temple tax, even more so in the key question of emperor worship,[47] the compromise achieved always remained fragile. The indissoluble tensions between Jewish Torah and Roman Nomos in terms of worshiping power as divine eventually led to the outbreak of the Jewish War in 66 CE. This began with the refusal to continue the twice-daily sacrifice on behalf of the Roman emperor in the Jerusalem temple, which had been instituted to replace Jewish non-participation in the rituals of emperor religion in the Diaspora.[48]

Paul's messianic integration of non-Jews as "children" of Abraham and his monotheistic God (Gal 3:29; 4:7) made this complicated situation even more difficult. Brewing especially in two areas was a dangerous conflict with Roman law and order:

47 Josephus, Antiquities 14 and 16 renders several decrees issued by Rome in order to protect the ancestral laws and privileges of Jewish groups within an often hostile polis-context.

48 Cf. Josephus, *Jewish War II*, 409-10; Kahl, *Galatians Re-Imagined*, 216; 209-243.

1. From a Roman perspective it is the emperor alone who unites and pacifies the *oikoumenē* of "Jews and Gentiles/non-Jews," i.e., the entirety of the nations subject to Rome. The Roman policy of integration was not aiming at uniformity and in general tolerated the cultural and religious identities of the conquered nations (*ethnē*), including their various deities, as long as they didn't interfere with Roman power. Judaism itself is an example of this flexible integration. Although such a "liberal" and pluralistic policy could also be used to play the different nations and ethnic groups against each other – Rome was a master of "Divide and Rule" (*divide et impera*) – on the whole, the Caesars were very successful in creating an "ecumenism from above" that was vertically structured and held together through the person of the emperor-god and the system of patronage/euergetism.[49]

On the other hand, Paul promotes an "ecumenism from below" that is integrated horizontally through mutual solidarity as One-an(d)-Otherness (instead of vertical patronage), as well as through the "body" of an executed outlaw Messiah who in a blasphemous way is attributed all the sacrosanct titles of emperor religion: Lord (*kyrios*), Savior (*sōtēr*), Son of God (*huios theou/divi filius*), as well as many other terms with both political and religious connotation like Faith, Grace, Peace, and Gospel.[50]

Furthermore, the community of Christ-believers cannot be categorized as "either this or that" within the established taxonomy and its normative dichotomies like Jew or Gentile/non-Jew, Greek or barbarian (cf. Rom 1:14), sinner and righteous that form the foundation of every positive Law. Already at the end of the 19th century this basic "anarchism" and "lawlessness" has been aptly described by William Ramsay, a British archeologist and eminent expert in matters of historical Galatia/Anatolia, and also a fervent admirer of the Roman Empire. In his opinion, Christians constructed a type of far-

[49] See e.g. Richard Gordon, "The Veil of Power" in: Horsley (ed.), *Paul and Empire*, 126-37and ibid., 88-95 (Richard A. Horsley).

[50] The "polemical parallelism" between imperial and Christ-terminology, a crucial point of reference for empire-critical hermeneutics of the New Testament until today, has first been stated by Adolf Deissmann a hundred years ago. His book *Light from the Ancient East*, New York 1995 (1927), 349 contains a lot of invaluable papyrological and epigraphical material.

reaching horizontal unity across borders that was based on solidarity and went against the vertical logic of Roman rule and imperial unity. This could not be tolerated, despite all the tolerance Rome usually had for the peculiarities of the conquered:

> (…) Christians still continued, no less than before, to maintain a unity independent of, and contrary to, the Imperial unity, and to consolidate steadily a wide-reaching organization. Such an organization was contrary to the fundamental principle of Roman government. Rome had throughout its career made it a fixed principle to rule by dividing; all subjects must look to Rome alone; none might look towards their neighbours, or enter into any agreement and connection with them. But the Christians looked to a non-Roman unity; they decided on common action independent on Rome....[51]

2. At the time of Paul, emperor religion – a phenomenon long underestimated in Pauline scholarship – had increasingly become an omnipresent way of communicating Roman Law among the colonized nations, especially in the Roman province of Galatia.[52] This makes Paul's "Gentile mission" politically suspect – not primarily as the worldwide proclamation of the Messiah Jesus, but as "universalizing" the Jewish-monotheistic refusal to worship Caesar as God *on the side of non-Jews.* This abstention in terms of emperor cult was accepted with regard to Jews and partially covered by the compromise solution of the daily emperor sacrifice in the Jerusalem Temple. Yet this was not acceptable in the case of non-Jewish Gentiles, including Galatians, who were still tainted by their lawless and barbarian past. Although through his dramatic *relectura* of Genesis, Paul boldly re-claimed them as "children of Abraham" in the full sense of ethnic belonging (Gal 3:1-31), this is not what they really were "according to the law," neither for Rome nor for Jeru-

[51] William M. Ramsay, *The Church in the Roman Empire before A.D.170*, London 1893, 356.

[52] Cf. Justin K. Hardin, *Galatians and the Imperial Cult: A Critical Analysis of the First-Century Social Context of Paul's Letter*, WUNT 2/237, Tübingen 2008; Thomas Witulski, *Kaiserkult in Kleinasien: Die Entwicklung der kultisch-religiösen Kaiserverehrung in der römischen Provinz Asia von Augustus bis Antoninus Pius*, Fribourg /Göttingen 2007; Michael Peppard, *The Son of God in the Roman World. Divine Sonship in its Social and Political Context*, Oxford 2011.

salem. Because they were uncircumcised they could not claim Torah-obedience, even if they, together with their Jewish brothers and sisters, gave glory and honor to "God alone," and like good Jews, abstained from the idolatry of worshiping Caesar as God.

In other words, the political flipside of Gentile-inclusive descent from Abraham, as Paul lays it out in Galatians (Gal 3:16), is an illegal extension of Jewish monotheism from circumcised towards uncircumcised Roman subjects. Paul deprives the Roman system of a most efficient "mass medium" to express and reproduce civil obedience, reorienting it instead towards the God of Israel and the Jewish Messiah, a "legally" executed insurgent and criminal in the eyes of Rome. The main antithesis of Galatians thus is not "Christ against the God/Law of Israel" but "Abraham's God-in-Christ against the Roman God and the Law of Empire." In an act of civil obedience, the Galatian communities gave to the God of Israel what belongs to Caesar, namely the unrestricted loyalty and the glorification by the subjugated nations in their entirety (cf. Gal 1:5)[53] This can easily be perceived as insurgence and rebellion.

In this situation it is very understandable if the opponents of Paul, quoting the law of Torah, urge the Galatians to get circumcised. This is not necessarily because of religious zeal but for very pragmatic reasons of protecting both the Jewish and Gentile messianic communities from the fallout of dangerously colliding with public order and Roman law. (cf. Gal 6:12). If the foreskin of the male Galatians has become the signifier of their political non-conformism, they either should opt for circumcision and full proselyte conversion, or they should return to their prior practice of civic and imperial religious observance that is expected from them as non-Jews. This always has been tolerated and respected by the synagogue with regard to sympathetic

[53] The term *ethnē* in Pauline writings, traditionally translated as "Gentiles," has outside the theological realm in 1st-century Koinē – Greek the general meaning of "nations." In this connotation it includes both Jews and non-Jews/Gentiles who all are "nations/ethnē" conquered by Rome. This has substantial implications for understanding the Jewish-Gentile integration in Paul as an integration of the *nations.* Cf. Lopez, *Apostle to the Conquered.*

God-fearing Gentile adherents.[54] Like good Lutherans, these voices demand to give God what belongs to God, and to Caesar what belongs to Caesar (cf. Lk 20:25).

Paul refuses both options for normalizing the "abnormal." Neither a return to the customary sacrifices and celebrations of imperial religion and its calendar that governs civic life (Gal 4:8-10),[55] nor circumcision of the Galatian men are acceptable solutions to him, even though the latter could give the Galatians the coverage of Torah for their "civil disobedience" with regard to emperor religion[56] and would make the non-messianic Jewish communities less suspect of gathering rebellious elements hostile to Rome (cf. Acts 17:6-7). Paul sees such acts of accommodation to "the Law" as outright hypocrisy (cf. Gal 2:18). Redrawing the lines that demark Jews from Gentiles damages the messianic integration movement at is core, as it happened in Antioch after the Jerusalem council (Gal 2:18). Torah is used in an oblique way that makes it, in fact, an agent and mediator of the Roman law of domination (Gal 3:19-20).[57]

54 Cf. Nanos, *Irony of Galatians,* 257-71.

55 That Paul's critique of the Galatians returning to the observance of "specials days, and months, and seasons, and years" in Gal 4:10 most likely refers to the imperial (rather than Jewish) calendar has already been observed by Stephen Mitchell, Anatolia, vol.2, 10; Justin Hardin (*Galatians and the Imperial Cult*, 122-27) and Thomas Witulski (*Adressaten des Galaterbriefes*, 158-68) support this thesis.

56 Circumcision as an "evasive action" to make the uncircumcised Christ-believers in Galatia less vulnerable and conspicuous in their abstention from the rituals of civic and imperial religion has been convincingly analyzed by Bruce Winter, *Seek the Welfare of the City: Christians as Benefactors and Citizens,* Grand Rapids 1994, 141-42.

57 For the assumption that this issue of Torah being "hijacked" by imperial *nomos* is the problem behind the notoriously opaque statement in Gal 3:19-20 about *nomos*/Torah (…it was ordained through angels by a mediator. Now the mediator is not of the One/*henos ouk estin*, but God is One/heis estin) see Kahl, *Galatians Re-Imagined*, 238, 282-83, 301.

5.3 Re-defining "works of the law" from an empire-critical perspective

This reading of Galatians from an empire-critical and postcolonial perspective makes it necessary to re-define the terms "law" and "works of the law" as the fundamental opposites of Pauline "justification by faith." The law that Paul abandons can be defined as the logic of "One-against-Other" in a threefold way:

-The logic of vertical and horizontal segregation between a dominant Self and an inferior Other in its countless variations, splitting society on the structural and personal, the individual as well as collective level. Wherever this logic is rooted in religion, it positions God as the "justifier" of the imperial Self and "Ego conquistador" (Enrique Dussel) with its "possessive individualism" (Ulrich Duchrow/Franz Hinkelammert).[58] In this classic Christian version of idolatry God is declared as the "God-with-us" or, as in the Self-idolization of emperor religion, the "Self-as-God." This inevitably results in the construct of a subhuman, undeserving and unworthy Other as counterpart of the super-Self.

-The logic of sin and of the "flesh" that turns this "lawless" Other established by the law into an object of "lawful" subjugation and (ab)use whose marginalization, objectification, exploitation, and extermination is *not* prohibited by the law.

-The logic of permanent Self-assertion that is ceaselessly geared towards combat and competition between Self and Other. The normalcy of "I" is defined as "*not* you," and of "mine" as "*not* yours." (Ton Veerkamp)[59]

This overall logic of "law" and its "works" as contested by justification theology in Paul's world is not primarily represented through Jewish Torah,

[58] Enrique Dussel, *Philosophie der Befreiung*, Düsseldorf 1989 (spanisch: [3]1985); Ulrich Duchrow/ Franz Hinkelammert, *Transcending Greedy Money. Interreligious Solidarity for Just Relations*, New York 2012, 21.

[59] Ton Veerkamp, *Die Welt Anders: Politische Geschichte der Grossen Erzählung*, Berlin 2012, 14.

but by Roman law as the *nomos* of empire. Torah as the law of Exodus and liberation from enslavement (Ex 20:1-5) is fundamentally opposed to this *nomos* of domination. Yet like any other religious law it can be drawn into its orbit, especially when it finds itself in a political space that is shaped and overdetermined by imperial law, as it was in the first century CE. Being hijacked by an alien law, however, is a danger Christian and Protestant theology today firstly needs to face with regard to its *own* tradition and "law" in terms of justification theology.

6. Conclusion

Wrestling with the overpowering force of tradition and authority in the (Catholic) church of his day, Luther prophetically tied the "alone" of grace and faith (*sola gratia/sola fide)* in his justification theology to the "alone" of scripture (*sola scriptura*). Thus, continually examining the Protestant tradition, guided by "scripture alone," becomes a core criterion of reformatory faith and theology, even where it challenges established Lutheran interpretations and traditions. Celebrating 500 years of Reformation turns into a hollow ritual historically and theologically unless it is embedded in a vivid culture of biblical debate. This was formative for the Reformation itself and is reflective of the permanent need for an ongoing Reformation of the church (*ecclesia semper reformanda*). Just as Martin Luther developed his reformatory re-discovery of Paul and the letter to the Galatians through intense grappling with the biblical text, today any meaningful theological engagement of the Reformation at its core needs to be measured against the depth and social relevance of its scriptural basis. This requires first and foremost a critical reexamination of Galatians as the most "Lutheran" of all Pauline letters – together with Luther, but also *beyond* Luther.

The established pattern of reading Paul and Galatians as the basis of Lutheran justification theology urgently needs to be reconsidered theologically, textually and historically. Paradoxically, it imprisons Paul in a binary Self-definition in rigid contrast to an Other. This precisely was the prime feature of his militancy *before* Damascus. However, this was transformed *through* his Damascus experience into a border-transgressing peace mission towards the Other, in mutual solidarity with the Other. The traditional misreading of Paul's law-critique as critique of Torah has become the hermeneutical basis for the "Babylonian captivity" of Galatians.

The paradigm shift currently taking place in Pauline Studies implies that the "apostle to the Gentiles" – in contrast to classic Western-Christian and Protestant attribution – was not a loyal Roman and a disloyal Jew. Instead he was a radical (if contested and marginal) Jew who was perceived as a threat by Rome because he galvanized a messianic movement among the nations under Roman rule. This is probably why he was executed during Nero's persecution as an "arsonist" together with many others of his sisters and brothers.[60] The messianic justice of the justification event that commissioned him as its emissary- across- borders was irreconcilable with the "right" of the Roman Empire. This is the point from which Reformation theology today needs to be re-thought in light of the authority of scripture.

[60] Kahl, *Galatians Re-Imagined*, 10-11.

Martin Luther and Reformation Theology: An East Asian Perspective

Paul S. Chung

A contextual and constructive interpretation of Martin Luther and Reformation theology in East Asian perspective is necessary in order to radicalize his insight into God's solidarity with those living poverty-stricken lives and to recognize the gifts of religious cultural diversity. Three distinctive interests remain undercurrents in Asian theological construction when it comes to political-economic responsibility, cultural reality of religious pluralism, and the web of life in fullness. These characterize emancipation, inculturation (or contextualization), and integrity of life as central for Asian theological imagination. Asian contextual theologies take issue with the Western hegemonic model of self-interested individualism and dominion embedded within the interplay between knowledge, power, and discourse. To what extent does a theological epistemology emerging from Martin Luther claim the triune God as the source of life in support of emancipation, inculturation, and fullness of life? Such a reading strategy challenges the structural reality of violence, injustice, and dominion in society, culture, and religion, which is perpetuated against humanity and the web of life in creation.

This chapter aims to hermeneutically and practically retrieve the prophetic potential of Reformation theology to set forth radical, new, and alternative possibilities of liberation, life for all creation in fullness, and recognize people of other cultures and faiths. Given this agenda, the chapter critically examines a Japanese colonial interpretation of Luther's theology of the cross (Kazoh Kitamori), as seen through the angle of minjung theology. A critical analysis of the Japanese colonial theology of God's pain helps us to understand to what extent the project of inculturation is undertaken in terms of a critique of ideology and is driven by solidarity with the life of the victims.

Furthermore, we shall investigate Luther's reflection of the triune God as the source of life and emancipation, exploring his hermeneutical-prophetic direction on behalf of emancipation, inculturation, and integrity of life in creation. This perspective, framed within a postcolonial orientation, provides new terrain for advancing the study of the future of Martin Luther and Reformation theology in East Asia. This process transcends Western modernist-neo-colonial epistemology, which is reproduced in the historical and political-economic realm in the context of increasing forces of economic globalization in Asia (for example, in Japan). The generalizing term "Asian" was embedded within the Japanese colonial context, which offered a counter force to Western imperialism in the late nineteenth and early twentieth centuries. The colonial character of "Asian" continued to shape the Japanese imperial understanding of God's pain with reference to Reformation theology.

1. Luther and God's Pain in Japanese Colonial Context

In a study of *Christian Theology in Asia*,[1] we observe that the churches in Asia have attempted to maintain their identity and integrity by articulating their own theologies. The terms "Asian," "Asian sense," or "Asian method" highlight the context, relevance, characteristics, and orientation of Asian theological works. A genealogical and archeological study of the unifying term "Asian" reveals its political and colonial usage within the context of Japan's nationalism and colonialism.

The Japanese colonial discourse of "Asian" might be traced to Japanese imperial theology and its reference to Japanese life in the Post-Hiroshima context. The first attempt to read Luther in this imperial direction was undertaken in the Japanese cultural context. Hence, I critically examine Kitamori's seminal book, *The Theology of the Pain of God*.[2]

In the wake of World War II, Kitamori (1916-98) explored the suffering of God in terms of a traditional Japanese Kabuki drama. The traditional and imperial Kabuki drama is rather shunned by those who wanted to break away from Japan's reprehensible colonial past. However, Kitamori utilizes Japanese cultural terms such as tsurasa (vicarious suffering), in order to propose a

[1] *Christian Theology in Asia*, ed. Sebastian C.H. Kim (Cambridge: Cambridge University Press. 2008), xi-xii.

[2] Kazoh Kitamori, *The Theology of the Pain of God* (Eugene: Wipf & Stock, 2005, Reprint).

theology of the cross. Given Luther's metaphor of "death against death" on the cross, Kitamori unfolds his theology in terms of "pain against pain." A notion of "God in pain" comes to the foreground in the sense that God embraces those who do not deserve to be embraced.[3]

Kitamori's theology of the cross operates by way of analogy in relation to pain, that is, *analogia doloris*,[4] incorporating the Japanese word tsurasa into the wounded heart of God.[5] Silence in God's mystery and tsurasa are the guiding metaphors for underscoring Kitamori's theological project, featuring God as the One who loves the unlovable through the sacrifice of Christ. Commenting on Kitamori's theology, Kosuke Koyama has shown that "embracing and enduring tsurasa becomes an intercultural correspondence to Luther's concept of 'God fighting with God'."[6] Kitamori utilizes tsurasa, rerooting the Christian narrative of a theology of the cross in the Japanese cultural matrix.[7]

Certainly, Kitamori takes deus absconditus in Luther's thought as the theological epistemology for understanding God's pain, because the hidden God is the fundamental principle of Luther's theology, from which all the rest of Luther's thought emerges.[8] Emphasizing the hidden God enmeshed in pain, Kitamori maintains that God's eternal decision to deliver the Son to the world becomes the hermeneutical bedrock for proposing the analogy of pain, which contrasts to the Roman Catholic (and Barthian) teaching on the analogy of being and analogy of faith.

Kitamori transforms Luther's teaching on justification imbued with justice into a mysticism of God's pain and silence in the fashion of the hidden God. In so doing, unfortunately, he expunges the social-critical and prophetic dimensions of the grace of justification in matters pertaining to Japanese colonialism, its historical responsibility, and guilt. Kitamori sidesteps the human

[3] *Ibid.*, 27.

[4] *Ibid.*, 56.

[5] *Ibid.*, 138.

[6] Kosuke Koyama, *Waterbuffalo Theology* (Maryknoll: Orbis, 1974), 120.

[7] *Ibid.*, 115.

[8] Kitamori, *The Theology of the Pain of God*, 107.

capacity to love and respect the righteousness and justice of *deus absconditus* only through *deus revelatus* (the revealed God) in his *resignatio ad infernum* (descent into hell), thereby the vicarious representative of those innocent victims. For Luther, Jesus Christ as a mirror of the Father's heart is also the first born among many brothers and sisters. Jesus Christ as the exemplary prototype stands with the tormented, because he is the one who suffers injustice among victims of violence, the forsaken among the forsaken.

Actually, Kitamori's book was completed at the very height of the war. Written during the war, Kitamori idealizes and even fetishizes the tragic suffering of the Japanese people, through which one perceives and comprehends the pain of God, while completely ignoring the innocent victims who suffered under Japan in other Asian countries. Kitamori completely eradicates the real victims of WW II, those suffering and murdered during the period of Japanese colonization. For instance, Japanese troops committed a series of atrocities in Nanjing during the Japanese War of Aggression against China. The brutal slaughter of innocent people, together with the rape and destruction of that ancient and beautiful city occurred over a period of six weeks between December 1937 and January 1938. A God identified with the pain of Japanese people remains questionable and even dangerous, because this God is mute and elusive about the outcry of all the real victims during the brutality of WW II.

2. God's Suffering in Solidarity with Minjung

The Japanese colonial reading of God's pain has faced a radical challenge from minjung theology, which refines the theology of the cross according to Jesus' socio-biography in deep solidarity with those who are marginalized, suppressed, and outcast. Minjung theology entails a strong critique of Japanese ideology, which emulated Western civilization in terms of colonialism, scholarship, and hegemony. A minjung theological reading of God's pain emphasizes Jesus' life connection with the ochlos-minjung, in which the gospel of the kingdom of God reinvigorates minjung-subaltern as the subject of history. Here Bonhoeffer's insight into a theological epistemology from below remains crucial to the radical horizon of the gospel. That is, "from the perspective of the outcast, the suspects, the maltreated, the powerless, the oppressed, the reviled—in short, from the perspective of those who suffer."[9]

Minjung theology is a postcolonial-liberative project in relation to the minjung-subaltern, which seeks to discover the globalization of cultures and histories within the structural violence of Western modernity in the aftermath of colonialism. It articulates the lingering effects of the colonial aftermath, while archeologically reading the previous history of the innocent victim, in order to remember the forgotten for our neo-colonial present. A project of inculturation in this regard endeavors to appreciate the distinctive character of culture for a thick description of the gospel narrative in the context of world Christianity. It debunks legitimatization of a racist, paternalistic, and neo-colonial system embedded within the civilization of the West. Thus inculturation as the critical and creative process aims at discovering and advancing Christian values that are already inherent in culture. It also entails a potential of emancipation from Western-centrism, archeologically discovering God's ongoing work in Christ and Spirit in a different culture. It enhances God's presence within the people, their culture, and history.

Challenging Kitamori's Japanese cultural-imperial reading of Luther, I have presented an interreligious hermeneutic for radicalizing Luther's theological insights in encounter with the Asian reality of minjung and Buddhist compassion through social engagement.[10] Faith, gratitude, and universal compassion in the Buddhist tradition do not stand in contradiction to Christian teaching. Rather, such a perspective needs to be appreciated and applied in any translation of the Reformation teaching of justification into East Asian language, culture, and religion. In a hermeneutical circle, the meaning of the living voice of the gospel is contextualized, while at the same time keeping a critical distance from the past colonial limitations and the current neo-colonial errors. Life together with the Other, grounded in faithfulness to the living and emancipatory Word of God, has priority over an individualist ontology in this prophetic project of interpretation and discipleship for ethical

[9] Dietrich Bonhoeffer, *Letters & Papers from Prison*, ed. E. Bethge (New York: Macmillan, 1971), 17.

[10] Paul S. Chung, *Martin Luther and Buddhism: Aesthetics of Suffering*. 2nd ed. (Eugene: Pickwick, 2008).

solidarity with the Other.[11] This theological project is grounded in an anamnestic reasoning and the subversive memory of Jesus, whose socio-biology for the gospel of the kingdom of God embraces his people – the *massa perditionis* (public sinners and tax collectors, thereby ochlos-minjung).

Driven by this postcolonial imagination, next we radicalize Luther's theological insights to make them more amenable to ecclesiology and theology in East Asia on behalf of emancipation, inculturation, and fullness of life in creation.

3. Martin Luther: The Triune God and the Church

For Luther, God is eternally a glowing oven full of love, who is fully revealed in Jesus Christ, "a mirror of the Father's heart." Jesus opens to us "the most profound depths of his fatherly heart and his pure, unutterable love."[12] The triune God, revealed as the fountain of love, speaks in terms of God's strange work, law, and the gospel.

In contrast to the Greek logos, the "word in Christian tradition is pure event, because the Word became flesh. Creation once took place through the word of God, such that the miracle of language is explained in the non-Greek notion of the creation. In his exposition of John's Prologue, Luther argues that God is the Word speaking in, with, and to God's self. God speaks because God is the Word – a force of communication – enabling communication within God's self and for the world. Luther conceived of God as the subject of divine speaking in promise, dialogue, and relation.[13]

This perspective characterizes God as the source of life, communication, and redemption, such that Trinity means a living, relational, and emancipatory God. God as the speaking subject upholds Luther's notion of gospel in the sense of the living voice of God. God is living, effective, life-giving, pro-

[11] Emmanuel Levinas, *Otherwise Than Being or Beyond Essence*, trans. Alphonso Lingis (Pittsburgh: Duquesne University Press, 2004), 37-38.

[12] Martin Luther, "Large Catechism," in Robert Kolb and Timothy J. Wengert, eds., *Book of Concord: The Confessions of the Evangelical Lutheran Church* (=BC) (Minneapolis: Fortress, 2000), 439-440.

[13] LW 52:45-46.

phetic, and redemptive in gospel, since God's Trinitarian being is framed in the internal structure of the speech-event in loving communion, that is, promise, dialogue, and participation.

The Word of God mediates God in self with God for us in the sense of *verbum relationis* (the word of relation), which comprehends faith and life of the world as linguistic, creational, and emancipatory. The Triune God comes to us in historical time: God the Creator, God the Redeemer, God the Sanctifier in God's salvific-missional drama, because "the Father gives us all creation, Christ all his work, the Holy Spirit all his gifts."[14]

God's act of speech to the church and the world is inseparably connected with the power of the Holy Spirit, who was actually poured out upon all flesh at Pentecost. With the gift of speech, people of every nation can understand each other. God's self-bringing to speech captures language, that is, the essence of language. This language is rooted in God's word-in-deed, that is, the Greek translation of the Hebrew notion of dabar into the logos.

The church is sent into the world and exists for the sake of the world, because the church as the assembly of saints, is created through the Word and the sacraments in the presence of the Holy Spirit. The Holy Spirit "[a]ffects faith where and when it pleases God in those who hear the gospel…not on account of our own merits but on account of Christ."[15] Luther characterizes the motherly character of the church, because it is "the mother that begets and bears every Christian through the Word of God" through the Holy Spirit. The Spirit illuminates and inflames our hearts.[16]

4. Hermeneutic of the Gospel and Interpretation

For Luther, Holy Spirit plays a normative role in the interpretation of the Scripture. There exists a dialectical and dialogical relationship between the character of the *verbum dei* (as spoken word) and the character of "writtenness" in the presence of the Holy Spirit. Insofar as gospel, as the living voice

[14] "The Large Catechism," BC 440.

[15] "Augsburg Confession," art. 5, BC 41.

[16] "Large Catechism," BC 436.

of God, is sung and proclaimed as an oral cry, it is a voice resounding in all the world, shouted and heard in all places through the proclamation of the Word of God. Luther's cardinal metaphor of "what promotes Christ" offers a hermeneutical principle in establishing dialogue with the world of the entire Scripture as well as the realm of creation. This is also the criterion for judging all scriptures regarding whether they are in agreement with what drives Christ.[17] Thus the concept of *viva vox evangelii* implies the priority of the spoken word (God's Saying; *dabar* in Hebrew) over the written word (the Scripture).

A scientific-critical investigation of Scripture retains its validity in qualifying Reformation theology as hermeneutical, critical theology for effectively communicating the meaning of the biblical narrative to people in the world. In his "Introduction to the Psalter" (1531) Luther further states that "there [in the whole Bible] you see into the heart of all the saints."[18] The humanity of the biblical authors and their limitations are not concealed, but actually uncovered and exposed to our exegetical investigation. The authors' historicity and sociopolitical situation in Scripture were shaped and influenced by their lives and voices, which were embedded within the socioeconomic and historical circumstances. This perspective helps us to comprehend that historically conditioned traditions and social connections remain influential factors in exploring and interpreting Scripture in a decisively political, prophetic, and socio-critical manner. Understanding assumes social and political agency in the interpretation of the effective involvement of God's Word in the life of world.

In light of God's communicative action, it is worth noting that Luther in the *Smalcald Articles* proposes that the "mutual colloquium and consolation of brothers and sisters"[19] is the fifth form of the gospel in relation to preaching, the sacraments, and the ecclesial office. Luther's understanding of the

[17] "Preface to the Epistles of St. James and St. Jude," in John Dillenberger, ed. *Martin Luther: Selections from His Writings* (Garden City, NY: Anchor, 1961), 36.

[18] Helmut Gollwitzer, *An Introduction to Protestant Theology,* trans. David Cairns (Philadelphia: Westminster, 1978), 58.

[19] "Smalcald Articles," BC 319.

Word of God is more rich and profound than Karl Barth in his threefold sense of the Word of God.

God's Word, understood interpersonally, retains an authority which is located in mutual colloquium. Luther adds the consolation of brothers and sisters, explaining this as a supplementary characteristic of God's Word. Thus Luther grounds his concept of the fifth form of the gospel in Matthew 18:20. "For where two or three are gathered in my name, I am there among them." God is understood as the one who is involved in the public and communicative life: "The Lord is witness between you and me forever…The Lord shall be between me and you, and between my descendants and your descendants, forever" (1 Sam 23:42). Luther therefore articulates the presence of God in the midst of God's people – Israel and the nations together (Zech 2:10-11; Ez 43:7; Joel 2:27).

Accordingly, Luther's hermeneutical theology in critical and prophetic relief is in accordance with Hebrews 1:1: "God spoke to our ancestors in many and various ways by the prophets." The word of God in Jesus Christ is indispensably connected with God's act of speech, which was undertaken throughout all the ages in their plural horizons of effect. The Hebrew way of expression remains in force, because God's word is related to a real thing or action, transcending the question of ontology. God's being is in God's word-in-deed, namely, speaking is doing, so that the word is the deed.[20] Luther is convinced of the necessity of interpretation, because Scripture is not merely the written word belonging to the past. Rather it is the living voice of God, which encounters us in our midst, here and now (Heb 4:12-13, 1 Cor 1:18, Is 55:10-11). Luther's creative engagement with the living and prophetic word of God can be undertaken over and against all normative and authoritative interpretation when previously established and placed over Scripture.

A notion of critical, contextual theology in this regard becomes indispensable, because the living word of God is not mechanically conveying or repeating certain words or statements from the Scripture to people in different times and places. Considering human life, language, and culture in the trans-

[20] F. W. Marquardt, *Das christliche Bekenntnis zu Jesus dem Juden: Eine Christologie 1* (Munich: Chr. Kaiser, 1990), 141-145.

lation of the biblical narrative, we observe that even the same word can be said differently in another context. Luther offers clear inspiration for advancing the relationship between God's word and interpretation through a contextual-constructive translation (or inculturation) of the biblical narrative, which remains central to the theological project of World Christianity today.[21] This perspective becomes arbiter in radicalizing Luther's insights, when it comes to political economic responsibility, integrity of life in creation, and recognition of the people of other cultures and faiths.

5. Gospel in the Midst of Political Witness

Luther's view of the gospel in the midst of political witness entails critical and prophetic potentials in critiquing and renewing the problems of social structure. As Luther argues against corruption by the powerful, "the princes" and "big shots" find it quite tolerable that the whole world should be criticized if only they themselves are exempted from this criticism. But they must certainly be criticized too, and anyone entrusted with the office of preaching owes it to them to point out where they act unjustly and do wrong, even if they protest that such criticism of rulers will lead to rebellion."[22]

Accordingly, the political realm belongs to political diakonia in faithfulness to God in terms of *parrhesia* (telling the truth in an audacious manner). For the sake of the freedom of the gospel, Luther spoke out against those who sought ideologically to misuse his theology of justification for a theology of revolution.[23] However, for Luther, the justified becomes a collaborator with God, because faith alone justifies. Once justified, we enter the active

[21] Lamin Sanneh, *Whose Religion Is Christianity? The Gospel beyond the West* (Grand Rapids: Eerdmans, 2003).

[22] Cited in Ulrich Duchrow, *Global Economy: A Confessional Issue for the Churches?* trans. David Lewis (Geneva: WCC, 1987), 7.

[23] Although his discourse – "suffering, suffering, cross, cross is the Christian right, no other" – was attacked during the Peasants' War (1524), Luther's radical critique of the state's violence must not be forgotten.

life of loving our neighbors.[24] Faith is active in love, seeking justice and prophetic diakonia in the public realm, because grace becomes, indeed, impulse and motivation for praxis and transforming activity.

The grace of justification, which entails the living Christ in union with us in Word and sacrament, makes the grace of justification and faith dynamically related to the service of the needy in the public sphere. Luther prophetically expresses Eucharistic theology in connection with anamnestic reason standing in solidarity with people who suffer: "Here your heart must go out in love and learn that this is a sacrament of love. As love and support are given you, you in turn must render love and support to Christ in his needy ones. You must feel with sorrow all the dishonor done to Christ in his holy Word, all the misery of Christendom, all the unjust suffering of the innocent, with which the world is everywhere filled to overflowing. You must fight [resist], work, pray, and – if you cannot do more – have heartfelt sympathy."[25]

The grace of justification, which is grounded in the sacramental dimension of God's promise and righteousness, underpins the church's responsibility in coping with the unjust suffering of the innocent by means of resistance, labor, prayer, and heartfelt sympathy. The celebration of the Eucharist reinvigorates the church's participation in God's mission, standing in solidarity with the unjust suffering of the innocent, in whom the risen Christ is present. A critical, emancipatory theology finds validity in witness to the God of justice in connection with the dangerous and subversive memory of Jesus, who is in deep solidarity with ochlos-minjung (Luke 4:18-19).[26]

As articulated in Luther's Commentary on the Magnificat (1520-1521), Mary actually became impoverished and was completely wrapped up in poverty. Without any human help, God alone may do the work.[27] Mary, as an

[24] Gollwitzer, *Krummes Holz – aufrechter Gang: Zur Frage nach dem Sinn des Lebens* (Munich: Kaiser, 1985), 313.

[25] "The Blessed Sacrament of the Holy and True Body and Blood of Christ, and the Brotherhoods" (1519), in *Martin Luther's Basic Theological Writings*, ed. Timothy F. Lull (Minneapolis: Fortress, 1989), 247.

[26] Craig L. Nessan, *The Vitality of Liberation Theology* (Eugene: Pickwick, 2013), 65-76.

[27] LW 21:328-29.

example of the grace of justification, shapes and underscores the church in terms of preferential service of the subaltern-minjung. She addresses the challenge of God's initiative against the patriarchal culture of the powerful, their hierarchical system, and institutionalized dominance. Luther, in a letter to Friedrich (March 7, 1522), expressed his new discovery of political theology with a theological turn: "The spiritual tyranny has become weak. That is only what I regard with my writings. Now, I see that God drives further, insofar as God works in Jerusalem and two regiments. I have learned newly that not merely spiritual, but also worldly power must obey the Gospel…It shows itself clearly in the story of the Bible."[28]

6. God and Economic Justice

Luther's view of the economic realm marks a promising field, as seen in his critique of the system and practice of early capitalism. Until the beginning of 1525 Luther was preoccupied with economic issues on the question of usury. Luther regards mammon as the chief example in opposition to God, fighting for the sake of the poor and needy against the "devouring capital" system, which dominated the social reality of the early capitalism at his time. For Luther, those who have everything needed (money and property) – without care for anyone else – have a mammon-god. They set their whole hearts on money and property: "This is the most common idol on earth."[29]

In the Old Testament, God's grace summons us to corresponding action, because faith in the God of Torah is active and effective in love and service of our fellow humans as well as in care for other creatures. Economy (oikonomia) is the law or the management of the household, which compounds oikos (household) and nomos (law or management). Since our relationship to God is influenced by economic realities, unjust economic conditions have the power to ruin the true worship of God, because worship of God is replaced by worship of mammon.

Luther's understanding of the Torah becomes a catalyst for appreciating the correlation between law and gospel for the sake of economic justice. His de-

[28] WA Br 2,461.61.

[29] "Large Catechism," BC 387.

liberation of the unity of the Word of God maintains that word and deed are one in God and the Hebrew word *dabar* is expressed as verbum facere ("to do" the Word). Torah in the Latin term *institutio* and *doctrina* (denoting command and promise) must be comprehended in the Jewish sense of the Bible as "divine instruction" rather than its translation as "law."[30]

Torah contains law/gospel, command/promise, judgment/grace, identifying the unity of the Word of God in such correlations. Luther comprehends faith in accordance with the First Commandment, which implies *Deum justificare* (giving God justice). When we act on faith in God's promise and accept God's forgiveness, we give God justice, the justification of God.[31] The Torah is more comprehensive than the accusing law, since the word of the covenant and the promise of salvation are the same as revealed in Jesus Christ.[32]

In faithfulness to *dabar* as God's effective word, Luther's discovery of the Torah can facilitate our understanding of the law-gospel hermeneutic in a more dynamic, living, and prophetic manner, especially in matters of the church's public responsibility and economic justice. For Luther, the Old Testament entails "certain promises and words of grace, by which the holy fathers and prophets under the law were kept, like us, in the faith of Christ."[33] Luther notices "the promises and pledges of God about Christ"[34] as the best thing in Moses, in whom there is a fine order, a joy about the gospel of

[30] Pinchas E. Lapide, "Stimmen jüdischer Zeitgenossen zu Martin Luther" in *Die Juden and Martin Luther – Martin Luther und die Juden: Geschichte, Wirkungsgeschichte, Herausforderung,* ed. Heinz Kremers, et al (Neukirchen-Vluyn: Neukirchener, 1985), 172.

[31] H. J. Iwand, *The Righteousness of Faith According to Luther*, ed. Virgil F. Thompson, trans. Randi H. Lundell (Eugene: Wipf and Stock, 2008), 21.

[32] In his *Table Talk*, Luther said: "The Hebrew drinks from the spring source, but the Greek from water that flows from the source. The Latin drinks from the puddles." WA Tr 525.

[33] "Preface to the Old Testament (1523, revised 1545)," in Timothy F. Lull and William R. Russell, eds. *Martin Luther's Basic Theological Writings* (Minneapolis: Fortress, 2005, 2nd edition), 114

[34] Luther, "How Christians Should Regard Moses," in *ibid*., 129.

Christ. Moses is a well of all wisdom and understanding.[35] Here is evangelical freedom or delight in appreciating and undertaking the gospel dimension of the law (paranesis), that is, an evangelically conceptualized notion of the law.[36]

Given this, Luther takes seriously the most internal core of the Torah, the Decalogue, for Christian faith. Luther's theological axiom of God versus mammon is elaborated in his critical analysis of economic issues in the context of the seventh Commandment of the Decalogue ("You are not to steal") as discussed in his Large Catechism (1529). Luther remains a prophetic voice for God's oikonomia versus the political reality of mammon. The economic reality, which is stamped by misusing the market in an arbitrary, defiant, and arrogant way, causes the poor to be defrauded every day, as new burdens and higher prices are imposed upon their life.[37]

Ulrich Duchrow makes a substantial contribution by maintaining that the economic arena is no longer simply an ethical problem for Luther, but has become a confessional problem. Confession to God and resistance against mammon is grounded in the confessional notion of status confessionis.[38] Luther takes issue with mammon as a system of totality, in which people want to be god of the whole world through mammon and to have themselves worshipped as such.[39] The concept of greed acts as a critical arbiter in Luther's theological thought, because greed contradicts truth and faith in God's promise. Luther's sharp critique of the devouring system of capital accumulation expresses a prophetic voice against the Christian character of early capitalism

[35] *Ibid.*, 121. During his stay in Coburg, Luther wrote his letter to Justus Jonas (June 30, 1530), stating that the Decalogue is the dialectic of the Gospel and the Gospel is the rhetoric of the Decalogue. Therefore we have, in Christ, all of Moses, but in Moses, not all of Christ. Luther became a new student of the Decalogue. WA Br 5,409, 26-29.

[36] H. J. Iwand, *Luthers Theologie, Nachgelassene Werke*, eds. H. Gollwitzer et al. (Munich: Chr. Kaiser, 1983), 203-204. For Luther, the original root of all good lies in taking delight in the Law of the Lord (Psalm 1).

[37] "Large Catechism," BC 417-418.

[38] "Formula of Concord," BC 516.

[39] Duchrow, *Global Economy*, 176.

in reference to colonialism in America.[40] In the practice of usury, speculation, and hoarding, Luther was keenly aware of the irrational and dangerous aspects of early capitalism, demonstrated by his ability to see clearly the political-economic alliance between the Catholic Church, Charles V, and the Fuggers. This perspective became inspiration for the church in East Asia to challenge the principalities and powers generated under the colonization of economic globalization and its tenet of possessive individualism today.

In this light, it is important to critically review Max Weber's evaluation of Luther's theology regarding economic justice. For Weber, Luther's concept of vocation has been interpreted as indifference to the spirit of capitalism, because the society is regarded as already produced and sanctioned by the divine order of creation. Accordingly, Luther's attack upon the great merchants of his time was neither biblically nor prophetically grounded. Rather Weber contended that Luther's critique of economic injustice was ironically claimed as a part of the spirit of capitalism, an expression of economic traditionalism. Thus Weber continued to argue that Luther lacked ethical rationalism, because he was not capable of maintaining the fundamental relationship between worldly activity and religious principle.[41]

Against Weber's misunderstanding, however, Luther himself considered the importance of economic life and justice in his theological deliberation of God and Torah, when it came to the connection between the first commandment and the seventh commandment. Luther's prophetic stance against the structures of mammon, which is grounded in God's justice and economic righteousness in the Old Testament, forms a substantial impulse for the church's responsibility for economic justice. Luther's stance for God versus mammon is biblically inspired, prophetically driven, and deeply embedded within the endeavor of creating fair and just life arrangements.[42]

[40] Karl Marx, *Capital, 1: A Critique of Political Economy*, trans. Ben Fowkes (London: Penguin, 1990), 649-650. Luther stands in line with the prophetic stance of Bartolomé de Las Casas (1484-1566) against Spanish mission and colonialism.

[41] Weber, *The Protestant Ethic and the Spirit of Capitalism*, trans. Talcott Parsons (Mineola, NY: Dover, 2003), 85.

[42] Paul S. Chung, *Church and Ethical Responsibility in the Midst of World Economy. Greed, Dominion, and Justice* (Eugene: Cascade, 2013), 38-40.

7. God's Universal Reign and Creatio Continua

Luther's teaching of justification can be seen in connection with God's universal reign, which acknowledges the dignity of people outside the walls of Christianity. God the Creator works all in all. God's ongoing act in the new creation (creatio continua) implicates divine power itself in preserving the creation and being present in creation's innermost and outermost aspects. God's on-going act of new creation in the world points to Luther's insightful concept of God, notably emphasizing the first function of law in reference to the gospel (and also sharpening our identity as created collaborators with God, as St. Paul teaches to in 1 Corinthians 3:9). St. Paul, in front of the Areopagus, bore witness to solus Christus, expressing his conviction that everyone lives, moves, and has his/her being in the universal reign of God (Acts 17:22, 27-28).

For Luther, God is wholly incomprehensible and inaccessible, as St Paul witnessed (Rom 11:33).[43] Divine majesty is reserved for God's self alone, since "God must therefore be left to himself in his own majesty."[44] This means that God works life, death, and all in all, keeping Godself free over all things. The hidden God, coupled with God's universal reign, works in the world through irregular grace. God is the Provider of all life arrangements, enhancing the integrity of life in creation in terms of political responsibility, economic justice, and recognition of the Other.

Theology of the cross, seen in connection with a theology of creation, finds its validity in upholding a theology of life in solidarity with those who are fragile, victimized, and vulnerable. This perspective characterizes theology of the cross as a theology in the flesh, which embraces fullness of life for creation and humanity in a holistic manner.

For Luther, a lively faith goes hand in hand with praise of God's beauty and glory in creation. All creatures are tools in the service of God's work, even behind "masks" (larva Dei), under which God hides God's activity. God

[43] *Luther and Erasmus: Free Will and Salvation,* eds. E. Gordon Rupp and Philip S. Watson (Philadelphia: Westminster, 1969), 330.

[44] *Ibid.*, 201.

remains free in the ceaseless activity with which God works all in all. The article of creation is one of faith. Faith in God's creation is faith in the triune God. Faith and justification correlate with ecological or environmental stewardship, which is indispensable for shaping and directing theology in a linguistic, creational, and emancipatory manner, transcending the limitations of Western modernity.

Luther's marvelous sense of the aesthetic dimension in creation is striking, because "the wonderful and most lovely music [comes] from the harmony of the motions that are in the celestial spheres."[45] This is a beautiful text for church and theology in East Asia, which is committed to keeping the aesthetic sense of creation intact for ecological stewardship and eco-justice. We are encouraged to listen attentively to the beautiful music of God coming from creation, because creation is conceived of as a linguistic and salvific phenomenon. God's work takes place in faithfulness, also in the realm of creation. Creation is the sphere of dialogue and communication occurring between God and the creatures. Given that creation is the communicative sphere, the world is to be understood as a text which is readable and decipherable, through which God may speak to us in a completely different manner than heard in the ecclesial sphere. This perspective finds validity in the East Asian sense of the web of life and of nature in a harmonious and holistic manner, which is crucial in Buddhist, Confucian, and Daoist visions of human life fully interconnected with other creatures and nature as a living organism.

8. Mission: Invitation and Dialogue

Luther's recognition of Others invites them to the gospel, while acknowledging that the non-Christian leads a morally mature life on the basis of the commands written upon all human hearts. Furthermore, Luther acknowledges in Abraham's faith journey that God becomes an advocate for Hagar and Ishmael. Luther's remark about Ishmael is striking at this point: "For the expulsion does not mean that Ishmael should be utterly excluded from the kingdom of God…The descendants of Ishmael also joined the church of

[45] LW 1:126.

Abraham and became heirs of the promise, not by reason of a right, but because of irregular grace."[46] Luther's Christological idea of grace does not stand in competition with God's embrace of the Other through irregular grace.

Bonhoeffer incorporates Luther's radical understanding of the gospel into his theology of the cross from below: "the curses of the godless sometimes sound better in God's ear than the alleluias of the pious."[47] The biblical radicalism of Luther's teaching of justification takes seriously such blasphemies more than many conventional hymns of praise.

Luther provides a hermeneutical way of speaking about God with all-embracing and inclusive force, while retaining a radical and particular direction. The dialectic between the exclusive tendency and an all-inclusive comprehensiveness enables Luther's language about sola (alone) to be closely associated with the term simul (at the same time). Sola, in the sense of biblical uniqueness, cannot be comprehended adequately without connection to God's universal simul in biblical openness toward the world. Thus gospel in the sense of viva vox evangelii, (more than proclamation) offers a living dynamism in underlying communication and translation of the biblical narrative through dialogue with the world.

Luther's teaching of justification, when seen in light of God's universal reign and irregular grace, has an inclusive dimension, which becomes obvious particularly in his commentary on 1 Timothy 2:4. Here the exclusive proposition is expressed in universal terms, because God causes all people to be saved.[48] Accordingly, Luther boldly appreciates pagan authority as a model to show the responsibility of secular authority. Luther was not reluctant to praise the Turkish state and exercise a critique of Christian authorities with unprecedented frankness.[49] As a gentle and rich Lord, God grants a great

[46] LW 4:42-44.

[47] Bonhoeffer, *Act and Being*, ed. Wayne W. Floyd, Jr., trans. H. Martin Rumscheidt (Minneapolis: Fortress, 1996), 160.

[48] LW 28:260. His reflection on Jesus' descent into hell also runs in this direction.

[49] Gerhard Ebeling, *Luther: An Introduction to His Thought* (Minneapolis: Fortress, 2007), 189.

measure of gold, silver, riches, dominion, reason, wisdom, languages, and kingdoms to those outside Christian religion.

Luther warns against misleading people of other religions through a forced conversion to Christianity by means of colonialism and domination.[50] Instead, mission can only be effective when it is performed with the continual renewal of the church and Christian existence, excluding the human purposes of dominion, cultural imperialism, and confessional rivalry. As Luther states: "it is not said, therefore, that God desires to convert everyone. St. Paul only declares of the Gospel that it is a cry, which he causes to go out over everyone. It is supposed to be pure blessing."[51]

This perspective supports mission as prophetic dialogue and inculturation, which is historically embodied in the case of Karl L. Reichelt (1877-1952) in his dialogue and collaboration with people of other faiths.[52] Luther's theology of conversion becomes arbiter in postcolonial formation of God's mission in recognition of the others. Our mission is to invite people to the mystery, love, and promise of God in the gospel of Jesus Christ for all, communicating its universal message and translating and interpreting it anew in different times and places. Luther's linguistic renovation and its dialectic of particular-universal becomes a driving force for upholding our public witness as prophetic dialogue within a pluralistic world of many religions, in support of interreligious solidarity for justice, peace, and integrity of creation.

9. Conclusion

In this study of Martin Luther and Reformation theology in East Asian perspective, we have sought to radicalize his insight into God as the Source of Life in solidarity with those who are fragile, vulnerable, and victimized. In so doing, we deepen Luther's recognition of the Other in a contextual and con-

[50] Volker Stolle, *Luther Texts on Mission: The Church Comes from All Nations*, trans. Klaus D. Schultz and Daniel Thies (Saint Louis: Concordia, 2003), 104-105.

[51] *Ibid.*, 29. Lutheran confessional theology states that "Conversion to God is the work of God the Holy Spirit alone." "Formula of Concord," BC 561.

[52] See Reichelt's legacy in connection with Tao Fong Shan Christian Centre, Hong Kong, China.

structive framework to undergird inclturation, emancipation, and integrity of creation. I conclude the East Asian interpretation of Luther by summarizing arguments for the future of Reformation theology as articulated in this chapter.

First, the Christian confession of Jesus Christ in the tradition of Reformation theology emphasizes the Son of God as the eternal and incarnate Word, who stands at the borderline between Israel and all nations, identifying himself with the lowest of the low among his brothers and sisters (Mt 25:31). This is characteristic of our understanding of the triune God as the Source of life and of God's emancipation in solidarity with and recognition of the subalterized – massa perditionis – for the kingdom of God has come in Jesus Christ.

Second, Luther's theology of justification needs to be extended and renewed in different times and places, especially in light of Luther's congenial notion of the gospel as the living voice of God. God as the Subject of speaking encourages us to acknowledge and respect the world of creation in which God continues to work and address. The Reformation teaching of justification should break through its encapsulation within Western possessive individualism under the colonization of the Empire; instead it should be reclaimed as way of expressing God's deep compassion in the death of Jesus Christ for all, reinforcing interreligious dialogue.

Third, a postcolonial reading of Reformation theology in East Asian context advances a project of inculturation, in order to undergird interreligious dialogue, adopting a new departure in the critique of an imperial version of Reformation theology or misuse of its scholarship in the service of the powerful in the ecclesial context of East Asia. In dialogue with Reformation theology, a theological project of inculturation entails prophetic-hermeneutical reasoning in revealing and clarifying the emancipatory and constructive values inherent in Asian religions and cultures. It archeologically focuses on what has been subjugated and foreclosed in the study of cultures and religions regarding the irregular side of history, society, and church. It is undertaken in terms of anamnestic reasoning in dangerous and subversive remembrance of Jesus's socio-biography with his people.

Fourth, theology of the cross, seen in light of a theology of creation, can overcome the previously tainted imagery between the cross and crusade in colonial age. This refers to a refurbishing of the theology of the cross for a theology of life (resurrection) seen in light of God's solidarity with the minjung and economic justice for all (theology in the flesh). This claims a postcolonial formation of theologia crucis as a radical critique of any cultural compromise with colonial or imperial directions. Through the Reformation notion of irregular grace, the goodness of creation is fulfilled and restored in God's grace of justification through divine reconciliation and solidarity with the innocent victim and wholeness (shalom) for all creation.

Fifth, the Lutheran insight into the living and emancipatory Word entails self-criticism and self-renewal for the project of inculturation, emancipation, and integrity of life, in order to deepen its prophetic-contextual horizon for political responsibility, economic justice, integrity of creation, and recognition of the Other. Law-gospel hermeneutics should be comprehended in a Torah-Gospel correlation, in which there is evangelical delight in doing Torah through prophetic words and economic justice for the world. This teaching can serve as a hermeneutical bedrock for articulating God's universal reign by sharpening the theologia crucis in terms of dialogue, recognition, and collaboration with people in the world. This reinvigorates interreligious dialogue in a practical direction for emancipation, inculturation, and ecological sustainability. For instance, universal compassion, social engagement, economic justice, and ecological sustainability in the Buddhist tradition needs to be appreciated in any contextualization of the Reformation teaching of justification, together with political-economic responsibility and social-ecological engagement, especially in the critical project related to a second Axial Age for "interreligious solidarity for just relations."[53] Through the process of interreligious dialogue, a fusion of horizons in a critical-emancipatory framework generates new meaning for the gospel of justification by faith, which is active in love and which seeks understanding and justice in the public realm across the globe.

[53] For this pioneering direction in interreligious dialogue based on a critical-emancipatory framework, see Ulrich Duchrow and Franz J. Hinkelammert, *Transcending Greedy Money: Interreligious Solidarity for Just Relations* (New York: Palgrave Macmillan,, 2012).

Common property for all who are needy: Eucharistic practice in the midst of economic injustice

Samuel Torvend

A woman went up to the priest after Mass and said, "Father, I went to communion without going to confession first." "How come, my daughter?" asked the priest. "Father," she replied, "I arrived rather late after the offertory had begun … For three days now I have had only water and nothing to eat … When I saw you handing out the hosts, those little pieces of white bread, I went to communion just out of hunger for that little bit of bread."[1]

1. Spiritual economy

The spiritual economy of the late medieval period[2] was spiritual in that it focused the Christian imagination on "the life of the world to come." It was an economy in that it sanctioned the exchange and purchase of spiritual goods in order to gain favor with the church and with God in the Christian's progress toward the "world to come." In this spiritual economy, participants were encouraged to invest whatever funds they possessed in good works which would gain merit in the sight of God and the church.

One of the prominent legacies of the Lutheran reform project was the insistence on asking questions, at times difficult questions, of what most people took for granted, what most people thought was normal. Thus, at the heart of the Ninety-Five Theses, Luther asks this troubling question: "Why doesn't the pope, whose wealth today is greater than the wealth of the richest

[1] Leonardo Boff and Clodovis Boff, *Introducing Liberation Theology* (Maryknoll: Orbis, 1987), 1

[2] 1350-1500

Crassus, build this one basilica of St. Peter with his own money rather than with money of the poor?"[3]

While the question was asked in a circular intended for conversation among the faculty of the University of Wittenberg, the theses themselves were quickly published and distributed widely throughout Germany and Western Europe. His theses regarding the practice of indulgence sales prompted some to wonder why a monastic professor, unknown outside his university town, was raising questions about a spiritual and economic practice that appeared to be sanctioned by the supreme head of the western church, a leader who claimed that his office was ordained by the will of God. Of course, one wonders what Luther was thinking when he sent a copy of his theses to the German archbishop who hired the indulgences sellers in the first place, that same archbishop who quickly forwarded Luther's questions to Pope Leo X.

Within six months of the publication of his theses, Luther was asked to explain his questions and comments which he did at Heidelberg in April, 1518.[4] He was subsequently interrogated, threatened, excommunicated, kidnapped and held under protective custody because he asked not only troubling theological questions, but also raised ethical concerns focused on the plight of the homeless and the hungry poor who were urged to "invest" what little they had in a spiritual economy sanctioned by late medieval church authorities. As Luther rightly intuited, participants in this "economy" were subject to a discourse of fear and coercion, a discourse that was intended to produce sales that would enable a church prelate to pay off the debt he had incurred in his move to purchase a church office from the Holy See.

While some of Luther's questions concerning a spiritual economy emerged in the Ninety-Five Theses, he continued to write, lecture, and preach on socio-economic concerns through 1540, six years before his death. Here are some of the questions he asked, questions embedded in those often

[3] *Luther's Works*, Vol. 31, Helmut Lehmann, gen. ed. (Philadelphia: Muhlenberg Press, 1957), 33; hereafter *LW*.

[4] *LW* 31:39-58.

overlooked texts[5] which treat of economic questions: Are the poor anonymous objects of Christian charity, essentially insignificant in the dispersal of financial contributions?[6] Does a charitable distribution of funds benefit the reputation of the donor rather than call attention to the deplorable plight of the poor, homeless, and hungry?[7] Is any response to those who suffer economically the responsibility of the few (e.g., religious professionals and the wealthy) or the many: all Christians, including city council members, magistrates, and rulers?[8] In times of crisis – drought, famine, war, natural disasters, and epidemics – is it the responsibility of political leaders to act swiftly and generously as advocates for those who suffer, especially those who have no means to recover from the effects of human-made or natural

[5] I mention "often overlooked texts" in reference to an anecdotal survey of U.S. Lutheran seminaries. While a number of Luther's biblical, sacramental, and theological writings are studied in required seminary courses, his economic and social ethical writings rarely enter the classroom. There are exceptions to this absence, but they are just that: exceptions. Consider a recent survey of one hundred ELCA clergy: only three had read at least one of Luther's economic writings while over sixty had no idea that such writings even existed.

[6] *LW* 35:68

[7] *LW* 35:69; see Louis Chatellier, *The Europe of the Devout: The Catholic Reformation and the Formation of a New Society* (Cambridge: Cambridge University, 1989), 133, in which, concerning late medieval charity, he notes: "It was not the poor person who counted but the act [of the donor] accomplished in the sight of God or for the good of the church." The person offering charity was the primary focus; a charitable act, a monetary investment, which, it was believed, would yield benefits, spiritual and social, to the benefactor.

[8] The Lutheran suppression of Benedictine monasteries and mendicant convents - for theological reasons - led to the dismantling of these centers of medieval social welfare that had endured for close to 1000 years. The emergence of the "evangelical" church order (Kirchenordnung) placed responsibility for the poor within the congregation and the "evangelical" town or city councils where Luther's reform was accepted, a responsibility rooted in his teaching on the priesthood of all the baptized. On the Wittenberg Order, see *Die evangelischen Kirchenordnungen des 16. Jahrhundert*, Emil Sehling, ed., (Tübingen: Mohr, 1902), 1:697-98; on the Leisnig Order, see *LW* 45: 161 ff.

disasters?[9] Is not the Christian voice to be heard publicly and with righteous indignation when lobbyists line the pockets of rulers with silver and gold and thus lure such leaders to serve only the private good of a business or corporation?[10] Who will prevent bankers from charging injurious interest rates on loans, interest rates that allow bankers to keep in perpetual servitude those who need a home, want to start a small business, or respond to an unexpected crisis?[11] Is it not the duty of the ruler or the courts to regulate banks and thus prevent corrupt banking practices?[12] In a state of emergency (e.g., war or natural disaster), who will stop merchants and corporations from artificially increasing prices on basic necessities?[13] Who will ensure an equitable sharing of food and drink based on need rather than social status or wealth?[14]

These questions were asked within a period of six years, between the publication of the Ninety-Five Theses in 1517 and the first evangelical "church

[9] See *LW* 7:158-159; *LW* 13:42-72; and *The Book of Concord: The Confessions of the Evangelical Lutheran Church,* Robert Kolb and Timothy Wengert, eds.; C. Arand, E. Gritsch, R. Kolb, W. Russell, J. Schaaf, J. Strohl, and T. Wengert, transs. (Minneapolis: Fortress, 2000), 450-451 (hereafter BC) in which Luther comments on the duties of princes toward their people in times of natural and human-made disaster (e.g., war).

[10] *LW* 45:241

[11] *LW* 2:263; *LW* 45:233-310; see also Ricardo Reith, "Luther on Greed," in *Lutheran Quarterly* 15 (2001): 336-351.

[12] At various times throughout his writings on trade and usury, Luther asks the reader to consider the need for government regulation of banking practices that favor the bankers and discriminate against the customer or promote deceitful practices. See *LW* 45:233ff.

[13] *LW* 45:272.

[14] Luther argues that the individual Christian, parents, churches, city councils, and rulers – shaped by the teaching of justification by grace and the equality established in baptism – are all responsible for the distribution of food and drink (i.e., the basic necessities for life) to those in need: infants and children, the chronically sick, the homebound elderly, widows, victims of human-made and natural disasters, and the unemployed. Rather than play one potentially responsible party off the other, as in much contemporary U.S. political discourse, he asked for a wider and integrated response to impoverishment.

order" produced, with Luther's direct consultation and approval, in 1523.[15] Luther's sermons, treatises, and letters in this period indicate his awareness of an array of pressing social and economic questions as well as his engagement with those who were most vulnerable and at his doorstep: the hungry poor in Wittenberg.[16] Catharina Lis and Hugo Soly suggest that at least 50

[15] The Kirchenordnung or "church order" developed rapidly throughout the cities of Germany where the "evangelical" reform was accepted. The first church order appeared at Wittenberg in 1522 (during Luther's Wartburg exile) with others following in Augsburg, Nürnberg, and Altenburg (in 1522), and then Kitzingen, Strassburg, Breslau, and Regensburg (in 1523). With the collapse of canon law in those regions of Germany where the Lutheran reform was accepted, rulers, city councils, and church leaders produced church orders which regulated the order of worship, education for children, and relief of the poor, destitute, and unemployed. The continuing publication of the critical editions of the German Lutheran church orders is currently under the supervision of the Heidelberger Akademie der Wissenschaften, Dr. Eike Wolgast, editor-in-chief. To date, nineteen volumes have been published in the series entitled *Die evangelischen Kirchenordnungen des XVI. Jahrhunderts.*

[16] It is in the Table Talks where Luther describes himself as an easy target for Wittenberg beggars: too easily he gave away the money earned by his spouse, Katarina von Bora. See Eberhard Schendel, "Martin Luther und die Armen", *Lutherische Kirche in der Welt* 36 (1989): 113-114. The incidence of poverty increased at the beginning of the sixteenth century. As poor peasants were freed from serfdom, the negligible form of economic protection found in a feudal economy – greater indebtedness to a vassal or lord – was lost. Many artisans and field workers who moved to cities in search of economic opportunity became a part of the urban poor. Lee Palmer Wandel suggests that at least 25 per cent of the population in Switzerland, Germany, the Lowlands, and France were continually underfed. See his *Always among Us: Images of the Poor in Zwingli's Zurich* (Cambridge: Cambridge University Press, 1990). For other assessments of poverty in late medieval and early modern Europe: *Aspects of Poverty in Early Modern Europe*, ed. Thomas Riis (Alphen aan den Rijn: Sijthoff, 1981); *Aspects of Poverty in Early Modern Europe II: Les réactions des pauvres à la pauvreté*, idem (Odense: Odense University Press, 1986); Carter Lindberg, Beyond Charity: *Reformation Initiatives for the Poor* (Minneapolis: Fortress, 1993) 17-67; Friedrich Luetge, "The Fourteenth and Fifteenth Centuries in Social and Economic History," *Pre-Reformation Germany*, ed. Gerald Strauss (New York: Harper & Row, 1972), 316-379; Michael, Mollat, *The Poor in the Middle Ages*, trans. Arthur Goldhammer (New Haven: Yale University Press, 1986); Merry Wiesner, "Making Ends Meet: The Working Poor in Early Modern Europe," *Pietas et Societas: New*

percent of the German population in the early sixteenth century lived on the edge of subsistence, uncertain as to where they would obtain an adequate amount of food to feed themselves on a daily basis.[17] Thus, as the reform grew in Germany, city councils were faced with an unexpected economic and social challenge: while eager to take over the land and resources owned by the Roman church and its monastic communities, the new "evangelical" Christians suppressed many of the institutions which had been the centers of poor relief for the previous millennium. With the disestablishment of cathedrals and the suppression of monasteries, who would care for the many living on "the edge of subsistence"?

2. The freedom of the Christian

One of the singular theological achievements of Luther's reform was to draw the Christian imagination from its late medieval fascination with the last judgment toward Christian life in this world. If the word of final judgment and justification by grace were spoken at baptism, the Christian life could then be lived within the dynamic of sin and grace here on earth. Indeed, the freedom of the Christian, given by God and guided by faith, is to be exercised in community and in service to the neighbor in need: "We conclude, therefore, that a Christian lives not in himself, but in Christ and his neighbor" ("Freedom of a Christian," 1520, WA 7; LW 31)

A growing concern for those who lived on the edge of subsistence, if not in destitution, was shaped by Luther's insistence that the late medieval spiritual economy be dismantled. This not only meant an end to the "investment strategy" of indulgence sellers, but also the breaking up of any practice that led the Christian people to believe they could secure a benefit from the church or from God through the purchase of spiritual favors, through the endowment of religious orders, cathedrals, or churches, or through the completion of spiritual works (e.g., pilgrimage, entering a religious order, corporal or spiritual

Trends in Reformation Social History, eds., Kyle Sessions and Phillip Bebb (Kirksville, MO: Sixteenth Century Journal Publishers, 1985) 79-88.

17 *Poverty & Capitalism in Pre-Industrial Europe* (Atlantic Highlands, NJ: Humanities Press, 1979) 53-96.

works of mercy). All of these spiritual and economic practices supported the notion that one could and must cooperate with God's grace as received in the sacraments: a cooperation that would demonstrate, on the Day of Judgment, the authenticity of one's commitment to Christian faith and life.

For Luther and his reforming colleagues at Wittenberg, such works or purchases suggested that the Christian's ultimate goal in life is union with God in heaven, a union nonetheless made perilous by the need to demonstrate a heartfelt and energetic cooperation with the grace received through the sacraments, especially the sacrifice of the Mass. While the Mass was understood theologically to be the generous offering of grace to the Christian soul as nourishment and strengthening in a life of virtuous living, in practice it had become "mere merchandise, a market, and profit-making business."[18] Against the view that life should be given over to preparation for an otherworldly existence, Luther argued that the Day of Judgment was not in the future but took place on the day of one's baptism into the death and resurrection of Jesus Christ. For it was in Holy Baptism that God offered the gift of justification by grace apart from any works. Thus, if the Christian were relieved of the need to spend his or her life cooperating with grace in hope of an eternal reward – investing in the present for a future benefit – then one's energies could be directed toward life on this earth, on faith active in love for the neighbor in need. As he claims in all three of the significant works of 1520,[19] God advances toward humanity with "life, health, and salvation," the late medieval movement of the Christian soul working toward heaven utterly reversed. Consequently, the Mass could no longer be interpreted as a sacrifice offered to God, but rather as the flowing of Christ and his grace into the life of the Christian and the Christian community, an overflowing of grace to be extended into daily life. Freed from the "market" as a "profit-making business," the reformed Mass could now serve as the inspiration of Christian generosity in the world, a generosity that would benefit those living on the edge of subsistence.

[18] *LW* 36:35.

[19] *Address to the German Nobility*, *The Freedom of a Christian*, and *The Babylonian Captivity of the Church*.

3. The reform of worship and social welfare

From his theological project, Luther engaged in the reform of worship and social welfare as set forth in his "Preface to the Ordinance of a Common Chest" (1523, WA 12; LW 45) and "The Fraternal Agreement on the Common Chest of the Entire Assembly at Leisnig" (1523, WA 12; LW 45). The reform of worship and welfare thus linked the free and equitable distribution of food and drink in the Lord's Supper with distribution of free food to the hungry poor which took place at the end of the reformed Mass. This is to suggest that there was an "economic" sensibility alive in the earliest Lutheran reforms of the Lord's Supper.

In 1522, the eleven villages which constituted the parish church of Leisnig, some sixty miles south of Wittenberg, asked for Luther's advice concerning worship and social welfare. In September, 1522, he travelled to Leisnig and met with members of the parish church and the two priests they had elected as their church leaders. After consultation with Luther, the members of the parish church created an Ordinance or Agreement which they then sent to Luther in January 1523, asking for his advice.[20] Luther responded enthusiastically to the proposed order, promised that he would send a reformed order for the celebration of the Mass,[21] and in early summer wrote a preface to the "Fraternal Agreement on the Common Chest of the Entire Assembly at Leisnig."[22]

The Leisnig church order was one of the first Lutheran responses to the growing number of persons who suffered with food insecurity, food deprivation, and malnutrition in Germany. The church order, a kind of Christian legislation regarding worship and welfare, established a link between this Lutheran response to the hungry poor and the reformed Mass. For in the juxtaposition of common worship and social welfare, the framers of the ordinance asked one very simple question: How is the one related to the other? Or this:

[20] Walther Brandt suggests that the two parish priests, Heinrich Kind and Johann Gruner, may have written the ordinance, though their authorship cannot be substantiated. See LW 45:163.

[21] "Concerning the Ordering of Divine Worship in the Congregation", *LW* 53:11-14.

[22] *LW* 45:169-194.

how might worship rightly lead to welfare? Or this: how might the ancient liturgy, now newly reformed, lead a Christian assembly to serve the homeless and the hungry? Indeed, in his "Preface" to the church order, Luther wrote: "Since [the] knowledge of Christ is so active and powerful among you that you have set up a new order of service, and a common fund after the example of the apostles [Acts 2:44-45; 4:32-35],[23] I have seen fit to have this ordinance of yours printed, in the hope that God will add his gracious blessing that it may become a public example to be followed by many others."[24] Indeed, at the outset of the preface, Luther praised the evangelical Christians at Leisnig for acceptance of the reformed Mass and the establishment of "a common fund after the example of the apostles." Set next to and flowing from "the breaking of the bread and the prayers" (Acts 2:42), Luther invoked the social practice of the early Christians: "All who believed were together and had all things in common; they would sell their possessions and goods and distribute the proceeds to all, as any had need" (Acts 2:44-45). Next to the sharing of bread was set the sharing of all things commonly held.

The Leisnig common chest – the collection and sharing of goods by the community for distribution "to all, as any has need" – was to be supplemented, in part, by the appropriation of monastic, mendicant, and ecclesial properties. The sale of said properties, the use of their incomes, or their transformation into schools for children or housing for the needy was to be accomplished without force or harm.

Devote all the remaining property to the common fund of a common chest, out of which gifts and loans could be made in Christian love to all the needy in the land, by they noble or commoners … Now there is no greater service

[23] "All who believed were together and had all things in common; they would sell their possessions and goods and distribute the proceeds to all, as any had need … Now the whole group of those who believed were of one heart and soul, and no one claimed private ownership of any possessions, but everything they owned was held in common. With great power the apostles gave their testimony to the resurrection of the Lord Jesus, and great grace was upon them all. There was not a needy person among them, for as many as owned lands or houses sold them and brought the proceeds of what was sold. They laid it at the apostles' feet, and it was distributed to each as any had need," *LW* 45:169.

[24] *LW* 45:169.

of God than Christian love which helps and serves the needy, as Christ himself will judge and testify at the Last Day, Matthew 25[:31-46]. This is why the possessions of the church were formerly called bona ecclesiae, that is, common property, a common chest, as it were, for all who were needy among the Christians.[25]

At the conclusion of the Preface, Luther hoped that his suggestions would diminish begging and the usurious practices that subject the poor and the needy to a lifetime of impoverishment. He also noted the effect of offering one's goods for the common good: when one gives freely and generously to others, the impulse toward greed can be quenched. He concluded by suggesting that if only one or two follow his advice, he would be content. Yet he remained somewhat dubious: "The world must remain the world … I have done what I can … God help us all to do what is right and to stand firm."[26]

The Agreement created by the Leisnig community followed Luther's Preface and, in its preliminary statement, claimed the congregation's capacity to appoint its own pastor "for the sole purpose of preaching God's word and administering the sacraments," to exercise its Christian liberty in conformity with the Scripture, and to undertake the care of the hungry poor. The right to call a pastor and care for their own needy, the Agreement noted, are rooted in "the eternal blessings won by our Lord and Savior Christ out of pure grace and mercy," and "our universal priesthood" – echoes of Luther's teaching on justification by grace and his redefinition of the spiritual estate. Since the Agreement set forth the community's commitment to social welfare, it declared at the outset that "all the internal and external possessions of Christian believers are to serve and contribute to the honor of God and the love of the fellow-Christian neighbor."[27] Where there is "eternal blessing," there is "brotherly love," and where there is such love, it comes to expression in deeds of kindness directed toward the needy. The love of Christ inspires Christian love of neighbor; the "Christian and evangelical Scriptures" guide social welfare.

[25] *LW* 45:172-173.

[26] *LW* 45:176.

[27] *LW* 45:177.

The Agreement then listed the ecclesial sources of income that, henceforth, would be donated to the common chest: hereditary lands, supplementary rents, toll income from church-owned bridges, cash, silver, jewels, rents from chapels, benefices, revenues, stores, income from masses for the dead, perpetual memorials, income from indulgence sales, alms, income and annuities from brotherhoods, and contributions, penances, or fines paid by craft guilds and peasant farmers to the church.[28] In the space of a few paragraphs, the Agreement named the myriad sources of income collected by the late medieval parish, monastery, convent, or priory. Some of this income was distributed to the hungry poor and the needy or used to support hospices and orphanages sponsored by cathedrals, parish priests, and monastic communities – the centers of social welfare in the late medieval world. At the same time, the list reveals the many and diverse sources that constituted the financial foundation of a spiritual economy focused on the purchase of spiritual "goods" and "services" that were believed to aid the dying and the deceased as they progressed toward their eternal reward "in heaven." Yet a surprising element, unmentioned yet quite clear, marks the Agreement: the list was inverted by the Leisnig community, its many revenues, rents, contributions, and fines now turned toward a common chest that would be used for the "preeminently spiritual undertaking [of caring for] the poor and the needy." Monies once devoted to the maintenance of chapel priests and their recitation of many masses, daily offices, and rosaries – which were believed to help the dead in their movement toward union with God "in heaven" – were now redirected to a common chest "on earth" where daily bread could be distributed to the hungry poor.

Supplementing the incomes previously derived from benefices, indulgence sales, and the annuities of the brotherhoods, the Agreement noted that each person in the parish should be urged to support the poor with voluntary contributions and bequests of property, cash, or jewels designated in a will. Likewise, the Agreement asked lay church officials and the pastor to exhort the community to bring offerings of food and other provisions along with coins so that the hungry poor might receive foodstuffs every Sunday. Whenever incomes or donations prove insufficient to meet the needs of the com-

[28] *LW* 45: 179-181.

munity, the Agreement mandated something not found in the 1522 Wittenberg Order: an annual tax on every household in the town and parish, "according to ability and means." From those who rented or resided with relatives or friends in the town and parish, a smaller collection was to be taken. Thus, the Agreement established a variety of sources that could be used to support the hungry poor and the needy: ecclesial revenues, voluntary contributions, bequests, and an annual graduated tax. Each citizen, each parishioner, was to contribute to the common welfare of all, especially the neediest: both a religious and civic responsibility.

> The parish assembly solemnly purposes and promises that to the honor of God and the love of our fellow Christians we shall never spare ourselves this trifling annual contribution in view of the fact that hitherto, since time out of mind, both residents and nonresidents throughout our common parish have by many methods and devices been overburdened and fleeced incessantly the year round with exorbitant and intolerable impositions and assessments. By the grace of God these practices have now been restored to the true freedom of the Christian spirit.[29]

Supervision of the common chest was the responsibility of the ten directors elected from the parish worshipping assembly: two nobles, two city council members, three town citizens, and three peasant farmers. To each group of directors, a key was allotted that opened one of the four locks binding the common chest. Thus, four representatives from each of the constituent groups would need to be present for the chest to be opened and the goods therein distributed. Meeting every Sunday, the directors shall review the books in which are recorded gifts to the common chest, the minutes of every meeting, and the disbursements of every Sunday and weekday when food and other provisions are distributed to the hungry poor and the needy.

Every Sunday, at the end of the reformed Mass and flowing from it, the directors were to distribute food and other provisions from the common chest to all in need. Should need arise during the week, the directors were to distribute food to the hungry. Likewise, the pastor, sacristan, and male and female school teachers were to receive an annual stipend and an appropriate

[29] *LW* 45:192.

allotment of food so that they might serve the community without worry or distraction. In addition to weekly and annual disbursements of food, grain was to be purchased and stored "for the general welfare of our parish" so that in times of scarcity a sufficient amount would be available for the entire city through purchase, loans, or free disbursement among those with little or no means. In effect, the Agreement established a theologically grounded program of social welfare, practiced primarily on Sunday, the Lord's Day, flowing from the celebration of the Holy Communion, in which the Christian worshipping assembly would see its contributions flowing to the hungry neighbor in need. Thus, on the Lord Day's, the day devoted to the resurrection of life from death, the Leisnig community kept the Lord's Supper which flowed into the feeding of the Lord's Poor.[30]

4. The Lord's Supper as a symbolic economic system

Is it possible that the reform of worship and welfare asks one to consider how a Christian vision of economic sharing might be informed by a "eucharistic economy"? Such a question asks one to consider the Lord's Supper

[30] For Lutheran and other Protestant social welfare initiatives, see Miriam Usher Chrisman, "Urban Poor in the Sixteenth Century: The Case of Strasbourg," *Social Groups and Religious Ideas in the Sixteenth Century* (Kalamazoo: Medieval Institute, 1978), 59-67; Ole Peter Grell and Andrew Cunningham, "The Reformation and changes in welfare provision in early modern Northern Europe," *Health Care and Poor Relief in Protestant Europe, 1500-1700.* Ed., Ole Grell and Andrew Cunningham (London: Routledge, 1997), 1-42; Carter Lindberg, "'There Should Be No Beggars Among Christians': Karlstadt, Luther, and the Origins of Protestant Poor Relief," *Church History* 46 (1977): 313-334; Charles Parker, "Calvinism and Poor Relief in Reformation Holland," *The Reformation of Charity: The Secular and the Religious in Early Modern Poor Relief.* Ed., Thomas Max Safely (Boston: Brill, 2003), 107-120; Mary Sprunger, "Mennonites and Sectarian Poor Relief in Golden-Age Amsterdam," *The Reformation of Charity*, 137-153; Lee Palmer Wandel, *Always Among Us: Images of the Poor in Zwingli's Zurich* (Cambridge: Cambridge University Press, 1990); William Wright, "A Closer Look at House Poor Relief through the Common Chest and Indigence in Sixteenth-Century Hesse," *Archiv für Refomationsgeschichte* 70 (1979): 225-238. Portions of this essay were published previously in "Those Little Pieces of White Bread: Early Lutheran Initiatives among the Hungry Poor," *Dialog* 52:1 (March 2013): 19-28.

(Holy Communion or Eucharist) as a symbolic economic system, "symbolic" in that it was and is charged with a variety of impulses and meanings. This is to suggest that Luther's sacramental reforms possessed a trajectory focused on life in this world and service to the neighbor in need.

Thus, one wonders: did this early Lutheran community see their participation in the reformed Mass as a "churchly" or "spiritual" practice and their commitment to care for the hungry poor as a "secular" or "worldly" matter? Or did this Christian assembly experience a seamless flow between the table of the Lord and the table of the poor? Consider Luther on the question:

> When you have partaken of this sacrament, you must in turn share the misfortunes of the fellowship … Here your heart must go out in love and learn that this is a sacrament of love. As love and support are given you, you in turn must render love and support to Christ in his needy ones. You must feel with sorrow all the misery of Christendom, all the unjust suffering of the innocent, with which the world is everywhere filled to overflowing. You must fight, work, pray and … have heartfelt sympathy … For here the saying of Paul is fulfilled, 'Bear one another's burdens, and so fulfill the law of Christ' [Gal. 6:2].[31]

And so another question: which is more important, worship or welfare, adoration or advocacy, sacrament or social action? Which is more important: breathing in or breathing out? Set next to and flowing from the proclamation of the Bible's many stories of hunger and feeding, of greed and generosity and their interpretation through preaching was the table filled with gifts of food and drink drawn from the earth and made available through human labor: there was the Leisnig table where food and drink were given away freely and with equity.

Indeed, it was in this sacramental giving where one might discern a relationship between eucharistic practice and economic sharing, a "eucharistic economy." For in the free giving of the bread fragment and the wine cup, each received the same amount and each received regardless of gender, race or ethnicity, socio-economic status, education, occupation, heritage or lineage, mental or physical capacity. Indeed, the central teaching on justification by grace would reject any and every claim to special treatment, to personal or

[31] *LW* 35:54.

cultural advantage over the other. In Holy Baptism, any claim to privilege as constructed in the larger culture was to be washed away. Thus, the Lord's Supper, the Holy Communion, renewed and confirmed the egalitarian dimension of Christian community – as articulated in the "Address to the German Nobility" – and at the same time announced the manner in which "goods" (i.e., food and drink) were to be shared at the Lord's Table and in the larger community.

It is this intuition – that the Lord's Supper sets forth an economic vision in which food and drink are shared equitably and according to need – which can prove so troubling for some, and so threatening for others, in a culture marked by consumerist sensibilities, in a culture so suffused with the capitalist goal to accrue as much as one can for oneself.[32] Indeed, I wonder if you share my dilemma, for I know that I am not and never will be free of my, of our, cultural formation in "acquisitiveness," of desiring more than we ever need, of holding on to that alleged treasure which a consuming culture deems valuable. And, so I wonder, and I ask you to wonder with me: could that formation in biblical story and equitable food practice actually serve as an act of resistance to a cultural formation in greed, which for Luther, nourished far too many forms of social injustice?[33]

5. The sacramental action

In addition to the historic Lutheran emphasis on forgiveness as the primary benefit of the Lord's Supper,[34] might other emphases emerge in the study of this sacramental action? While some Lutherans and other Christians now

[32] For current Lutheran reflection in North America on the relationship between sacramental practice and ethical action, see Gordon Lathrop, "Remember the Poor: The Public Implications of Eucharistic Sending," unpublished ms., given at Valparaiso University (March 25, 2008); Carter Lindberg, *Beyond Charity: Reformation Initiatives for the Poor* (Fortress, 1993); Cynthia Moe-Lobeda, "Globalization in Light of Luther's Eucharistic Economic Ethics," *Dialog* 42:3 (2003):250-256; Martha Stortz, "Practicing What It Means: Welfare Reform and the Lord's Supper," in *Currents in Theology and Mission* 26:1 (February 1999): 19-32.

[33] Reith, "Luther on Greed," in *Lutheran Quarterly* 15 (2001): 336-351.

[34] Luther, "The Small Catechism," in *BC* 362.

recognize a relationship between the Supper and care for the hungry poor, does Luther's early criticism of growing mercantile capitalism and its proclivity to control goods for the sake of the few and for their profit alone open the way to consider a relationship between eucharistic sharing and the commitment to a just and equitable distribution of goods and wealth in the world today?

This is to suggest that the practice of the Eucharist may well disclose a Christian way to share the gifts of God's earth, in the economy of God. The presider, in breaking apart the loaf of bread, must ensure that there are sufficient fragments for all who come with hands open to receive bread. Those who sip from the one cup need be mindful of others who will also drink from the cup: not drinking too little, not drinking too much. Each one who comes to the Lord's Table receives the same amount. The bread and wine are not distributed in quality or size according to one's gender or orientation, one's race, ethnicity, or nationality, one's socio-economic or educational status, one's political commitments. The comfortable worker cannot claim more than the unemployed. The wealthy citizen of a developed country cannot take bread from the hands of worker. Rather, bread and wine are given equitably to all because they are in need, because they want to eat and drink.

In many churches, those who come to eat and drink at the Lord's Supper rightly say "Amen" as bread and wine are offered. And even if no such word of assent is uttered, they very eating and drinking is, in truth, an assent to the reception of this bread and this wine. Yet such assent, through word or act, is not only the recognition that bread and wine are "given for you." It is the recognition of and an assent to an equitable practice, to this generous sharing of Christ's body and blood among those who are hungry and thirsty. It is a reception not only of the words but also the practice. And if this is so, would not such participation in this eucharistic practice, this "eucharistic economy" cause one to wonder why there remains an inequitable and unjust distribution of earth's many gifts, those gifts which, in faith, the churches claim are God's and not ours?

Luther wrote that greed is a disobedient and unbelieving scoundrel, a ravenous consumption of what rightly belongs to all. The early Lutheran linking of sacrament and social welfare thus continues to serve as both memory and challenge in a world where the open hands of many wait to be filled with bread fragments. Indeed, the skeptical voice of the prophet asks: Who benefits from keeping the hungry poor both hungry and poor?

Re-Radicalizing Justification

Cynthia D. Moe-Lobeda

1. Introduction

Lutheranism(s) and Lutheran claims about justification were born of courageous resistance to political-economic-cultural power arrangements that prevented people from experiencing and trusting God's gift of unconditional and unstoppable love as the central guiding reality of life in all of its aspects. To Luther, the centrality of neighbor-love, as a fruit and consequence of God's love, had implications for economic life that radically contradicted the emerging capitalism of his day. How is it that a tradition sprung from such roots could have remained largely (though not entirely) complicit with political-economic-cultural power arrangements of modernity that also impede the reception of and trust in God's grace as the heart of life, and the normative guide for economic life? Conversely, how could Lutheranism and Lutheran understandings of justification be re-reformed to claim the heritage of resistance, specifically in relationship to political-economic-cultural systems that defy God's call to love neighbor as God loves, both interpersonally and in relationship to social structures?

In response to these questions, I argue that dominant streams in Lutheran traditions have tended to claim the "safe" half of Luther's key discoveries while ignoring or subordinating the "dangerous" half. Specifically:

1) In describing justification, we[1] have claimed the first of "two kinds of righteousness" while tending to ignore the "second kind of righteousness" which – according to Luther – is "fruit and consequence" of the first and results in "living justly with neighbor."

[1] "We" in this paragraph refers in general terms to dominant trends in North Atlantic Lutheranism of modernity and post-modernity. I am well aware that these trends do not represent all streams of Lutheran traditions.

2) We uphold Luther's call to charitable sharing but ignore his call to renounce economic systems that create wealth for a few while harming the poor.
3) We tend to claim Christ as gift of grace but not Christ as gift of God's actual presence dwelling within us.
4) We uphold Luther's admonishment to obey secular authorities, while ignoring his admonition to disobey them when they demand ways of life that betray allegiance to God before all else or betray God's call to love neighbor as God loves.

Thus, while Luther dared to face the fire, we theologically rationalize fleeing from it. In that flight, we draw especially on claims about justification that represent part but not all of Luther's radical discoveries about justification. This critique bears hopeful and life-giving potential. It is the potential of Lutheranism(s) to drink from the wellsprings of our radical heritage – especially in re-understanding justification – in order to build ways of life that first trust the gracious love of God and then embody it by living toward economic justice for all.

Two methodological assumptions inform this work. First, it reflects my understanding that theological inquiry as a critical constructive discipline entails three elements. They are: 1) critique of where the tradition has betrayed the gospel or served the causes of death, destruction, or domination; 2) retrieval of suppressed or ignored elements of the tradition that are capable of igniting the fire of the gospel in our day; and 3) reconstruction for the sake of being faithful to God. These elements may be sequential or they may be interwoven. Here, they are threaded together throughout.

Secondly, this chapter is grounded in an assumption regarding theological work in the Lutheran heritage. Lutheran inquiry into justification often focuses on asking what the message of justification by grace through faith means in each new time and place. I presuppose that inquiry into justification also should ask how dominant understandings of justification have undermined the proclamation and hearing of the gospel, including its radical political-economic-cultural-ecological implications, and then should build on what is learned through that crucial critical query.

2. Luther's Subversive Claims

Luther's faith claims shook the foundations of the constructed world – the reigning political-economic-theological power arrangements and ideological assumptions that shaped the terms of social life in his day. From Luther's theological perspective, these assumptions and power alignments had a disastrous impact on God-human relations; they deceived and distracted people from remembering who they are *coram deo* (before God) and *coram mundo* (before the world). His intense hermeneutic of suspicion was levied at whomever or whatever – including institutions, worldviews, and hegemonic powers – he thought distracted people from hearing the Word, remembering who they were as both objects and agents of Christ's love, and living according to that promise. This compelled Luther to challenge the "basic institution for the coordination, hegemony, and reproduction of the existing system," the ecclesiastical power structure.[2]

The transformative power of his claims lay in his commitment to disclose and refute whatever dynamics prevented people from hearing and trusting the gracious love of God given to them, for them, and through them. This meant convincing people that they could do nothing to earn God's love and salvation because it was given freely and only freely, and also convincing them that as people freely saved by God, they had an infinitely meaningful calling in the world. This calling included loving neighbor, and it had startling implications for noncompliance with the early emerging capitalism of Luther's day.

2 Leonardo Boff, "Luther, the Reformation, and Liberation," in: *Faith Born in the Struggle for Life: A Re-reading of Protestant Faith in Latin America Today,* ed. Dow Kirkpatrick, trans. L. McCoy, Grand Rapids 1988, 203. Luther's subversive moves were within the arena of religion; his primary intent was not to change social, political or economic structures except where those obscured the Word. Yet, as Boff points out, while Luther's intent was to challenge theological falsehood, his religious convictions had implications in virtually all dimensions of human life. Challenges to the power structure by Luther took many forms. For example: what was held to be salvific, he named oppression and bondage (indulgences, works, poverty and charity); what–other than God alone–was seen as worthy of trust, he named as betrayal (the papacy and salvific works; wealth); what was held to be divinely ordained, he disclosed as human construct (the papacy); what demanded allegiance and conformity so that allegiance and obedience did not go to Christ alone, he denounced (the pope).

We consider in this essay four tendencies in later Euro-Western Lutheranism that have truncated our ability carry forth that intensely reforming impulse – the impulse to find and refute dynamics that prevent hearing and trusting God's gracious love given to all, given both to be received and to be shared into the world in public and private life. Each of the four tendencies involves a central claim related to justification made by Luther, a claim having two folds or faces. I first summarize these four claims, and then argue that North Atlantic Lutheranism has tended to embrace only the parts of his Earth–shaking claims that do NOT disrupt the reigning power alignments of our contexts, but rather reinscribe them. We conclude with the hope and moral-spiritual power to be found in recognizing this dynamic and reclaiming the faithful subversive face of Luther's central faith claims.

2.1 Two Kinds of Righteousness[3]

Luther rattled the world with his radical claim that God, rather than human works, make us righteousness. His essays, "Two Kinds of Righteousness" and "The Disputation concerning Justification" reveal what is entailed in God's gift of righteousness in two kinds. The first kind of righteousness places us in a radically different relationship with God; we are totally forgiven and become righteous in God's sight. This occurs by the grace of God alone through faith alone on account of Christ.

After this first gift, we are placed in radically different relationship with people by "second kind of righteousness ... our proper righteousness"[4] which is the "product ... fruit and consequence" of the first. The second kind of righteousness is in essence "that manner of life spent profitably in good works." Luther goes on to define the moral life in terms of relationality in three spheres: "living soberly with self, justly with neighbor, and devoutly

[3] Significant portions of this section and the section entitled "Christ as Indwelling Presence" are taken from Cynthia Moe-Lobeda, *Healing a Broken World: Globalization and God,* Minneapolis 2002, ch. 4. The ideas in these two sections are developed far more fully in that chapter.

[4] This and the following brief quotations in this paragraph are from Martin Luther, "Two Kinds of Righteousness," in *Martin Luther's Basic Theological Works,* ed. Timothy F. Lull, Minneapolis 1989, 157, 158, 157, 158, 158.

toward God." Our proper righteousness "does not seek its own good, but that of another, and in this its whole way of living consists ....This righteousness follows the example of Christ in this respect (I Pet. 2:21) and is transformed into his likeness (2 Cor. 3: 18)." Luther insists in "Two Kinds of Righteousness" that we receive – not earn – two kinds of righteousness. His "*Disputation Concerning Justification*" iterates the two kinds of righteousness, their cause-effect relationship, and love as the essence of the second kind.[5]

Luther's understanding of justification is, thus, transformative. Justified sinners gradually are changed – individually but only in communities of faith – by the gratuitous righteousness of Christ. They are transformed into people who increasingly seek the well-being of others. They are in fact "made one with all others" by union with Christ.[6] The radical implications for economic life will become evident shortly.

Luther's notion of justification as transformation does not contradict the centrality of sin in his theology. The terrible and condemning reality of sin as constituent of human being is integral to his theology of justification. Luther understands sin as incurvatus in se (self-turned in upon self), the human proclivity to do everything for the promotion of self, out of concern for self, and using resources claimed as one's own rather than as gifts of God. "Man is so self-centered that he uses not only the physical but also spiritual gifts for his own advantage and seeks his own advantage at every opportunity."[7] Sin is thus fundamentally "unbelief" manifest as failure to trust God for all and to attribute all to God.[8] Luther argues (against the Aristotelian theological tradition, which held discipline as a morally significant counteractive to the condition of sin) that this condition is absolutely inescapable by human effort. Human beings are bound to this condition of sin, cannot make their way out

[5] Luther, "Disputation concerning Justification," in *Luther's Works* 34, ed. Lewis W. Spitz, Philadelphia 1960, 161-162.

[6] Luther, "The Blessed Sacrament of the Holy and True Body and Blood of Christ, and the Brotherhoods," in *Lull*, 251.

[7] Luther, "Lectures on Romans," *Luther's Works* 25, ed. Hilton C. Oswald, St. Louis 1972, 260.

[8] Luther, "The root and source of all sin…is unbelief in the inmost heart." in *Luther's Works* 35, 369.

of it. Humans can be freed from this condition only by God, as undeserved gift from God. God can grasp and turn the sinner. Thus the terrible pervasiveness and inescapability of sin is linked to the incredible beauty and power of grace. Luther claims that failure to acknowledge the gravity of sin is failure to know the truth about Christ.[9] I will argue shortly that, in Luther's theology, it is the power of the indwelling Christ and Spirit that "turns" sinners from se *incurvatus in se*, empowering them gradually, although never perfectly, to love with the actual love of Christ within.

One of Luther's most important contributions, in my estimation, is his insistence that justification as transformation is not justification as moral perfection, now or ever in earthly life. Luther's notion of human moral agency grounded in God's gift of righteousness and the indwelling Christ is accompanied by no illusions of human perfectibility. Christians remain simultaneously sinners and righteous. They are "rusty tools, being polished by God for as long as they live."[10] The import of Luther's claim – that human fallibility inevitably persists together with the morally transformative power of justification – is its coherence with lived reality. Luther is describing a key dimension of the human condition.

Luther's understanding of what happens to people when they are made righteous by God coheres with his central convictions regarding the relationship of works to salvation – works do not and cannot cause salvation. They follow from salvation. This claim refutes medieval morality which held that human works were meritorious for salvation.

This claim refutes also the common tendency in later Lutheranism to discount that indeed works are a vital part of the life of those who are justified by Christ. Luther's claim regarding the relationship between works and salvation, which does not lend itself to systematic formulation, is seen in the following excerpts from sermons and treatises. Concerning thesis 2S of the "Heidelberg Disputation," he argues: "Not that the righteous person does

[9] See "Against Latimus, " *in Luther's Works* 32, 137-260.

[10] Martin Luther, *D. Martin Luthers Werke: Kritische Gesamtausgabe,* Weimar 1883, known as the *Weimar Ausgabe* (*WA*), 2.413.27, cited by George W. Forell, *Faith Active in Love,* Minneapolis 1954, 92.

nothing, but that his works do not make him righteous, rather that his righteousness creates works. His grace and faith are infused without works. After they have been imparted the works follow.... ln other words, works contribute nothing to justification.... The works which he does by faith are not his but God's.... Christ is his wisdom, righteousness....that he himself may be Christ's action and instrument."[11] Luther expresses in a lecture on Genesis that "Faith is followed by works as a body is followed by its shadow."[12] In "The Freedom of a Christian ..." he declares that "faith in Christ does not free us from works hut from false opinions concerning works, that is from the foolish presumption that justification is acquired by works."[13]

The form of works" relevant here are the works that embody "love to our neighbor." Luther writes in his "Sermon on the 4th Sunday after Epiphany:" "God makes love to our neighbor an obligation equal to love to himself."[14] In "The Sacrament of the Body and Blood of Christ-Against Fanatics" Luther identifies "two principles of Christian doctrine.'' The first principle is that Christ gave himself that we may be saved, and we are saved by no effort of our own. The second "is love ... as he gives himself for us ... so we too are to give ourselves with might and main for our neighbor." Luther insists on the inseparability of the two: they are "inscribed together as on a tablet which is always before our eyes and which we use daily."[15]

That is, God gives the unearnable gift of forgiveness regardless of how broken we may be, and then sends us forth to be God's hands and feet while remaining sinners. We become God's "rusty tools" (italics mine), Christ for

[11] Luther, "Heidelberg Disputation," in *Lull*, 46-47.

[12] Luther, "Lectures on Genesis, *WA* 44, 135, 2, cited by Forell, *Faith*, 56. "We should not simply think, 'All I have to do is to believe and everything is taken care of, I do not have to do any good works.' No, we must not separate the two. You must do good works and help your neighbor so that faith may shine outwardly in life as it shines inwardly on the heart." Luther, "Sermon on John 6:48," cited by Forell, ibid.

[13] Luther, "Freedom of a Christian," in *Lull*, 625.

[14] Luther, in *Sermons of Martin Luther vol. 7*, ed. John Nicholas Lenker, Grand Rapids 1983, 68-69.

[15] Luther, "The Sacrament of the Body and Blood of Christ – Against Fanatics," in *Lull*, 331.

the other through love for our neighbor. According to Luther, our shortcomings in fulfilling this calling are vast. Vaster yet is God's unfailing forgiveness of them. Those shortcomings and that forgiveness do not detract from the centrality of active neighbor-love in the Christian life.

2.2 Neighbor Love as Guide for Economic Life

For Luther, that norm of neighbor-love – as the heartbeat of the second kind of righteousness – pertains to every aspect of life for the Christian, including economic life. According to him, economic activity is intrinsically an act in relationship to neighbor, and all relations with neighbor are normed by one thing: the Christian is to serve the neighbor's well-being, while also meeting the needs of self and household. Economic practices that undermine the wellbeing of the neighbor (especially of the vulnerable) are to be rejected and replaced with alternatives. About this Luther was vehement and specific.

Luther's was a time of "economic revolution gradually transforming Germany from a nation of peasant agriculturalists into a society with at least the beginnings of a capitalist economy."[16] Consequences included high prices, growing disparity of wealth, and increasing poverty, especially of those with low or fixed income. The poor "were a cheap labor pool for an expanding profit economy"; "Poverty was a growing social problem that the medieval tradition of almsgiving and personal charity was incapable of addressing."[17] Increasing "large" scale international trade required capital which sought profitable investment, feeding the emerging capitalist economy. Thus, the ethics of capital transactions were in public discussion.

In this context, Luther helped to establish a local social welfare system that provided material goods and created jobs for the unemployed. He theologically denounced certain aspects of the emerging capitalist economy that exploited the poor of his day – including the autonomy of capital from political constraints – and admonished preachers to do the same.[18] Hear Luther in his

[16] Walter I Brandt, "Introduction," to "Trade and Usury," in *Luther's Works* 45, 233.

[17] Carter Lindberg, *The European Reformations,* Cambridge 1996, 114, 111.

[18] See for example, Luther, "Admonition to the Clergy that They Preach against Usury," *WA* 51.367, cited in Ulrich Duchrow, *Alternatives to Global Capitalism,* Utrecht 1995, 220-221.

comments on the tenth commandment in the Large Catechism: Speaking of the "free public market," he writes, "Daily the poor are defrauded. New burdens and high prices are imposed. Everyone misuses the market in his own willful, conceited, arrogant way, as if it were his right and privilege to sell his goods as dearly as he pleases without a word of criticism."

Luther taught that widely accepted economic norms and practices that undermined the widespread good or the well-being of the poor ought be eschewed in daily practice and replaced with alternatives. As alternatives, Luther established norms for everyday economic life that prioritized meeting human needs over maximizing profit as the central aim of economic life. To illustrate: Christians, according to Luther's economic norms, must refuse to charge what the market will bear when selling products if so doing jeopardizes the well-being of impoverished people.[19] Christians may not buy essential commodities when price is low and sell when it is high, for so doing endangers the poor.[20] In this vein, he argued that economic activity should be subject to political constraints. "Selling ought not be an act that is entirely within your own power and discretion, without law or limit." Civil authorities ought establish "rules and regulations," including "ceilings" on prices, he insisted.[21]

Finally, Luther admonishes pastors regarding their roles and obligations in the face of economic practices that exploit the vulnerable. Pastors are to "unmask hidden injustice, thus...opening the eyes of the secular authorities for their mandate to establish civil justice."[22] Luther goes so far as to admonish clergy to preach (for Luther, that is to speak the living Christ) against

[19] I use the term "impoverished people" rather than the more common term "the poor" at the suggestion of colleagues from the Global South who prefer the former term as a way of indicating that people are not poor by chance but rather are poor because systems that enrich some sectors of humanity impoverish others.

[20] Luther, "Trade and Usury," in *Luther's Works* 45, 261, 247-251. See also the entirety of "Trade and Usury," in *Luther's Works* 45, 244–308, and Luther's comments on the first, fifth, sixth, seventh, and ninth/tenth commandments and on the fourth petition of the Lord's Prayer in the Large Catechism.

[21] Luther, "Trade and Usury," in *Luther's Works* 45, 249-50.

[22] Heiko Oberman, cited in Lindberg, *European Reformations*, 116. See for example, Luther, "Admonition to the Clergy that They Preach against Usury," ibid.

usury and to withhold the sacrament from a usurer unless he repents, for he is "damned like a thief, robber and murderer."[23]

In short, according to Luther, neighbor-love, as the norm for public life, has at least three dimensions:

*love manifest in service to neighbor, even if it may bring great danger to self and family;[24]

*love manifest in disclosing and theologically denouncing oppression or exploitation of those who are vulnerable, where it is perceived;[25] and

*love manifest in ways of living that counter prevailing cultural norms where those norms exploit the vulnerable or defy God in some other way.

Loving in these forms, we embody Luther's "second principle of Christian doctrine" ("…to give ourselves with might and main for our neighbor"), and his second kind of righteousness.

2.3 Christ as Indwelling Presence[26]

These startling moves in economic life presuppose significant moral agency in the believing community. That is, they presuppose that believers will exercise the moral wherewithal to reject cultural norms and trends that defy God's Word regarding who they are in relationship to God and others. This means rejecting the opportunity to maximize profit at the expense of the vulnerable other, for harming neighbor in this way would transgress neighbor-

[23] Luther, "Admonition to the Clergy that They Preach against Usury," ibid.

[24] See, for example, Martin Luther, "Whether One May Flee from a Deadly Plague," *Luther's Works* 43, 115–138.

[25] Luther's perceptions of where injustice lay however were severely limited by a number of contextual factors. See the section of this chapter entitled "Obey and Disobey Temporal Authority."

[26] Isolating a single term or concept by which to signify this multidimensional notion in Luther's theology is difficult. "Indwelling Christ," "union with Christ," "Christ mysticism," and a nuanced understanding of *theosis* (participation in God) all capture a portion of the significance for Luther. Some Luther scholars at the University of Helsinki use the term "union with Christ." Close reading of Luther leads me to lean on "indwelling Christ" as the term best conveying the implications of his conviction that Godself in the form of Christ is given by God to indwell and transform the faithful, and to create communion and union of love and service among them.

love and the second kind of righteousness. For Luther, this moral power was not a humanly generated virtue. Rather it comes to us as the presence of Christ dwelling within the community of believers. The centerpiece of this moral agency, for Luther, is the crucified and living Christ dwelling in and gradually transforming the community of believers, the form of Jesus Christ taking form in and among those with faith. Christians as objects of Christ's love become subjects of that love. Faith is both "faith in Christ" and "faith of Christ." The indwelling Christ, mediated by practices of the Christian community, transforms the faithful toward a manner of life that actively loves neighbor. The moral life is simultaneously gift and imperative, a mystical as well as physical reality, ontologically communal while also individual, and a necessary outflow of the sacraments.

Nuanced differently in various works, this role of Christ is evident both in theological treatises and in sermons. (The writings of Luther upon which my understanding of "union with Christ" draws most heavily are: "Freedom of a Christian," "The Blessed Sacrament of the Holy and True Body and Blood of Christ and the Brotherhoods," "Two Kind of Righteousness," "Disputation concerning Justification," "The Heidelberg Disputation" and the five sermons cited in this essay.[27]) Luther indicates four related aspects of what I refer to as "the indwelling Christ." They are Christ dwelling in the faithful, Christ transforming the faithful into servant of all, Christ rendering union and communion among the faithful, and Christ rendering the faithful "divine" or "partaker in the divine." All involve the Holy Spirit.

The following excerpts from sermons and treatises, read together, reveal these aspects of the indwelling Christ. "[T]his is ... one of the exceedingly great promises granted to us poor miserable sinners, that we should become partakers of the divine nature, and should be so highly honored as not only to be loved by God through Jesus Christ ... but should even have the Lord Himself dwelling completely in us."[28] Regarding one in whom God dwells, Luther says: He "makes daily progress in life and good works ... is useful to God and man: through him ... men and countries benefit ... such a man's

[27] The sermons are found in the 8 volume series, *Sermons of Martin Luther*, ed. John Nicholas Lenker, Grand Rapids 1983.

[28] Luther, "Third Sermon of Pentecost Sunday," in *Lenker* 3, 316-317.

words, life and doings are God's."[29] Likewise, 'Filled unto all the fullness of God means ... full of God ... adorned with his grace and the gifts of his Spirit ... who illuminates us with his light, lives within us, saves m with his salvation, and enkindles love within us ... having God and all his blessings dwelling in us in fullness and being effective to make us wholly divine."[30] "For through faith Christ is in us, indeed, one with us.'‘[31] Through Christ's love, "we are to be changed and to make the infirmities of all other Christians our own; we are to take upon ourselves their form and their necessity, and all the good that is within our power we are to make theirs, that they may profit from it. ... We are changed into one another and are made into a community by love."[32] "Christians are indeed called and made the habitation of God, and in them God speaks, and rules, and works."[33]

It is crucial to note four points at which Luther's understanding of the indwelling Christ departs profoundly from medieval theology.

We become dwelling place of Christ not as cause of salvation but as effect of salvation.

We become God's abode not through our effort or perfection, but rather through God's gracious gift of Godself to dwell in the person through faith and to transform the person by love into love in Christ's form. That is, the believer is united with God through dissimilitude not similitude; Christ unites with sinners. As Reformation historian Stephen Ozment explains, Luther assailed the fundamental axiom of medieval theology: the conviction that "likeness" to God is the sine qua non for union with God, and hence for salvation.[34] The principles that likeness was achievable by human

[29] Ibid., 317.

[30] Luther, "Sermon on the 16th Sunday after Trinity," in *Lenker* 8, 279-80.

[31] Luther, "Heidelberg Disputation," in *Lull*, 47.

[32] Luther, "The Blessed Sacrament of the Holy and True Body and Blood of Christ, and the Brotherhoods," in *Lull*, 251.

[33] Luther, "Third Sermon for Pentecost," in *Lenker* 3, 321.

[34] Stephen Ozment, Luther and the Late Middle Ages: The Formation of Reformation Thought," in *Transition and Revolution: Problems and Issues of European*

effort and was the indispensable condition for salvation underlay monastic practice, mysticism, and the sacramental system of the church. Saving faith was formed by sacramentally infused grace in concert with human effort toward godliness or perfection.[35] Luther absolutely rejected this move toward similitude between creature and creator on the basis of creaturely effort as the basis of salvation.

Moral transformation as "union with Christ" is gift, as opposed to either obligation or reward. Though Luther occasionally employs language of obligation with reference to the moral life, far more often he speaks the language of gift, and never does he speak of the Christian moral life as reward.

Christ may be received only after the person has utterly despaired of his or her own ability to justify self.

The relevant point here is that this presence of Christ within believers and the believing community is the active love of Christ for the world working within human beings. That love, as we have seen above, is astoundingly public in its commitment and freedom to serve the neighbor's well-being while also meeting the needs of self and dependents. For Luther, it is this indwelling presence of infinite love that enables the Christian to disclose and theologically denounce economic norms that exploit the vulnerable or defy God in some other way, and to generate alternative ways of living.

While other aspects of his theology supply the obligation to embody love for neighbor in both private and public life, the indwelling Christ and indwelling Spirit supply the courage. Resistance to hegemonic authority, where that resistance is life-threatening, requires courage. For Luther, the most powerful courage known to humankind is generated by Christ and the Spirit living in the faithful. In his "Sermon for the Sixteenth Sunday after Trinity," Luther speaks of the power, strength, and courage that may be imparted to the faithful by the immanent presence of Christ and Spirit. Christ is brought into the faithful by the Holy Spirit; Christ and Spirit indwell together. "The Hebrew word for spirit," Luther preaches, "might well be rendered 'bold,

Renaissance and Reformation History, ed. Robert M. Kingdom, Minneapolis 1974, 109-129.

[35] Ibid., 117-119.

undaunted courage.'"[36] We are made, he argues, "far more powerful through the Holy Spirit, and are undaunted by the world, the devil, death, and all kinds of misfortune."[37] This empowering courage is, according to Luther, greater and more powerful than any other force on Earth. This courage empowers the risky moves entailed in neighbor-love where it transgresses exploitative economic norms and practices.

2.4 Obey and Disobey Ruling Authorities

Luther's understanding of what constituted exploitation and injustice, however, was severely limited by a number of contextual factors including: 1) his anti-Semitic, Constantinian, and patriarchal worldview; 2) the nonexistence, in the pre-modern conceptual world, of the concept of organized social structural change; and 3) his conflating the orders of society with the orders of creation. These factors, among others, led Luther to assume a divinely ordained social hierarchy, align himself with the political powers that enforced it, and admonish obedience to temporal authority – in the form of civil authorities, masters (for servants), and parents – as obedience to God. According to this norm of obedience, Luther considered rebellion against civil authority to be evil, more evil than murder, for rebellion against civil authority, he concluded, attacks the divinely established head and interferes with the divinely ordained function of rulers.[38] Rebellion against civil authority could be, in Luther's estimation, demonic.[39] Thus, in some arenas, Luther was aligned with terrible injustice which he did not perceive to be injustice and that he supported theologically. This is seen most clearly in his demonizing

[36] Luther, "Sermon on the 16th Sunday after Trinity," in *Lenker* 8, 275.

[37] Ibid. This sermon goes on to say: "This is the Holy Spirit's office," he writes, "to rule inwardly in the heart… making it burn and create new courage so that a man grows happy before God . . . and with a happy heart serves the people." See also the "Third Sermon for Pentecost Sunday," in *Lenker* 8, 316-317, and "Freedom of a Christian".

[38] See especially "On Temporal Authority: To What Extent It Should be Obeyed" and "Treatise on Good Works," in *Luther's Works* 44.

[39] In his first "Letter to Elector Frederick," of 1522, *Luther's Works* 48, Luther attributes to Satan: disruption of society, chaos, and violent rebellion against either church (as was occurring in the case at hand) or state (as Luther feared might happen). Luther is referring to the disturbances at Wittenberg, which Luther attributed to Karlstadt's teaching while Luther was at the Wartburg.

of Jewish people, and his denunciation of the peasant uprising and of the "radical" reformers.

Notable therefore is Luther's astonishing exception to this norm of obedience. He firmly admonished disobedience to temporal authorities when they demand ways of life that betray allegiance to God – including God's call to embody neighbor-love – above all else. As a public theologian and a theologically political figure uncritically committed to and theologically justifying a norm of obedience to civil authority, Luther demanded one exception to that norm. Where obedience to civil rulers contradicted obedience to God or to conscience in line with God, or where the demand of civil rulers "tends toward the suppression of the Christian faith, the denying of the divine word," Christians, he taught, were "to resist them at least with words," and to "obey God ... rather than men."[40] In his "Letter to Frederick," Luther states: "Human authority is not always to be obeyed, namely when it undertakes something against the commandments of God; yet it should never be despised but always honored." According to Luther in 1523, that resistance could take the form of words, and of refusal to hold certain beliefs or to obey the proclamation that certain books could not be read or possessed.[41] Yet by 1531, in "Dr. Martin Luther's Warning to His Dear German People," the mandate to resist became stronger. This "warning" contains one of Luther's strongest statements that where rulers disobey God or call Christians to disobey God, the rulers are to be resisted.[42] To not disobey civil authorities could jeopardize

[40] Luther, "Temporal Authority," in *Lull*, 658; ibid.; 699.

[41] Ibid., 686.

[42] "Whoever does obey him [the emperor] can be certain that he is disobedient to God and will lose both body and soul eternally in the war" (30). "Dr. Martin Luther's Warning to His Dear German People" in *Luther's Works* 47, ed. Franklin Sherman, Philadelphia 1971, 3-55. Here Luther overturns his earlier prohibitions against armed resistance, against self-defense, and against resisting injustice done to self. This treatise was written under extreme circumstances: Emperor Charles was calling people to arms on behalf of the Pope against the Protestants. Luther believed that the gospel itself and the souls of the German people were at stake, jeopardized by the imperial dictate. Luther's alteration in political ideology, theology of temporal authority, and accompanying norms seems to be terribly difficult to him. He says he is "now speaking as if in a

people's salvation, and resistance could take even armed form because civil authorities were jeopardizing the proclamation of the gospel and demanding that people disobey God. Where rebellion against civil authorities was for any other reason, it was wrong. In essence, where Luther finds the proclamation, hearing, and remembering of the gospel to be at stake on a large scale, he calls for resistance to civil authorities.

2.5 Held together: subversive moral agency

Held together, these four sets of claims were and are subversive. They are subversive precisely because they entice people to remember who we are as both objects and agents of God's love, and they empower people for living according to that promise. That is, these claims provide both the reason and the moral-spiritual power to defy political, economic, cultural, and ecclesiastical authorities and norms where those norms demand us to ignore, distrust, or contradict God's gift of right relationship with God and with neighbor. That includes economic practices, policies, and systems that demand people to harm the vulnerable in order to maximize profit for self. To illustrate: The second kind of righteousness – with neighbor-love at its heart – would not allow Christians to comply with economic norms that maximize profit at the expense of impoverished people. We could not, for example, abolish worker protections in the quest of higher corporate profit. We could not allow profit to accrue based on failure to pay living wages and to provide health care benefits. Neighbor-love would demand Christians to speak out against extractive industries that destroy communities in order to benefit a relative few. This is not strange given that Luther himself vehemently denounced aspects of the emerging capitalist economy that he considered harmful to economically vulnerable people. The moral-spiritual power and "bold undaunted courage" for such transgressive and evangelical moves are – according to Luther – given to us by the power of Christ and Spirit dwelling within the believing community.

dream, as if there were no God" (13). He sounds tormented. My impression is that he is moved to these reversals also by his passionate love for "his dear German people."

3. Embracing the Safe Side.....Obscuring the Word

The subversive nature of these four faith claims, however, disappears if only the first and non-disruptive part of each is adopted. Lutheran traditions in the ensuing 500 years have swerved toward adopting only the parts of each claim that did NOT disrupt but rather tended to reinscribe the reigning power alignments and their ideological underpinnings of later contexts. This includes the context of the current global neo-liberal economy.

3.1 Two Kinds of Righteousness

Lutheran traditions have eagerly adopted and "first kind of righteousness" as the core of the Gospel. We are indeed made right with God by God's grace alone through faith alone on account of Christ. God loves, fully accepts, and saves us despite our short fallings – however terrible they may be – and does this freely. Nothing that we do can change this saving reality. Centralizing this truth claim is one of Lutheranism's great contributions to humankind. It has meant life to me; I stake my life on this claim. To minimize it would be to betray Luther and the gospel itself.

Yet, to uphold this first form of righteousness without upholding the second also betrays both Luther and the gospel. Such has been the tendency of North Atlantic Lutheranism. While Luther insisted that two kinds of righteousness were inseparable, we have allowing the second to slip out of consciousness.

We have welcomed being made right with God without seeing that we are also to be make right with neighbor, set on a course of living justly with neighbor that shapes all facet of life, both public and private.

While the first kind of righteousness threatened the dominating authorities of Luther's day, it is the second kind that would threaten the life-shaping power structures of ours – the reigning form of advanced global market economy. The second kind of righteousness could not tolerate growth at all costs and profit maximization for the wealthy despite its consequences for the impoverished.

3.2 Neighbor Love as Guide for Economic Life

Lutherans have been admirable in adopting the call to love neighbors in need by giving generously through such efforts as providing schools, health care, personal assistance, welfare relief, resettlement for refugees, housing for homeless people, food for hungry people, development assistance, and more. Historically and contemporarily, this is a good and faithful aspect of the Lutheran heritage. It represents the first of Luther's three forms of loving in economic life. The other two, however, North Atlantic Lutheranism, has tended to ignore.

It is far more risky to love by "disclosing and theologically denouncing oppression or exploitation of those who are vulnerable," and by transgressing "prevailing economic norms that exploit the vulnerable." These forms of love would call into question nearly every economic move we make (buying, selling, investing) in the currently reigning form of global market economy. Loving in these ways would invite us to align our lives with the rapidly expanding global movement to create more socially equitable and ecologically sustainable economic principles, policies, and practices.

Lutheran diaconal ministers from around the world, gathered for a "Global Consultation on Diakonia," express this impetus to add justice to service in the work of love. In a compelling Epistle," they declare:

> We acknowledge with gratitude the many kinds of diaconal work that the Church has carried out through the centuries, and which necessarily continues in our own day. This work is now challenged to move toward more prophetic forms of diakonia. Inspired by Jesus and the prophets who confronted those in power and called for changes in unjust structures and practices, we pray that God may empower us to help transform all that leads to human greed, violence, and exclusion." "While diakonia begins as unconditional service to the neighbor in need, it leads inevitably to social change that restores, reforms and transforms.[43]

Luther, I have a hunch, would rejoice.

3.3 Christ as Indwelling Presence

Accepting Christ as means of gracious forgiveness of all sin, as God's way of making us right before God, is a hallmark of Lutheran tradition. This un-

[43] "An Epistle from the LWF Global Consultation on *Diakonia,*" 1.

derstanding is a profound gift that Lutheranism has offered to the broader church and the world.

Our weakness lies where we have ignored or minimized Christ also as indwelling presence. Accepting the Eucharist and baptism as means of grace in which God offers forgiveness, we have not tended to preach and teach Eucharist and baptism also as means of Christ's infinite power of love actually coming to abide within us. This weakness stems in part from the Augsburg Confession and the Formula of Concord. In contrast to Luther, himself, these confessional documents, in discussing justification, emphasize the gift of grace which makes us righteous before God, but not the gift of Christ's indwelling presence which enables the second kind of righteousness – our relationships to neighbor changed toward neighbor-love.

Not naming, claiming, and knowing this gift of Christ's indwelling presence, we are "off the hook" from taking seriously what it implies for how we live in relationship to political, economic, military, and cultural systems that may exploit, displace, or even kill neighbors. If we take seriously that the God of justice-making love – who, in the form of a Palestinian Jew, defied the norms of the Roman Empire – lives within us, then are we not compelled to counter the norms of oppressive economic empire? Trusting the presence of Christ truly within us means trusting that infinite love, unstoppable even by torture and death, is a part of our very being. Standing up against exploitation of vulnerable neighbors becomes an act of Christic love breathing within us.

3.4 Obey and Disobey Ruling Authorities

Lutherans – at least in Euro and Euro-American traditions – have tended to uphold Luther's admonishment to obey secular authorities. That propensity contributed to the church's complicity the fascism in mid-century Germany. In the United States, it has contributed, likewise, to the church's relative silence in the face of public policies that have vastly widened the gap between rich and poor.

We have not however, given equal weight to his astonishing exception to that norm. It is the call to disobey temporal authorities when they demand ways of life that betray allegiance to God – including God's call to embody neighbor-love – above all else, or that obscure the proclamation, hearing, and remembering of the gospel. Ways of economic life that enable some to flourish at the cost of degrading or destroying countless others in our backyards and across the globe betray allegiance to the God of justice-making love. And they block our proclamation that God loves all and is working and willing toward abundant life for all.

3.5 Held together

Held together, these moves to embrace the safe side of Luther's claims while ignoring the risky side open the door to privatized understandings of justification and of gospel-based liberation. Liberation is from the inner demons produced by the effort to justify oneself according to the meritocracies of our day, but not from the systems of oppression that daily cost countless people their lives, livelihoods, or communities. Freedom from the law becomes the freedom from the law of individual meritocracy, but not from the law of empire. Justification changes my relationship with God, but has little to do with how I relate to neighbors through economic, political, or military systems.

That is, these moves detach Luther's world-shaking claims related to justification from their political-economic-ideological implications. Choosing the safe side of his claims enables us to live a privatized form of gospel, escaping from its implications for the public or political side of life. They enable us to see the gospel as freedom from private sin and despair, but not as freedom from systemic sin. Both the moral mandate and the gift of moral power to "love neighbor" as a political, economic, and ecological vocation resulting from justification slip from consciousness.

Luther was convinced that the greatest abuse of the church in his day was that "God's word has been silenced."[44] People were prevented from hearing the Word and, through it, remembering who they were coram deo (as recipients of God's love) and coram mundo (as agents of that love). Luther's liberating faith claims uncovered and refuted the belief systems and power structures responsible for this obscuring of God's Word and this corroding of the trust in God that the Word sowed. I would argue that by adopting only the safe side of his theological truths, we too obscure God's liberating Word about who we are in relationship to God (recipients of God's love) and in

[44] David W. Lotz, "The Proclamation of the Word in Luther's Thought," in *Word and World* 3. 4 (1983), 344.

relationship to others (as agents of that love). We, thereby, truncate the power and meaning of justification.

This is a tremendously hopeful assertion.

4 Faithful Response, Great Hope

It is hope-filled because it means that Lutherans are blessed with an incredible gift, a gem of unspeakable worth. It is the invitation to re-affirm our most closely held beliefs and open our hearts and minds to the vast and life-giving potential that they hold beyond what we may already have realized. We may, in communities of faith, prayerfully and daringly risk living into new vistas of the gospel's power. They are in the terrain of public life, terrain that Jesus walked at great cost and in which Luther was a daring and faithful traveler.

With Luther, we may venture boldly into long-ignored aspects of his claims, aspects that disrupt the power alignments and ideological gods of our day. If we trust God's love by holding firmly to the second kind of righteousness as well as the first, welcoming neighbor-love's call to renounce systemic injustice and build life-giving alternatives, embracing the power of Christi love abiding in us, and disobeying power structures that demand us to transgress the call to love neighbor as self, then we can more truly be "God's hands and feet on Earth." We will more faithfully honor Luther's daring, risky, evangelical discoveries about what it means to be justified by God's grace. And we will be a force to challenge systemic injustice and build more socially just and ecologically sustainable alternatives. In these ways, we trust God's gracious and transformative Word and embody it in the world. "The Word of God," Luther said, "wherever it comes, comes to change and renew the world."[45]

In these faithful ventures and modes of living the gospel we will be fallible, faulty, at times fearful, and encumbered by the incessant lure of *incurvatus in se* – as was Luther and as (he vociferously assures us) are human be-

[45] As cited by Mary Solberg in *Compelling Knowledge: A Feminist Proposal for an Epistemology of the Cross*, Albany 1997.

ings. This includes humans justified by the gracious love of God. That we are "rusty" tools makes us no less precious tools in God's sight and in God's liberating work on Earth.

Beyond Luther to Ethical Reformation: Peasants, Anabaptists, Jews

Craig L. Nessan

In the last decades attention has been given to the emergence of what political analysts have characterized as "identity politics." Although the critical discussion of this phenomenon, pro and con, may be recent—especially in an increasingly polarized political climate—the reality of identity politics is ancient.

At the 500th anniversary of the Reformation we must reckon with three tragic cases from the theological ethics of Martin Luther, repenting of how Luther's devolution into "religious identity politics" misled him to horrific conclusions, whose consequences continue to plague the world centuries later. These three cases involve Luther's stances against the Peasants, the Anabaptists, and the Jews. Rather than standing for their protection under the laws of society according to "neighbor politics," Luther resorted to religious rhetoric and appeals to violence that reverberate until today.

The logic of Luther's two strategies paradigm should have led him to different conclusions.[1] Luther articulated the centrality of neighbor love for ethics according to his concept of the two strategies, especially in his treatise "The Freedom of a Christian". However, in his polemic against the peasants, Anabaptists, and Jews, Luther operated according to a religious identity politics that negated the Greatest Commandment: to love God and one's neighbor as oneself (Mt 22:34-40). Instead of defending these oppressed groups

[1] Luther's two kingdoms paradigm is here reconstructed as God's "two strategies." Cf. Craig L. Nessan, "Christian Political Responsibility: Reappropriating Luther's Two Kingdoms," in Paul S. Chung, Ulrich Duchrow, and Craig L. Nessan, *Liberating Lutheran Theology: Freedom for Justice and Solidarity in Global Context* (Minneapolis: Fortress, 2011), 46-52.

according to the imperative of neighbor politics, they were targeted as enemies through the hermeneutic of a vicious religious identity politics. Luther's ethical conclusions require critique, deconstruction, and repudiation toward the reconstruction of theological ethics as neighbor politics.

1. Religious Identity Politics Today: Abortion, Homosexuality, and the State of Israel

In the United States the religious identity politics of the Christian religious right provides background for analyzing Luther's own religious identity politics against the peasants, Anabaptists, and the Jews. Three primary examples of religious identity politics by the Christian religious right involve stances on abortion, homosexuality, and the State of Israel. In religious identity politics the warrants for arguments come primarily, if not entirely, from sources of religious authority. Religion serves as a particularly powerful source for identity politics, insofar as those motivated by religious belief claim divine authorization for their cause.[2]

For the Christian religious right, warrants come primarily, if not entirely, from the Bible. Based on absolute claims about the plenary inspiration of the Bible and appeals to biblical literalism, the Christian religious right positions itself as an interest group with divine endorsement for its political agenda. There is a virtual one-to-one correspondence between the Biblicist arguments of the Christian religious right and its political agenda regarding abortion, homosexuality, and the State of Israel. This is a characteristic of all religious identity politics. Religious identity politics is motivated to maintain purity regarding its interpretation of God's will based on appeals to divine revelation in Holy Scripture. Due to veritable certainty about the truth of their conclusions, there is little or no room for compromise in relation to the possible needs of those neighbors, who might be negatively affected by their religious agenda. This also means there is virtually no ideological space for "neighbor politics."

[2] Cf. Cressida Heyes, "Identity Politics," *Stanford Encyclopedia of Philosophy*, <http://plato.stanford.edu/entries/identity-politics/>, August 1, 2013.

Religious identity politics is central to the political agenda of the Christian religious right in relationship to abortion, homosexuality, and the State of Israel. In religious identity politics there is a direct linkage between a particular interpretation of the Bible and the warrants that are drawn for pursuing a particular political agenda. The ostensible one-to-one correspondence between biblical interpretation and a clearly defined political program lends passion to religious identity politics. Because God has purportedly authorized this agenda through divine revelation, the consequences for those negatively affected by such an agenda are discounted, sometimes even dealt with through sarcasm or ridicule.

Contrast religious identity politics with "neighbor politics." Neighbor politics is also grounded in religious or ideological motivations. However, neighbor politics resists the reduction of ethical deliberation to a one-to-one correspondence between divine authorization and political agenda. Neighbor politics introduces complexity into ethical deliberation and the emerging political agenda. The needs of all neighbors, especially those most negatively affected by a given political stance, are taken seriously in ethical deliberation.

The reductionist approach of the Christian religious right is overcome by including a range of other neighbors: not only the rights of an unborn child but the situation of the mother, father, extended family, and a host of other social, economic, and contextual factors; not only the norm of marriage between a man and a woman but the rights of gay and lesbian persons, the situation of their families and friends, and a host of other practical matters, civil rights, and legal issues; not only the sovereignty of the State of Israel but the legitimacy of its laws and policies, especially as these oppress the Palestinian people and negatively interact with other Mid-Eastern countries. Neighbor politics entails a differentiated method of ethical deliberation, weighing many competing factors that affect a range of other persons—including also the needs of creation and its creatures!—in arriving at a course of action.

Employing the distinction between religious identity politics and neighbor politics, we will examine how Luther himself, in controversy with particular religious opponents, departed from his otherwise clearly articulated neighbor politics to assume the posture of religious identity politics, in order to oppose and defeat particular religious foes. Notwithstanding that the religious opponents themselves—peasants, Anabaptists, and Jews—may have employed their own versions of religious identity politics, Luther's reversion to religious identity politics in his rhetoric, controversies, and writings against these groups not only had disastrous ethical consequences in his own time but his positions continue to undermine the integrity of Lutheran theological and ethical heritage 500 years later.

2. Religious Identity Politics in Luther: Peasants, Anabaptists, and Jews

Three particular instances of religious identity politics call into radical question the legitimacy not only of Luther's ethics but his entire theology: his writings against the peasants, the Anabaptists, and the Jews. The ethical integrity of the Lutheran Reformation is severely questionable, if the conclusions drawn by Luther in these three cases in the sixteenth century are not repudiated. Where did Luther go wrong? Is it possible to draw upon Luther's own theological arguments to arrive at other conclusions? One key for interpreting, criticizing, and deconstructing Luther's thought involves unmasking how religious identity politics undermined the foundations of neighbor politics as grounded by his concept of the two strategies. Only by confronting Luther's reasoning against the peasants, Anabaptists, and Jews is it possible to turn his thought toward a consistent neighbor politics.

2.1 Luther against the Peasants

Luther's writings against the peasants need to be understood within the historical context and currents of the early 16th century. The Reformation was a nascent movement, dependent upon favorable protection by the German princes who sheltered Luther and fostered the reforms undertaken through his theological program. Peasant uprisings had occurred in Europe already in the 14th century.[3] The German Peasants War began in 1524 and climaxed in March-May 1525. The poverty, economic suffering, and consequent social problems facing the German underclass were extreme. Theological and prac-

[3] For this and the following, see Martin Brecht, *Martin Luther: Shaping and Defining the Reformation 1521-1532*, trans. James L. Schaaf (Minneapolis: Fortress, 1990), 172-173.

tical reforms introduced by Luther raised legitimate expectations that the living conditions of the peasantry would also be remediated.

Luther took a prophetic stance against the practice of usury.[4] Initially Luther exercised measured support for the peasants' cause. Because Luther saw that the grievances of the peasants belonged to the responsibility of the civil authorities, he rejected their attempts to appeal to spiritual and biblical arguments as rationale for rebellion.[5] To a certain degree Luther may have operated according to a neighbor politics, holding that the peasants' call to arms would lead to their destruction. Once the crisis began to deteriorate into violence, however, Luther lacked imagination for a solution other than a return to the status quo. He defended the prevailing political order against the demands of peasants, arguing vehemently for the obligation of civil rulers to crush their efforts to reform society through violent revolutionary change. "Luther only partially grasped the complexity of the situation, and this must have had an influence on his judgment and reaction."[6] Revolt appeared to Luther as a sign of the arrival of the apocalypse.

Brecht comments on The Fundamental and Proper Chief Articles of All the Peasantry and Those Who Are Oppressed by Spiritual and Temporal Authority, otherwise known as the Twelve Articles, published in March 1525:

> The common accusation that the gospel causes revolution was rejected. In desiring the gospel, the peasants were not revolutionaries. However—and this was a veiled threat—one could expect God to support his oppressed people. All of the articles were supported by Bible references in the margin.[7]

Although many peasant leaders, including the authors of *The Twelve Articles* desired peaceful change, violence broke out against rulers and monaster-

[4] Ulrich Duchrow, "Property, Money Economies, and Empires: Contexts of Biblical, Reformation, and Contemporary Ecumenical Theology," in Chung, Duchrow, and Nessan, *Liberating Lutheran Theology*, 173-181.

[5] Johannes Heckel, *Lex Charitatis: A Juristic Disquisition on Law in the Theology of Martin Luther*, trans. ed. Gottfried G. Krodel (Grand Rapids: Erdmans, 2010), 78-80.

[6] Brecht, 173.

[7] Brecht, 174.

ies at the end of March, culminating in April. Upon receiving this document in April, Luther prepared a response, *Admonition to Peace: A Reply to the Twelve Articles of the Peasants in Swabia*, which was published in early May. Luther was not persuaded of the Christian character of the peasant movement and was convinced that if the temporal order was threatened that the conditions would no longer allow the continuation of the Reformation.

Luther linked inseparably the maintenance of the existing civil order with freedom to proclaim the Gospel. While acknowledging the legitimacy of some peasant demands, Luther believed that God would be the judge of unjust rulers and argued against the use of violence by the peasants, particularly mindful of the precedents by Müntzer and Karlstadt.[8]

> Now you can see how far these false prophets have led you astray. They still call you Christians, although they have made you worse than heathen. On the basis of these passages even a child can understand that the Christian law tells us not to strive against injustice, not to grasp the sword, not to protect ourselves, not to avenge ourselves, but to give up life and property, and let whoever takes it have it. We have all we need in our Lord, who will not leave us, as he has promised [Heb 13:5]. Suffering! Suffering! Cross! Cross![9]

Luther advised the peasants not to seek economic justice through force but to appeal to God for aid. He referred to his own example of protest in relation to pope and emperor and how he never fomented rebellion or took up the sword.[10]

The failure of Luther to advocate more strongly against the economic conditions suffered by the peasants, and instead his admonishing them to suffer and bear the cross, reveals something about his own self-interest in this conflict. The temporal order that protected his own reformation agenda would not tolerate, Luther reasoned, the kinds of material reforms demanded by the

[8] *LW* 46:24-28.

[9] *LW* 46:29.

[10] *LW* 46:31.

peasants. The turn to violence would jeopardize the temporal status quo and give occasion to suppression of everything thus far accomplished. Luther had scarce imagination for a reformation that moved beyond the feudal political order toward participatory social and economic justice, even though his theology formally acknowledged the requisites of the left hand kingdom. Luther writes against the third article:

> This article would make all men equal, and turn the spiritual kingdom of Christ into a worldly, external kingdom; and that is impossible. A worldly kingdom cannot exist without an inequality of persons, some being free, some imprisoned some lords, some subjects, etc....[11]

Moreover, Luther rejected the appeals to Scripture by the peasants as a kind of religious identity politics, countering with his own form of religious identity politics, to oppose their demands. Especially galling to Luther were the appeals to Scripture by the peasants to justify rebellion.[12] Luther feared that chaos would engulf Germany should the peasants persist on their violent course and recommended arbitration as the necessary alternative.[13]

Events overtook the publication of Luther's *Admonition to Peace* as he received reports of an escalation of violence on the part of the peasants in early May. Therefore Luther amended his earlier treatise, adding a devastating new section, *Against the Robbing and Murdering Hordes of Peasants*. Luther charged the peasants with violating their obligation of obedience to the rulers. Because they had turned to violence, Luther implored the authorities to crush the peasant rebellion:

> For rebellion is not just simple murder; it is like a great fire, which attacks and devastates the whole land. Thus rebellion brings with it a land filled with murder and bloodshed; it makes widows and orphans, and turns everything upside down, like the worst disaster. Therefore let everyone who can, smite, slay, and stab, secretly or openly, remembering that nothing can be more poisonous, hurtful, or

[11] *LW* 46:39.

[12] *LW* 46:34-36.

[13] *LW* 46:42-43.

> devilish than a rebel. It is just as when one must kill a mad dog; if you do not strike him, he will strike you, and a whole land with you.[14]

While Luther appealed to the rulers to negotiate where possible, the thrust of his argument was aimed at freeing their consciences to respond to the revolt with all necessary force to maintain good order. Even against those who against their own will had been compelled to join the rebellion, the rulers should "stab, smite, slay. If you die doing it, good for you! A more blessed death can never be yours, for you die obeying the divine word and commandment in Romans 13 [1, 2], and in loving service to your neighbor, whom you are rescuing from the bonds of hell and the devil."[15]

Luther's defense of the established political and economic order was consistent with his concept of good government. As also in his writings against the Anabaptists and the Jews, Luther's imagination was bound by the constraints of his time regarding the requisites of political and economic justice. Caught in the rush of unfolding events, Luther's writings against the "robbing and murdering hordes" appear even more vicious to later generations, who know how these words also have contributed to the suppression of other movements for social change, such as advocated by liberation theologies.[16]

Even in the face of excesses by the rulers and the abiding resentment by the peasants, Luther remained adamant in righteousness about his stance. For example, Luther published four letters of Müntzer under the title, *A Dreadful Story and a Judgment of God against Thomas Müntzer*, to defend his views about how God judges rebels.[17] Luther made frequent reference to Müntzer in many of his later writings to justify his position in the peasants uprising: "I killed Müntzer; his death is on my shoulders. But I did it because he wanted to kill my Christ." Luther remained convinced that his role in the peasants'

[14] *LW* 46:50.

[15] *LW* 46:54-55.

[16] Craig L. Nessan, *The Vitality of Liberation Theology* (Eugene: Wipf & Stock, 2012), 149-150.

[17] Brecht, 184-185, who also includes the following quote.

war, advising the authorities to negotiate with their subjects and calling them to arms in the event of rebellion, was justified.

Already in 1525, Luther was prepared to defend his position, composing *An Open Letter on the Harsh Book against the Peasants*. God so ordered the world that subjects owed obedience to their lords and those in authority owed wrath to disobedient subjects: "The peasants would not listen; they would not let anyone tell them anything, so their ears must now be unbuttoned with musket balls till their heads jump off their shoulders. Such pupils need the rod."[18] While Luther counseled mercy for those who surrendered, he defended his stance according to the two kingdoms:

> There are two kingdoms, one the kingdom of God, the other the kingdom of the world. I have written this so often that I am surprised there is anyone who does not know it or remember it. Anyone who knows how to distinguish rightly between these two kingdoms will certainly not be offended by my little book, and he will also properly understand the passages about mercy. God's kingdom is a kingdom of grace and mercy, not of wrath and punishment. In it there is only forgiveness, consideration for one another, love, service, the doing of good, peace, joy, etc. But the kingdom of the world is a kingdom of wrath and severity. In it there is only punishment, repression, judgment, and condemnation to restrain the wicked and protect the good. For this reason it has the sword and Scripture calls a prince or lord "God's wrath," or "God's rod" (Is 14).[19]

Luther in this case tragically failed to grasp the rudimentary obligation of the left hand kingdom to provide sufficient livelihood for the underclass. God had to teach the peasants the value of maintaining law and order, and instruct the lords "to rule justly and to keep order in their territories and highways."[20] While the peasants were interpreted according to the categories of rebels, thieves, murderers, and evildoers, Luther seemed oblivious that those in authority could be accused of the same through their establishment of structural

[18] *LW* 46:65.

[19] *LW* 46:69-70.

[20] *LW* 46:75.

injustice.[21] It is at this juncture that Luther's teaching about the two kingdoms requires severe criticism and revision, if it is salvageable at all. "What we miss completely is any sign of understanding for the oppressed and their problems."[22]

2.2 Luther against the Anabaptists

Luther's stance against the Anabaptists was based on his opinion that they were engaged in monastic withdrawal from the world. He criticized the Anabaptists, as he did monks, for attempting to "climb into heaven" to escape civil society and thereby failing to fulfill the basic obligations of neighbor love. Luther's views were, moreover, negatively affected by his inability to differentiate the views expressed by revolutionary leaders like Müntzer in the peasants' revolt from other Anabaptists.[23] The lack of first hand knowledge about the Anabaptists, due in part to lack of contact with actual representatives of the movement, led Luther to make generalizations that failed to take seriously many key features of Anabaptist thought and practice.[24]

Luther's stance against the peasants was driven both by his antipathy against their biblical appeals for their revolutionary cause and his fear of the loss of political support for his own reformation, should the rulers see a connection between Luther's program of reform and the peasants' demands for economic justice through revolt. In response to the religious identity politics of the peasants, Luther's retreated from neighbor politics to his own version of religious identity politics in order to oppose them. Luther's primary argument against the Anabaptists was that they, as Enthusiasts (Schwärmer), fomented the same seditious agenda as Müntzer. Luther was troubled by the apparent success of the Anabaptist movement, especially among the lower

[21] *LW* 46:80-81.

[22] Brecht, 188.

[23] For this and the following references to Luther's 1528 treatise see, John S. Oyer, *Lutheran Reformers against Anabaptists: Luther, Melancthon, and Menius and the Anabaptists of Central Germany* (The Hague: Martinus Nijhoff, 1964), 249-252.

[24] Luther was, furthermore, overly beholden to the harsh rhetoric of Melancthon, against perceived Anabaptist errors.

classes. He feared civil unrest would jeopardize the protection by the princes of his theological and practical reforms.

Although Luther's most extensive discussion of the Anabaptist movement was *Von der Widertauffe an zwen Pfarherrn, ein Brief* (1528), his writings are filled with critical and disparaging comments against them.[25] The conservative character of Luther's reformation is demonstrated by his defense of Roman Catholic theology against the Anabaptists regarding the Lord's Supper, forgiveness of sins, the pastoral office, the Creed, and especially baptism.[26] Luther rejected Anabaptist views of baptism on several counts.

First, he criticized their reliance on the faith of the believer as the prerequisite for baptism.

> They cannot get out of the predicament but must reduce to mere human works even Baptism and the Sacraments, which are God's Word and institution. Thus the Anabaptists claim that Baptism is nothing if one is not previously sanctified. They do not want to acquire holiness through and from Baptism, but by their piety they want to make Baptism holy and wholesome.[27]

Thereby Luther distanced himself from the proposal of rebaptism by Balthasar Hubmaier. Second, he rejected the Anabaptist claim that infant baptism made the believer uncertain about the validity of his/her own baptism.

> This is the true remembrance, to hear the Word of Christ. Thus all Sacramentarians and Anabaptists are Pelagians.[28]

To allow free choice in matters of the Gospel made salvation conditional on human will.

Third, Luther criticized the motives of the Anabaptists as a stance taken merely for the sake of opposing the pope. Fourth, Luther criticized the Anabaptist reliance on Mark 16:16 ("The one who believes and is baptized will be saved") for making baptism too subjective.

[25] *WA* 26: 139-?

[26] Oyer, 117-121.

[27] *LW* 14:39.

[28] *LW* 17:256.

> One must be on one's guard against the Anabaptists and the schismatic spirits, who speak sneeringly of Baptism and aver that it is mere water and of benefit to no one. They gaze at this sacred act as a cow stares at a new door. For they behold a poor preacher standing there, or, in an emergency, a woman who baptizes. They take offense at this and say: "Well, what can Baptism accomplish.[29]

By contrast, Luther defended infant baptism as historic church practice, quoting other Scripture texts for his position (for example, Mt 19:14).[30] Because baptism is done at God's command, not according to human faith, infant baptism is efficacious and valid as a sacrament of the church.

Fifth, Luther charged the Anabaptists with works righteousness in their approach to baptism.[31] The act of performing baptism itself became among the Anabaptists a kind of monastic demonstration of good works.

> These are the ravenous wolves in sheep's clothing, who have corrupted Christianity in every age. Until recently they were called monks; now they are the Anabaptists, the new monks.[32]

The Anabaptists' subjective approach to baptism, together with their biblical literalism, led Luther to identify the Anabaptists as Enthusiasts (Schwärmer).[33]

Luther's writings took an ominous turn when he identified the Anabaptists as blasphemers, a punishable crime. For example, in his *Commentary on Psalm 82* from 1530 Luther wrote:

> If some were to teach doctrines contradicting an article of faith clearly grounded in Scripture and believed throughout the world by all Christendom, such as the articles we teach children in the Creed—for example, if anyone were to teach that Christ is not God, but a mere man and like other prophets, as the Turks and the Ana-

[29] *LW* 22:173.

[30] Cf. *LW* 3:103.

[31] Cf. *LW* 21:254.

[32] *LW* 21:258-259.

[33] Oyer, 124.

> baptists hold—such teachers should not be tolerated, but punished as blasphemers. For they are not mere heretics but open blasphemers; and rulers are in duty bound to punish blasphemers as they punish those who curse, swear, revile, abuse, defame, and slander.[34]

Roland Bainton comments: "In 1530 Luther advanced the view that two offenses should be penalized even with death, namely sedition and blasphemy."[35]

Bainton describes Luther's endorsement of Melancthon's stance against the Anabaptists in two *Gutachten* from 1531 and 1536:

> In a memorandum of 1531, composed by Melancthon and signed by Luther, a rejection of the ministerial office was described as insufferable blasphemy, and the disintegration of the Church as sedition against the ecclesial order. In a memorandum of 1536, again composed by Melanchthon and signed by Luther, the distinction between the peaceful and the revolutionary Anabaptists was obliterated....Luther may not have been too happy about signing these memoranda. At any rate he appended postscripts to each. To the first he said, "I assent. Although it seems cruel to punish them with the sword, it is crueler that they condemn the ministry of the Word and have no well-grounded doctrine and suppress the true and in this way seek to subvert the civil order." Luther's addition to the second document was a plea that severity be tempered with mercy.[36]
>
> In 1540 he is reported in his Table Talk to have returned to the position of Philip of Hesse that only seditious Anabaptists should be executed; the others should be merely banished. But Luther passed by many an opportunity to speak a word for those who with joy gave themselves as sheep for the slaughter.[37]

[34] *LW* 13:61.

[35] Roland Bainton, *Here I Stand: A Life of Martin Luther* (New York: Mentor, 1950), 295.

[36] Bainton, 295.

[37] Bainton, 295.

Luther's invective against the Anabaptists contributed to defamation of character and charges of sedition and blasphemy.

> That seditious articles of doctrine should be punished by the sword needed no further proof. For the rest, the Anabaptists hold tenets relating to infant baptism, original sin, and inspiration which have no connection to the Word of God, and are indeed opposed to it….From all this it becomes clear that the secular authorities are bound…to inflict corporal punishment on the offenders…we conclude that the stubborn sectarians must be put to death.[38]

Such conclusions were justified by a harsh religious identity politics that claimed the executions of the Anabaptists were warranted because they were of Satan:

> Such is the religion of the Anabaptists today, although day by day they are betraying that they are possessed by the devil and are seditious and bloodthirsty men.[39]

> The Anabaptists were Satan's minions in a vast cosmic struggle. The Lutherans could detect the demonic character of their opponents by their doctrine and also by their secrecy in spreading their ideas. They preferred darkness to light.[40]

Such opinions became embedded in the authoritative writings of the Lutheran Church in the Book of Concord. They were only finally repudiated by the Lutheran World Federation in 2010 with the confession: "So Lutherans, following the example of the returning exiles in Nehemiah 9, dare to ask for forgiveness for the harm that their forebears in the sixteenth century committed against Anabaptists, for forgetting and ignoring this persecution in the intervening centuries, and for all inappropriate, misleading and hurtful por-

[38] Martin Luther as quoted by Johannes Janssen, *History of the German People from the Close of the Middle Ages*, trans. A.M. Christie (St. Louis: Herder, 1910), 222-223.

[39] *LW* 27:88.

[40] Oyer, 250.

traits of Anabaptists and Mennonites made by Lutherans authors, in both popular and academic publications, to the present day."[41]

2.3 Luther against the Jews

The conventional view—that Luther began his career with certain openness and generosity to the Jews in anticipation of their conversion to the Gospel, who only later in life turned toward animosity and hatred against them—is demonstrably false.[42] From his early writings onward, Luther demonstrated contempt for the Jewish people, not only on biblical grounds but especially due to their rejection of Jesus as the Christ both in the New Testament and especially in rabbinic Judaism.[43] Although one could not have predicted that his utterances against the Jews would lead finally to Auschwitz, the legacy of anti-Semitism ignited by his pen and perpetrated by his followers is the most disastrous of all Luther's ethical missteps.

Luther knew precious little about living Judaism: "He had neither Jewish conversation partners nor Jewish friends. His knowledge of Judaism was primarily dependent on what he read, and those readings were dominated by overtly anti-Jewish treatises, some of which were written by Christians and some by Jewish converts."[44] Luther consistently maintained the view that the Jews were an apostate people, based on their failure to receive Jesus as their Messiah, and therefore blameworthy for their own subsequent mistreatment in Christian history. He employed the argument that for 1500 years the Jews had been living in defiance of the Gospel of Jesus Christ. The only reasonable explanation was "that they had been handed over by God to the Devil. Thus their resistance to the gospel—and their resistance to admitting the reason for their exile—was willful and unforgiveable."[45]

[41] Healing Memories: Reconciling in Christ. Report of the Lutheran-Mennonite International Study Commission (Geneva: Lutheran World Federation, 2010), 102.

[42] Brooks Schramm and Kirsi I. Stjerna, eds., *Martin Luther, the Bible, and the Jewish People: A Reader* (Minneapolis: Fortress, 2012), 5-10.

[43] Eric W. Gritsch, *Martin Luther's Anti-Semitism: Against His Better Judgment* (Grand Rapids: Eerdmans, 2012), 35-36.

[44] Schramm and Stjerna, 5.

[45] Schramm and Stjerna, 6.

The Jewish people had abandoned their status as the "chosen people" due to their rejection of Jesus as Christ.

> For Luther, the promise to Abraham's seed was in reality the promise of the Seed, that is the Messiah/Christ (Gen 3:15). The physical seed of Abraham, the Jews, were God's chosen instrument in Old Testament times to bear that promise. But Abraham's true descendents/seed, even in the Old Testament times, were always those who believed in the promise of the Messiah and not those who relied on the physical descent. This is the fundamental error, and sin, of the Jews, who trust as it were that they have been born into grace, that they are bound to God by birth, and thus that God owes them God's benevolence. For Luther, this constitutes a theological obscenity, because the grace and benevolence of God can only be accessed by faith, and it has never been otherwise.[46]

Luther rejected Jewish "choseness" according to the terms of the old covenant, which led him to view the Jews as the apostate people. The Jews are fully culpable for their sins. The curse uttered by the Jewish crowds at the crucifixion of Jesus rightly falls upon the apostate Jews for all time: "His blood be on us and on our children! (Mt 27:25)."

Already in Luther's early Psalm lectures (1513-1515), there is evidence of this fundamental posture against the Jews.[47] Commenting on Psalm 1, Luther wrote: "For to deny that it is a sin to have crucified the Lord is worse than to have perpetrated the sin itself, that is, to do the crucifying. Therefore the last error and the last sin are unforgiveable."[48]

> To this very day they crucify him within themselves, as the apostle accuses them (Heb 6:6), because they keep the truth pierced through and continue to stab it with their extremely hard iron lies (which are their goads). Thus to this day they do not know what they are doing,

[46] Schramm and Stjerna, 7.

[47] The following citations follow the material documented in Schramm and Stjerna.

[48] *LW* 10:13.

just as they did not know then. They scourge, stone, and kill the prophets and scribes in the same way as did their fathers.[49]

The "1500 years of Jewish apostasy and exile" myth was embedded already in Luther's thought at this early stage. Regarding Psalm 78 Luther commented: "[God] made this a firm policy, and He punishes them permanently without ceasing, not in passing, like the godly, but over and over again. As a road is usually not made by one passing but by incessant footsteps, so by incessant tracks and signs of God's wrath, which we see in them, He has now, as it were, made a road, a road worn and indeed made firm."[50]

Luther held out hope that some Jews would be converted through the preaching of the Gospel as it was newly proclaimed through the reformation. In his *Commentary on the Magnificat* (1521), Luther wrote:

> When Mary says, "His seed forever," we are to understand "forever" to mean that such grace is to continue to Abraham's seed (that is, the Jews) from that time forth, throughout all time, down to the Last Day. Although the vast majority of them are hardened, yet there are always some, however few, that are converted to Christ and believe in Him...We ought, therefore, not to treat the Jews in so unkindly a spirit, for there are future Christians among them, and they are turning every day.[51]

Luther did not hold that all Jews would remain reprobate until the eschaton. However, conversion was the condition placed upon their being accepted. This view was elaborated in *That Jesus Christ Was Born a Jew* (1523): "If we really want to help them, we must be guided in our dealings with them not by papal law but by the law of Christian love. We must receive them cordially, and permit them to trade and work with us, that they may have occasion and opportunity to associate with us, hear our Christian teaching, and

[49] *LW* 10:19.

[50] *LW* 11:80.

[51] *LW* 21:354-355.

witness our Christian life. If some of them prove stiff-necked, what of it? After all, we ourselves are not all good Christians either."[52]

One fascinating treatise for understanding Luther's Old Testament hermeneutics and thereby his concept of Judaism is *How Christians Should Regard Moses* (1525). Here Luther addressed the question: what from the Law of Moses, that is, the Old Testament still applies to Christians? He offers a threefold answer, each point related to his theological concept of law and Gospel. First, the Mosaic laws that conform to the natural law remain binding for Christians. All other laws, ceremonial or ritual specific only to Israel, are no longer binding.[53] Second, the Law of Moses is binding wherever it conveys Christ and the promise of the Gospel (for example, Gen 3:15 or Deut 18:15). Third, the Law of Moses is useful for instructing Christians through examples of righteous living, for instance, Abraham. While retaining key aspects of the Old Testament for Christian faith and life, Luther's hermeneutical method accords with his judgment of rabbinic Judaism as being apostate in the period following the New Testament.

In his correspondence, sermons, treatises, and biblical commentaries, Luther perpetrated to the end of this life a basic posture against the Jews. Commenting in 1538 on Genesis 17, Luther argued: "God does not lie. His promises are true and firm. They do not promise that some dregs of a people will come from Abraham; they promise kings and peoples. Where, then, has the kingdom remained during these 1500 years? Where have their laws remained, the institutions of the fathers, and their worship? What else are the Jews today than a body miserably torn to pieces and scattered throughout the world?"[54]

Luther's body of work against the Jews culminated in the treatise, *On the Jews and Their Lies* (1543). Contrary to conventional interpretations, his shocking recommendations to both civil authorities and clergy about how to deal with the Jews cohere with Luther's stance throughout his career.[55] The

[52] *LW* 45:229.

[53] Cf. *LW* 35:165.

[54] *LW* 3:150.

[55] Cf. Schramm and Stjerna, 99-163.

occasion for this writing was a rabbinic rebuttal of his own arguments against the Jews, which Luther earlier had published as Against the Sabbatarians (1538). At the same time, Luther was offended by slanderous claims against Jesus and his mother which were transmitted in a certain medieval Jewish text and by the information conveyed to him by a Jewish convert.[56]

Luther asserted his views regarding the Jewish problem of this own time, whether Jews should be tolerated or expelled. While he would prefer for Jews to take up residence in lands not occupied by Christians, Luther argues that the Jewish blasphemies can no longer be tolerated.

> What shall we Christians do with this rejected and condemned people, the Jews? Since they live among us, we dare not tolerate their conduct, now that we are aware of their lying and reviling and blaspheming. If we do, we become sharers in their lies, cursing, and blaspheming. Thus we cannot extinguish the unquenchable fire of divine wrath, of which the prophets speak, nor can we convert the Jews. With prayer and the fear of God we must practice sharp mercy to see whether we might save at least a few from the glowing flames. We dare not avenge ourselves. Vengeance thousand times worse than we could wish them already has them by the throat. I shall give you my sincere advice…[57]

In *On the Jews and Their Lies* Luther makes his infamous proposals regarding policy against the Jews by both civil authorities and the clergy.[58] To the civil authorities Luther recommends the following measures: burn down synagogues, destroy Jewish homes, confiscate prayer books and Talmudic writings, forbid rabbis to teach, abolish safe conduct for Jews, prohibit usury by Jews, and enforce the Jews in manual labor. To the pastors and preachers he commends: burn down synagogues; confiscate prayer books, Talmudic writings, and the Bible; prohibit Jewish prayer and teaching; and forbid Jews

[56] For this and the following, see Schramm and Stjerna, 164-165.

[57] *LW* 47:268.

[58] *LW* 47:268-272, 285-287. Cf. the chart outlining the following measures in Schramm and Stjerna, 165.

to utter the name of God publicly. To the end of his life and even in his final public utterance, Luther advocated harsh treatment of the Jews.[59]

The force of Luther's public testimony against the Jews took on a life of its own over the centuries.[60] The path leading from Luther to Kristallnacht and Auschwitz is long and twisted. But one can arrive there from here.

> In our post-Holocaust context, and knowing more than Luther did about just how far human beings—including Christians—can go down the road of Jew-hatred, we are following the tracks that are shameful and that require honest remembering. Because of the atrocities of the Nazi era, and because of ongoing expressions of anti-Semitism in our time as well, it is only proper to bring to continued inspection and prayerful reflection words such as Luther's, so that we better continue to tell the truth, repent, and strive for justice and protection of the dignity of life, in accordance with the worthy principles of our respective religions.[61]

Only in 1994 did the Evangelical Lutheran Church in America adopt a statement repudiating Luther's anti-Jewish writings and their legacy.[62]

3. Fallacy in Luther's Ethical Theology

Luther's ethical theology is embedded in the late medieval apocalyptic worldview that pitches God in a life versus death, cosmic battle against Satan.[63] Because the end of the world was drawing near, the Devil had intensified efforts to gain control of the world through those who sought to deceive and delude many from believing the Gospel of Jesus Christ. The peasants,

[59] See Admonition against the Jews (1546) in LW 58:458-459.

[60] Gritsch, 97-137.

[61] Schramm and Stjerna, 204.

[62] "Declaration of ELCA to Jewish Community," <http://www.elca.org/Who-We-Are/Our-Three-Expressions/Churchwide-Organization/Office-of-the-Presiding-Bishop/Ecumenical-and-Inter-Religious-Relations/Inter-Religious-Relations/Christian-Jewish-Relations/Declaration-of-ELCA-to-Jewish-Community.aspx>, August 14, 2013.

[63] Heiko Obermann, *Luther: Man between God and the Devil* (New York: Doubleday, 1992).

Anabaptists, and Jews were among those (though not the only ones!) through whom Satan was raging on the eve of the Apocalypse. Luther saw himself justified in waging war against these enemies of God.

Luther's writings against the peasants, Anabaptists, and Jews expose a tragic fallacy in Luther's ethical theology and pose penetrating and incisive questions that must be answered. Is there anything worth salvaging from the wreckage of Luther's intemperate and vilifying utterances, which not only have led to the suffering and death of many in the 1500s but also have contributed to the hatred, persecution, and even murder of countless vulnerable people in subsequent centuries? How might Luther's legacy of contempt and destruction as executed in the name of Jesus Christ finally be brought to an end? Is there any alternative to the outright rejection of Luther's theology, when the ethical consequences have been so lethal? Four correctives are imperative.

First, it is necessary to deconstruct Luther's binary thinking against enemies. While the apocalyptic battle between God and Satan was the framework for Luther's theology, wherever opponents become identified as Satan's minions, all things become possible as means to their destruction. Luther experienced spiritual attack (Anfechtung) with vivid reality. The devil and demons raged as agents, threatening his cause on every side. The danger, to which Luther succumbed, like the danger befalling contemporary expressions of religious identity politics, involved demonizing opponents. Once others are objectified through dehumanizing categories, every form of eliminationism is legitimated.[64] Luther's rhetoric against the peasants, Anabaptists, and Jews deprived them of their status as neighbors worthy of protection under the aegis of the law. It is imperative to guard theology against constructing binary opposites that authorize evil against those deemed less than human.[65]

[64] Daniel Jonah Goldhagen, *Worse than War: Genocide, Eliminationism, and the Ongoing Assault on Humanity* (New York: Public Affairs, 2009), 14-21.

[65] David Livingstone Smith, *Less than Human: Why We Demean, Enslave, and Exterminate Others* (New York: St. Martin's Press, 2011), 250-262.

Second, it is necessary to apply suspicion, based on the universality of human sinfulness, to one's own arguments. Luther constructed a thoroughgoing doctrine of the universality of sin. Even those justified by grace through faith in Jesus Christ continue to labor under the reality of sin. Resisting Christian perfectionism, Luther insisted that Christian existence in this world always remains *simul justus et peccator* (simultaneously saint and sinner). However, in times of intense conflict Luther exempted himself from this cautionary proviso. Rather than acknowledging the limits of his own perspective and the possibility of this own fallibility, Luther assumed ethical absolutism against his enemies. It is imperative to guard theology against the demonization of others through genuine humility about the limitations of one's own ethical perspective due to the universality of sin, also among Christians.

Third, it is necessary without exception to safeguard by rule of law the status of neighbors, including those neighbors with whom we are in conflict for religious or ideological reasons. Luther advocated that by defending neighbors from harm, civil government contributes to preserving the common good. The primus usus legis belongs inherently to God's left hand kingdom/strategy. However, in his own brand of "enthusiasm" (Schwärmerei), Luther advocated harm against those neighbors—peasants, Anabaptists, and Jews— whom he opposed for religious reasons. Thereby Luther suspended his own theological logic about the proper function of government and succumbed to religious identity politics, summoning civil authorities to engage in violent action against certain neighbors, not only because he opposed their politics but especially due to their religious convictions. Although it is anachronistic to expect Luther to adhere to any modern doctrine of separation of church and state, the nascent foundation for such a doctrine is implicit in his own teaching about the two kingdoms/strategies. By failing to uphold the responsibility of the civil authorities for protecting neighbors according to the first use of the law, including those he opposed for religious reasons, Luther neglected the primary function for which God instituted government. It is imperative to restrain religious institutions from doing harm to religious enemies by upholding a universal rule of law that provides physical protection of all neighbors and safeguards their rights.[66]

Fourth, it is necessary to repent of past failures not only by the confession of sins but through the restoration of right relationships with those who have been harmed. The 500th anniversary of the Reformation affords the occasion for the dominant Protestant churches to confess the sins of their forbearers against peasant, Anabaptist, and Jewish peoples at the time of the Reformation and to repent of the legacy of persecution in the subsequent centuries. Although there have been declarations of guilt[67] and processes of reconciliation[68] in recent ecumenical relations, the Reformation anniversary provides a kairos not only for solemn acts of contrition but the possibility for truth and reconciliation processes throughout the Lutheran communion, whose goal is the restoration of right remembering[69] and restoration of right relationships with the living generation of Anabaptist and Jewish people. While such truth and reconciliation processes needs to begin with formal actions by denominations and global church organizations, they also need to extend to local communities and congregations. From the side of Lutherans, this process needs to begin by remembering the history documented in this chapter and acknowledging the harm caused to millions of human beings as Luther's writings have contributed to an historical trajectory of defamation, persecution, and acts of physical harm, even murder. How can truth telling about the

66 *Universal Declaration of Human Rights*, Article 18, < *http://www.un.org/en/documents/udhr/*>, December 26, 2013.

67 "Declaration of ELCA to the Jewish Community," adopted April 18, 1994, <http://download.elca.org/ELCA%20Resource%20Repository/Declaration_Of_The_ELCA_To_The_Jewish_Community.pdf>, December 26, 2013.

68 "Action on the Legacy of Lutheran Persecution of "Anabaptists," adopted by LWF in July 2010, <http://www.lwf-assembly.org/uploads/media/Mennonite_Statement-EN.pdf>, December 26, 2013.

69 "Right Remembering in Anabaptist-Lutheran Relations," Report of the Evangelical Lutheran Church in America-Mennonite Church USA Liaison Committee (Chicago: Department of Ecumenical Affairs, 2004), <http://download.elca.org/ELCA%20Resource%20Repository/Right_Remembering_In_Anabaptist_Lutheran_Relations.pdf>, December 26, 2013.

Lutheran heritage in relation to the peasants, Anabaptists, and Jews lead toward reconciliation with neighbors from these traditions in our times?[70]

4. Reconstructing Luther's Two Strategies as Neighbor Politics, Beginning with the Least

The Gospel of Jesus Christ, proclaimed as Word and administered as sacraments, sets Christians free from the power of sin, death, and the devil and free for service of the neighbor. According to an ethics of the cross, Christian neighbor love pays particular attention to those neighbors who are the most vulnerable and in need of protection. The right hand (spiritual) strategy involves the work of God to accomplish salvation by grace through faith in Jesus Christ alone. This grace is not "cheap."[71] The death and resurrection of Jesus Christ takes place in the life of every Christian person as death to sin and resurrection to new life in discipleship. The Christian life entails participation both in God's right hand strategy of sharing the good news with others through evangelical listening and speaking the faith[72] and through engagement in God's left hand strategy of service to neighbors. The neighbors God gives us to serve as Christians include 1) members of our families, 2) those we encounter through our daily work, 3) those served through the efforts of religious institutions, and 4) those that we serve through collective political action.[73] It is this fourth group to whom we devote special attention in relation to the failures of Luther's social-political ethic.

One acute danger facing Christian social ethics is religious identity politics. This is patently manifest in the contemporary agenda of the Christian

[70] Cf. *From Conflict to Communion: Lutheran-Catholic Common Commemoration of the Reformation in 2017* (Leipzig: Evangelische Verlagsanstalt/Bonifatius, 2013), 236-237, which includes a call for "Lutheran confession of sins against unity" in relation to both Roman Catholics and Anabaptists/Mennonites.

[71] Cf. Dietrich Bonhoeffer, *Discipleship*, ed. Geffrey B. Kelly and John D. Godsey, trans. Barbara Green and Reinhard Krausss (Minneapolis: Fortress, 2001), 53-56.

[72] Richard H. Bliese and Craig Van Gelder, ed., *The Evangelizing Church: A Lutheran Contribution* (Minneapolis: Fortress, 2005), 133-137.

[73] Craig L. Nessan, *Shalom Church: The Body of Christ as Ministering Community* (Minneapolis: Fortress, 2010), 22-25.

religious right with reference to abortion, homosexuality, or the State of Israel. Drawing a one-to-one correspondence between claims to biblical authority and an absolutist ethical stance, religious identity politics brackets out the complexity of the issues and narrows the range of neighbors needing to be served. Although his time and context were clearly different, Luther's social ethics succumbed to the logic of religious identity politics in his absolutist positions against the peasants, Anabaptists, and Jews. While there are resources in Luther's thought that could have reframed his arguments into a consistent neighbor politics, in the end his appeals to Scripture led him to harsh condemnation of his religious enemies with grave consequences for their protection by the civil authorities.

Given Luther's failure to defend the peasants, Anabaptists, and Jews as neighbors who deserved the protection of civil law, we must, as an act of repentance, reconstruct his thought with more thoroughgoing consistency regarding the two distinct, yet dialectically related kingdoms, which describe God's ways of working in the world. It is crucial, first, to understand that these kingdoms are not to be interpreted spatially. One fundamental error, leading to a range of misunderstandings about the two kingdoms, imagines them according to a spatial metaphor, which inevitably leads to understanding them as separated and disconnected.[74] Therefore it is constructive to speak not of two "kingdoms" (Reiche) but of two "strategies" (Regimente). God has two distinct but indispensable strategies for ruling the world. Both are necessary to serve God's purposes of guarding against evil and bringing forth the kingdom of shalom.[75] These two strategies must be viewed in dialectical, not contradictory, relationship to one another. God is ambidextrous in ruling the world with two hands: through the spiritual strategy of the Gospel on the right and the civil strategy, entailing the first use of the law, on the left.[76]

[74] Walter Altmann, *Luther and Liberation*.

[75] Cf. Paul Althaus, *The Ethics of Martin Luther*, trans. Robert C. Schultz (Philadelphia: Fortress, 1972), 52-53.

[76] Althaus, 54-56.

Second, in the left hand strategy the civil law encompasses all people, not only Christians. All people "dance in God's masquerade," fulfilling their obligations to neighbors in the four stations belonging to the left hand strategy—through family, daily work, religious institutions, and political responsibility—whether they explicitly acknowledge God as the One whom they serve or not. God employs secular rulers as agents in this left hand strategy, whether these are the princes and lords of Luther's late medieval world or the elected officials in modern democracy. The scope of the enacted civil law, if the law is to be equitable and just, must protect and safeguard all people, without exceptions based on race, class, gender, sexual orientation, or any other marker, including religion. It is the fallacy of religious identity politics, whether by Luther at his time or by contemporary representatives of the religious right, to exempt certain neighbors from equal protection under law on the basis of their appeals to religious (biblical!) authority.

Third—and in contradiction to the special pleading of religious identity politics—if there is bias exercised by Christians in the left hand strategy, it is not against those who fail to share a "Christian" religious worldview, but rather on behalf of those whom Jesus named "the least"—the hungry, thirsty, homeless, sick, or imprisoned ones—the most vulnerable, those at the margins of society in need of particular political advocacy (cf. Matt 25:31-46). What legitimates political engagement on behalf of the oppressed (including increasingly the oppression of the natural world) are not appeals to religious (biblical) authority. Rather, when Christians are involved in political advocacy, they are compelled to employ public arguments that aim to persuade all reasonable people about the legitimacy of a particular course of action apart from special pleading based on religious (Biblicist!) authority. The work of politics entails constructing coalitions to influence the balance of power in league with all those who share concern for the neighbor, beginning with the least. Religious identity politics must yield to a consistent neighbor politics, with the welfare of the neighbor as the sole concern of Lutheran social ethics, not religious self-righteousness.

Fourth, when civil authorities violate their God-given responsibility to protect and safeguard the rights of the people (especially minorities), Christians are called to engage in direct political action to make the government accountable for the proper exercise of its civil responsibility. According to Bonhoeffer:

> There are thus three possibilities for action that the church can take vis-à-vis the state": first (as we have said), questioning the state as to the legitimate character of its actions, that is, making the state responsible for what it does. Second it is service to the victims of the state actions. The church has an unconditional obligation toward the victims of any societal order, even if they do not belong to the Christian community. "Let us work for the good of all." These are both ways in which the church, in its freedom, conducts itself in the interest of a free state. In times when the laws are changing, the church may under no circumstances neglect either of these duties. The third possibility is not just to bind up the wounds of the victim beneath the wheel but to seize the wheel itself. Such an action would be direct political action on the part of the church. This is only possible and called for if the church sees the state to be failing in its function of creating law and order, that is, if the church perceives that the state, without any scruples, has created either too much or too little law and order. It must see in either eventuality a threat to the existence of the state and thus to its own existence as well.[77]

With this third possibility Bonhoeffer offers the needed correction to Luther's religious identity politics: the church must call for the state to fulfill "its function of creating law and order," not to impose its peculiar religious agenda on the state. Bonhoeffer (alongside the other conspirators) exercised this form of political responsibility by following the ultima ratio of planning cout d'etat against the dictatorship, a measure Luther never imagined within the legitimate scope of Christian political responsibility.

The limits of Luther's social ethics are profound. Luther's political reasoning and advocacy against the peasants, Anabaptists, and Jews must be rejected and repudiated. His counsel and conclusions reverberate across subsequent history in the arguments and actions of those who have appealed to his precedent, both by their rhetoric and through acts of persecution and violence. Only by deconstructing the logic of religious identity politics, both

[77] Dietrich Bonhoeffer, "The Church and the Jewish Question," in Dietrich Bonhoeffer, *Berlin 1932-1933*, ed. Larry L. Rasmussen, trans. Isabel Best and David Higgins (Minneapolis: Fortress, 2009), 12:365-366.

then and now, can Luther's ethical framework be reconstructed in service of a neighbor politics that has its sole purpose in defending the weak from harm and safeguarding the welfare of the most vulnerable in society, regardless of their religious convictions.

JESUS THE REVOLUTIONARY: RADICALIZING CHRISTOLOGY AFTER BONHOEFFER

Peter Goodwin Heltzel

1. Introduction

Vital to the task of Radicalizing Reformation today is the construction of a prophetic post-colonial Christology that emphasizes the subjugated Jewish flesh of Jesus of Nazareth. Since Martin Luther's theologia crucis, Jesus Christ has been at the center of Protestant theology. Yet, in Lutheran theology there was a focus on the justification of individuals by faith in Jesus Christ. Dietrich Bonhoeffer maintains the Christological focus of Lutheran theology, but deepens it through arguing that Jesus is a cosufferer with the suffering and oppressed in the present. Reggie Williams agues in *Bonhoeffer's Black Jesus: Harlem Renaissance Theology and an Ethic of Resistance* that Bonhoeffer's baptism into the black church in Harlem helped him connect the suffering of Jesus and the suffering of the oppressed, be they blacks in America or Jews in Germany. After Harlem, Bonhoeffer emphasizes Jesus as a revolutionary prophet, the "One for Others," who descends into the suffering of others to bring healing and hope.

Bonhoeffer's Christology "from below" offers an important trajectory for black liberation theology in the Americas. Emphasizing Jesus as a Jewish peasant who was part of a minority group in an age of Roman Empire, black and liberation theology in the Americas, connects Jesus the Jewish prophet to the struggle for racial and economic justice in the Americas. In the black theology of James Cone, Jesus' Jewishness becomes the basis of the "black Christ," the presence of Jesus in the movement of people engaged in the black freedom struggle. Cone's emphasis on the historical social location and suffering of Jesus, as well as Jesus' identification with the oppressed, is an important starting point for any theological project that is concerned with the suffering of humanity and the liberation of the oppressed in the here and now.

2. Bonhoeffer's Black Jesus: Radicalizing the Reformation through a Prophetic Christology

While on a Sloane Fellowship at Union Theological Seminary in 1930-1931, Dietrich Bonhoeffer (1906-1945) was transformed by his encounter with prophetic black Christianity. Unable to get ordained until he was 25 years old, Bonhoeffer decided to travel to New York City to attend Union Theological Seminary for post-doctoral theological studies. However, after taking courses at the seminary, he resolutely concluded, "there is no theology here.... The students - on the average twenty-five to thirty years old - are completely clueless with respect to what dogmatics is really about."[1] Deeply disappointed in the quality and depth of the theological conversation at Union Theological Seminary, he found the spirit and fire in the black church in Harlem much more to his liking.

One Sunday, Albert Franklin Fisher, a black Union student from Birmingham, Alabama, invited Bonhoeffer to join him for morning worship at Abyssinian Baptist Church. Bonhoeffer's baptism into the black church changed his life forever. It was in a big black Baptist church in Harlem that Bonhoeffer heard the powerful preaching of Rev. Adam Clayton Powell, Sr. (1865-1953) who preached good news to the poor. Rev. Powell's pulpit was the site of a powerful proclamation of Jesus the Liberator of the oppressed. At a time when blacks were being lynched across America, Powell passionately preached against social sin, suffering and injustice, offering a horizon of hope for poor people in Harlem.

Bonhoeffer was inspired and challenged by Rev. Powell's prophetic sermons and the ecstatic worship of Abyssinian Baptist Church, where he had a transformational encounter with the "Black Jesus" that was lifted up from the

[1] Dietrich Bonhoeffer, "150. To Superintendent Max Diestel" (December 19, 1930) Barcelona, Berlin, New York: 1928-1931. English ed., *Dietrich Bonhoeffer Works* (Minneapolis: Fortress, 2008), 10: 265. Hereafter cited as DBWE. I would like to thank Nkosi Anderson, Gottfried Brezger, Jamall Calloway, J. Kameron Carter, James Cone, Willie Jennings, Jennifer M. McBride, Christopher Morse, Jan Rehmann, Hans Schwarz, and Reggie Williams for their comments on this chapter.

pulpit.[2] According to Reggie Williams, Rev. Powell's sermons "A Hungry God" and "A Naked God" offered an innovative interpretation of Matthew 25:31-46, having a lasting impact on Bonhoeffer's theology and ministry.[3] Powell helped Bonhoeffer to see that God in Jesus Christ is present in our fellow humans who are hungry, thirsty, naked and in prison. Arriving shortly after the Great Depression (1929-1939), Bonhoeffer saw abject poverty in the black community in Harlem in the context of brutal racial violence in Jim Crow America.

Rev. Powell's preaching crystalized the insight that Jesus is a cosufferer hidden in black suffering, revolutionizing the young Bonhoeffer's Christology. Since Jesus suffered for all people who suffered, the Gospel offered hope of a "this-worldly" liberation for the oppressed. In New York City, Bonhoeffer saw the dramatic disparity between the lives of rich whites and poor blacks. This black border W. E. B. Du Bois described as the color line. As a border stalker, Bonhoeffer crossed the color line in the US, descending down the hill from a white elite educational community in Morningside Heights into the black heart of Harlem.

At Abyssinian Baptist Church, Bonhoeffer experienced the Christ community that he dreamed of in his dissertation *Sanctorum Communio*, completed in 1927, writing: "Christians can and ought to act like Christ: they ought to bear the burdens and sufferings of the neighbor. . . . It must come to the point that the weaknesses, needs, and sins of my neighbor afflict me as if they were my own, in the same way as Christ was afflicted by our sin."[4] The black Baptist church was a safe haven in a white supremacist society for African Americans to claim their self-worth in Christ Jesus and be spiritually nurtured in a community of revolutionary friends.

In the 1930s, mainstream white American Christians who remained silent about lynching and racism, were effectively preaching the Gospel of a white

[2] See Reggie Williams, *Bonhoeffer's Black Jesus: Harlem Renaissance Theology and an Ethic of Resistance* (Waco, TX: Baylor University, 2014).

[3] Reggie Williams, *Bonhoffer's Black Jesus*, 101-115.

[4] Dietrich Bonhoeffer, *Sanctorum Communio: A Theological Study of the Sociology of the Church*, DBWE 1: 178-180.

Jesus, offering religious justification for the racial hierarchy. In contrast, Rev. Powell spoke boldly about Jesus the prophet who was leading the black freedom struggle. Powell's message connected catalytically with the growing African American community in Harlem. From 1890-1930, 2.5 million African Americans from the South migrated to Northern cities searching for opportunity and freedom. During this period the black population of New York City grew 66 percent. Since the South was fiercely religious, thousands of migrating Southerners joined Northern congregations, including Abyssinian Baptist Church, bringing their folk orality, soulful music, and creative writing to Harlem. In the 1920s, the Harlem Renaissance erupted with new art forms to express black soul. For example, Countee Cullen's poem "The Black Christ" was an artistic attempt to reimagine Christianity in the context of white supremacy. During turbulent times, Harlem musicians made new music with swing and soul. The spirituals, blues and jazz music hearkened a prophetic intercultural future.

It was black spirituals that moved Bonhoeffer the most. A pianist who loved classical music, Bonhoeffer was drawn into the blue note and soul of the spirituals he sang at Abyssinian. The spirituals unveil a liberative worldview of a people under oppression. In a world of segregation and suffering, God is with us. We are not alone. In the music, preaching, dancing, literature and visual art, the black spirit comes to life through a principle of improvisation.[5] Black art was created as a form of survival, a ritual of resistance.

Drawing on forms and fragments of their African past, and the tragic experiences of the Middle Passage, slavery and segregation, blacks in Harlem in the 1930s were forging a form of faith-filled art that was authentically black. The prophetic imagination of black Christians rejected the rule of the Egyptians, praying for God to come down and liberate them, a people enslaved like Israel. This was a worldview forged by a people whose African ancestors had to improvisationally survive in the hull of the slave ship underneath a

[5] See my discussion of improvisation in jazz music in *Resurrection City: A Theology of Improvisation* (Grand Rapids: Eerdmans, 2012), esp. 13 ff.

white commanding crew.[6] For a people subjected and suffering, it was God and God alone who was the source of their life and liberation. The spirituals sung by blues-soaked souls would echo in in Bonhoeffer's soul for years to come, witnessing to a faith as strong as martyrs.

While attentive to Jesus' concern for the poor in the Gospels, in Harlem Bonhoeffer was baptized into blackness. The descent of Bonhoeffer into the lives of the downtrodden and disinherited, stabilized his privileged and prestigious position as a white theologian of German descent. Bonhoeffer began to see Jesus hidden in the lives of the poor and oppressed. As a lay leader in the church Bonhoeffer taught a group of boys in Sunday School, led a boys club at the Harlem YMCA, and taught a mid-week Bible study to women. From the cries of young boys who could not find a quiet place to study, to the voices of black women in Harlem who shared with him a black woman's interpretation of the Bible, to the call and response during the Sunday sermon, Bonhoeffer heard the cries of blacks with their backs against the wall. It was at Abyssinian Baptist Church that Bonhoeffer realized what was at stake in the black freedom struggle for survival—the very truth of the Gospel itself, a message that was supposed to be good news to the poor (Isaiah 61:1; Luke 4:18).

Bonhoeffer's baptism into black Christianity in Harlem challenged him to deepen Martin Luther's claim that Christ is for us (pro nobis). While Luther developed the idea of God in Jesus Christ being for us primarily in the doctrine of soteriology, Bonhoeffer deepened and radicalized this motif applying it to ecclesiology and ethics. Reading Barth's commentary the Epistle to the Romans in 1924 inspired Bonhoeffer to reclaim his Lutheran roots with a bold Word of God theology, but in Harlem Bonhoeffer was faced with a new challenge: What relevance did God's Word of Grace have to the concrete lives of the poor and oppressed?

In Harlem, black folks were the poor. As a lay leader at the nation's largest black Baptist church, Bonhoeffer began to reflect on race as a theological problem. As Williams writes "Bonhoeffer remains the only prominent white

[6] See Willie Jennings' discussion, "The Story of the Slave Ship," in *The Christian Imagination: Theology and the Origins of Race* (New Haven: Yale University Press, 2010), 171-180.

theologian of the twentieth century to speak about racism as a Christian problem....The black Jesus became a discursive figure representing God with and for the despised and rejected of all humanity."[7] Bonhoeffer was the first white western theologian who tried to de-center himself and wrestle theologically with a subaltern Christian tradition on its own terms – prophetic black Christianity in the United States. Bonhoeffer was a radical reformer because he dared to think about black church tradition as a source of theology, offering the possibility of a prophetic Protestant theology.

J. Kameron Carter argues that Bonhoeffer's sojourn in Harlem and the Caribbean—the Black Atlantic—initiated him into blackness as oceanic reality like the Middle Passage. An ecumenical mode of existence, the blackness into which Bonhoeffer was baptized into in Harlem left him inextricably bound to black people's historic struggles for freedom, giving him the prophetic fire to return to Germany to courageously fight for the freedom of Jews during the German Third Reich. Carter writes, "to read Bonhoeffer in this way is to reckon with his blackness, if I may risk such a heterodox thought for Bonhoeffer studies and theological studies, or his having been seized by an in-sovereign blackness, by the between, by the force of relationality, that renegade movement of the future of blackness."[8] Through the lens of the black church, Bonhoeffer was better able to see the sin of racism and the possibility of a prophetic anti-racist Christian witness.

3. Bonhoeffer and the Black Social Gospel in Berlin

Bonhoeffer brings the spirit and fire of America's black social gospel movement back to Germany, courageously confronting the racist Volk ideology that was going viral across his nation. Bonhoeffer and his friend Franz Hildebrandt coauthored a Lutheran catechism that confessed and renounced the sin of racism: "God has arranged it so that all races of humanity of the earth come from one blood (Acts 17:26). Therefore, a definite ethnic pride in

[7] Reggie Williams, *Bonhoeffer's Black Jesus*, 139.

[8] J. Kameron Carter, "Paratheological Blackness" *South Atlantic Quarterly* (2013): 112 (4): 608 n. 4; 589-611.

flesh and blood is a sin against the Holy Spirit."[9] After experiencing the black-white racial divide in America, Bonhoeffer saw the biblical invocation of humanity being united by one blood as the foundation for his own struggle leading the prophetic Church in Germany to resist Nazi ideology and to treat Jews with love and respect.

After his ordination on November 15, 1931, Bonhoeffer asked the Superintendent of the Evangelischer Kirchenkreis if he could be assigned to a poor neighborhood similar to Harlem. In February 1932, Bonhoeffer began his service as a Parish priest at Zionskirche in Stadtmitte. Charles Marsh writes, "after his full-immersion baptism in Harlem, this move to an urban parish felt like a homecoming of sorts."[10] A loving and committed youth pastor, Bonhoeffer was charged with spiritually caring for thirty young boys in the church which the Senior Pastor had no time or interest to care for. Bonhoeffer dove into his new job, listening to the boys, playing sports with them, and teaching them the Bible and the Lutheran Catechisms. Charles Marsh writes, "In the second semester, Bonhoeffer started inviting his confirmands in groups of two and three, to Herr Heide's boardinghouse, where he served them supper, read them scripture or recounted Bible stories, played for them recordings of classical music and Negro Spirituals, even taught them chess. Sometimes he would tell a story from his travels. Evenings usually concluded with 'a short spell of catechizing'"[11] Bonhoeffer built beloved community among the poor young men as a parable of the Kingdom, seeking to bear communal witness to Christ for the Other in the spirit of his Sunday School class in Harlem.

During this period Bonhoeffer undertakes a focused study of Jesus' Sermon on the Mount with its simple, direct call to a life of love and justice (Matthew 25). Jesus' call was not simply to love the neighbor, but to love the enemy. It is from this encounter with Jesus' radical teaching of non-violent love in the streets of a poor neighborhood in Berlin that Bonhoeffer's prophetic

[9] As quoted by Reggie Williams, *Bonhoeffer's Black Jesus*, 114.

[10] Charles Marsh, *Strange Glory* (New York: Alfred A. Knopf, 2014), 147.

[11] Charles Marsh, *Strange Glory*, 148. Cf. Reggie Williams, *Bonhoeffer's Black Jesus*, 113-115.

Christological ethic is deepened and becomes more concrete. Rooted in Jesus' Jewishness, Bonhoeffer cultivates a Christ-centered ethic of responsibility in deep solidarity with the Jewish freedom struggle.

4. Die *Judenfrage* in Lutheran Theology

In April of 1933, Bonhoeffer speaks out against the Nazi regime, arguing that the church should not simply "bandage the victims under the wheel, but jam the spoke in the wheel itself." While Karl Barth drafted the Barmen Declaration, Bonhoeffer helped to draft the Bethel Declaration with his colleagues Hermann Sasse, Gerhard Stratenwerth, George Merz, Hans Fischer, and Wilhelm Vischer. While these confessional documents rejected German Christian's complicity with the Nazi regime, they did not mention Die Judenfrage nor did they boldly reject the Aryan paragraph. As a result Bonhoeffer signed neither document. The Reich Church's adoption of the anti-Jewish clause portended more manifestations of anti-Semitism in the years ahead.

On May 6, 1939 the Nazi government established an Institute for the Study and Eradication of Jewish Influence on German Church Life, which was opened in the castle of Wartburg, where Martin Luther translated the New Testament into German in 1521.[12] The Institute funded three groups of scholars who sought to dejudaize the Bible, the catechism, the liturgy, and the theology of Christianity in Germany. Alon Confino writes,

> The institute reflected the popular appeal of the German Christian movement among Protestants in the Third Reich and of the idea of a Germany without Judaism. It commingled Nazi ideas about the Aryan

[12] For a thoughtful analysis of the establishment and research agenda of the Institute for the Study and Eradication of Jewish Influence on German Church Life at the University of Jena in Thuringia, Germany, see Susannah Heschel, *The Aryan Jesus: Christian Theologians and the Bible in Nazi Germany* (Princeton: Princeton University Press, 2008), esp. 67-105; Cf. Susannah Heschel, "Transforming Jesus from Jew to Aryan: Protestant Theologians in Nazi Germany", Albert T. Billgray Lecture, University of Arizona, 1995.

> race with Christianity, while pastors, scholars, and church and state institutions lent its message support and legitimacy.[13]

Dejudaizing Jesus went hand and hand with reestablishing him as a white Aryan super hero. Severing its historic connection to Judaism, western theology replaced Jewish identity with 'whiteness' as the primary matrix for interpreting and practicing Christian faith.[14]

German anti-Semitism has roots in Martin Luther's theology itself that draws on a broader tendency toward supersessionism in European Christianity. Luther's firebrand penchant for doctrinal critique through character assassination turned from the papal authority of the Roman Catholic Church toward that of the Jewish people. In the latter half of Luther's career as a reformer, he published an infamous treatise, *The Jews and their Lies* (1543) a scathing defamation of Jewish culture, including a rationale for why it actively assailed and purged from his land. In offering advice to the Princes, Luther writes of the Jews:

> First to set fire to their synagogues or schools and to bury and cover with dirt whatever will not burn, so that no man will ever again see a stone or cinder of them. ... Second, I advise that their houses also be razed and destroyed. ... Third, I advise that all their prayer books and Talmudic writings, in which such idolatry, lies, cursing and blasphemy are taught, be taken from them. ... Fourth, I advise that their rabbis be forbidden to teach henceforth on pain of loss of life and limb. For they have justly forfeited the right to such an office by holding the poor Jews captive with the saying of Moses (Deuteronomy 17 [:10 ff.]) in which he commands them to obey their teachers on penalty of death, although Moses clearly adds: 'what they teach you in accord with the law of the Lord.' Those villains ignore that. They wantonly employ the poor people's obedience contrary to the law of the Lord and infuse them with this poison, cursing, and blasphemy. ... Fifth, I advise that safe - conduct on the highways be abolished completely for the Jews ... Sixth, I advise that usury be prohibited to them. ... Seventh, I commend putting a flail, an ax, a hoe, a spade, a distaff, or a spindle into the hands

[13] Alon Confino, *A World without Jews: The Nazi Imagination from Persecution to Genoncide* (New Haven: Yale University Press, 2014), 147.

[14] For an elaboration of this claim see J. Kameron Carter, *Race: A Theological Account* (Oxford: Oxford University, 2008).

> of young, strong Jews and Jewesses and letting them earn their bread in the sweat of their brow, as was imposed on the children of Adam (Gen 3[:19]).[15]

Luther argued that the Jews were no longer the chosen people, and advocated outright violence against them, including destroying their synagogues and homes, seizing their prayer books and other property, and preventing Rabbis from preaching. Luther's advice to the Princes is clear - do not grant Jews protection and fellowship because they were deceptive and dangerous. Seeing them as false prophets, Luther wanted them expelled from the polis conceived as a "Christian" sphere.

In Martin Luther we see a flowering of the Christian tradition of anti-Judaism, and his intervention against the Jews marks an important transition from the anti-Judaism of the Medieval Catholic Church to what Heiko Oberman calls the racial anti-Semitism of modernity.[16] One of the towns that Luther lived in had expelled the Jews ninety years earlier, reflecting the theological and cultural tradition of placing the guilt of Christ's murder on Jews. Like many Christians in the 16th century, Luther was a supersessionist, seeing Christianity as the fulfillment and completion of Judaism, and expecting their conversion. Indeed, in his early writings Luther saw them as allies against the corruption of the Catholic Church (while still considering them blasphemers for rejecting the divinity of Jesus.) But Luther became increasingly bitter toward the Jews as it became clear they were little more likely to convert to his Protestant revolution than the old order of Catholicism.

Luther's theology exposes the way in which the Christian theological imaginary can reject its Jewish origins, while simultaneously furthering the pro-

[15] Luther, The Jews and Their Lies (1543), in *Luther Works* 47:268-272.

[16] While Heiko Oberman argues that Martin Luther was not an anti-Semite, he thinks that Luther's theology created the conditions for the emergence of racial anti-Semitism, writing "If Luther could forsake the buffeted race as God's disinherited people, then indeed there was no room left for Jews as Jews. Opposition to Judaism in effect became opposition to Jews. From this point on, the image of the Jew, just as it stood, was no longer proof against conscription into the unfamiliar service of racial anti-Semitism." Heiko A. Oberman, *The Roots of Anti-Semitism: In the Age of Renaissance and Reformation* (Philadelphia: Fortress Press, 1984), 50.

ject of whiteness in the project of Western Civilization. The European colonial idea that whites were superior to the indigenous populations of Africa and the New World is theologically rooted in the problematic idea that the Christian was superior to the Jew.

Racism is rooted in supersessionism, an interpretation of the New Testament that sees God's relationship with Christians as replacing God's covenant with the Jews.[17] Christian "replacement theology" - the idea that Christianity replaces Judaism - is a heresy that must be denied and continually struggled against within the church.

Through the corrupting influence of anti-Semitism, modern German theology began to transform Jesus from a Jew into an Aryan. While theologians like Karl Barth and Dietrich Bonhoeffer tried to resist the Nazi regime, most of the Christian leaders in Germany betrayed Christianity's prophetic ideals, standing by silently as the Nazi's propaganda machine forwarded an Aryan Jesus as a theological justification for German nationalism.[18]

Shorn of his Jewishness, Jesus becomes 'white' in much 20th century German theology. Severing its historic connection to Judaism, western theology often replaces Jewish identity with 'whiteness' as the primary matrix for interpreting and practicing Christian faith. As the primary privileged social marker in the modern world, whiteness refers to the racial identity of people of European descent who are the primary beneficiaries of the power and privileges of the social institutions that continue their power.

[17] See J. Kameron Carter, *Race: A Theological Account.*

[18] See Stefan Arvidsson, *Aryan Idols: Indo-European Mythology as Ideology and Science.* Trans. Sonia Wichmann (Chicago: University of Chicago, 2006); Zygmunt Bauman, *Modernity and the Holocaust* (Cambridge: Polity 1988); Robert P. Ericksen and Susannah Heschel, ed. Betrayal: *German Churches and the Holocaust* (Minneapolis: Fortress Press, 1999); George Mosse, *Nationalism and Sexuality* (Madison: University of Wisconsin Press, 1985); Leon Poliakov, *The History of Anti-Semitism, vol. 1* (Oxford: Oxford University Press, 1985); idem, *The Aryan Myth* (London: Sussex University Press, 1974); Paul Lawrence Rose, *Revolutionary Anti-Semitism in Germany from Kant to Wagner* (Princeton, N.J.: Princeton University Press, 1990); Gershom Scholem, *From Berlin to Jerusalem: Memories of My Youth*, trans. Harry Zohn (New York: Schocken, 1971).

At issue is the structural and cultural links between the German and American Christian world, indeed, the wider racial world as it operated by way of a discourse of western civilizational ambitions and cultural (sometimes called "manifest") destiny. Hitler is instructive because he exemplifies precisely the problem of how the project of Western civilizing has made use of Christian concepts and thus at the cultural level or the level of social structures has been nothing less than a problematic project of salvation - where salvation here is ordered around a false "God-Man," the white masculine.[19] Indeed, it is this dynamic - the hegemony of the white masculine - that Christian theology must continue to struggle against.

In vigorous opposition to the ideology of anti-Semitism advanced by many German Christians, Bonhoeffer joined the Confessing Church Movement, seeking to reclaim Christianity's Jewish roots through working for deep solidarity with the Jews who were being murdered by the Nazi regime. His prophetic Christology would lead him, step by step, into the conspiracy to kill Hitler and end the Nazi's violent murders of the Jews. Because of his activism in the resistance movement, Bonhoeffer was arrested on April 5, 1943 and taken to Tegel prison.

5. Fragments of the Future from Prison

During his imprisonment in Germany for his resistance against Hitler and the Nazi regime, Bonhoeffer imagined what a religionless Church would be. It was vital that the church after the War stand with the victims. Bonhoeffer writes:

> The hungry person needs bread, the homeless person needs shelter, the one deprived of rights needs justice, the lonely person needs community, the undisciplined one needs order, and the slave needs freedom. It would

[19] On the notion of a false "God-Man," which echoes what in classical Christian theology has been called the Christological problem, see more recently by J. Kameron Carter, "An Unlikely Convergence: W. E. B. Du Bois, Karl Barth, and the Problem of the Imperial God-Man," *CR: The New Centennial Review* 11.3 (2012): 167–224.

> be blasphemy against God and our neighbor to leave the hungry unfed while saying that God is closest to those in deepest need.[20]

The bearing of the sins and burdens of others to which Jesus calls the church is nothing less than a concrete imitation of Jesus' own life, a cruciform life, one that was fundamentally disruptive and that cannot be contained in the categories of religion.

Since Jesus was in full solidarity with the suffering and oppressed throughout his ministry, Christians are called to seek solidarity with the suffering. Bonhoeffer calls for a prophetic Christianity that will "see the great events of world history from below, from the perspective of the outcasts, the suspects, the maltreated, the powerless, the oppressed and reviled, in short from the perspective of the suffering."[21] Constructing Christian doctrine from the perspective of the suffering offered a new horizon for prophetic Protestant theology. In this, the church should find itself not only in solidarity with those on the underside of history, but intentionally marching up to the frontlines of the struggle against the powers and principalities. In other words, the church's identification with those who suffer is nothing short of an apocalyptic gesture meant to highlight the fact that the current age, in which the few are on top while the many suffer below, has met its end in Jesus Christ. This unjust state of affairs is passing away. The world is being turned upside down

[20] Dietrich Bonhoeffer, "Ultimate and Penultimate Things," *Ethics*, DBWE 6: 163. Discussing theology "from below" is a common construction in contemporary liberation theology, but Bonhoeffer had a more nuanced view of the von oben / von unten distinction. In his essay "The 'Ethical' and the 'Christian' as a Topic," Bonhoeffer argues that "the orientation from above to below...is an essential quality of the ethical, even though it is so highly offensive to the modern mind." (Bonhoeffer, *Ethics*, DBWE 6: 372). Since Bonhoeffer thinks the command of God comes from above to below, he finds the theological movement "from above to below" to be important ethically. Christopher Morse argues that "heaven's at-handedness" addresses this tension in Bonhoeffer's theology, as the reality of heaven, while not of this world, is coming into the world. All of our ethical action is oriented by the coming Kingdom of God. Christopher Morse, "Responsibility in the Real World: Bonhoeffer", in *The Difference Heaven Makes: Rehearing the Gospel as News* (New York: T & T Clark, 2010), pp. 86-98, esp. pp. 87 and 96.

[21] Dietrich Bonhoeffer, "After Ten Years: A Reckoning made at New Year 1943", *Letters and Papers from Prison.* ed. Eberhard Bethge (New York: Collier Books, 1953), 17.

and the church's identification with those who suffer witnesses to this fact in both word and deed.[22]

6. The Jewishness of Jesus: Black Theology and the Interrogation of White Supremacy

By following Reggie Williams' lead, interpreting Bonheoffer's prophetic Christology through his experiences with the black church in Harlem unveils an important trans-Atlantic theological encounter. Because of violent initial encounters between Europeans and dark skinned people in the "New World," colonial Christianity cast a long, dark shadow on the Americas. Bonhoeffer's baptism into blackness was a holy disruption of America's colonial Christian matrix, offering an apocalyptic sign of healing and hope. Bonhoeffer the pro-reconciliation ecumenist began to bridge the black-white and American-German divide. Bonhoeffer's life and legacy opens up the possibility of a reconstitution of revolutionary spirit today, transgressing the boundaries of race and religion.

Dietrich Bonhoeffer embodied revolutionary spirit as he led the Confessing Church toward deep solidarity with the Jews, while courageously confronting the racism of the Third Reich and the Christians who were complicit with the Fascist regime. Bonhoeffer's life and theology provides an important bridge between Martin Luther's Reformation in Germany and James Cone's Reformation in America. Martin Luther was a revolutionary in that he reclaimed the power of the Gospel of Grace in the context of its captivity in Catholic Christendom. In the same revolutionary spirit, James Cone reclaimed the prophetic power of the Gospel of Liberation in the context of its captivity in the white supremacist church in America.

Dietrich Bonhoeffer's dream of costly discipleship is echoed in Cone's call for liberation as the project of freedom. Bonhoeffer reclaimed Jesus' Jewishness in his prophetic confrontation with the Aryan Jesus proclaimed by German Christians. After Bonhoeffer, Jesus' Jewishness remains a theological problem and a racial problem. Following Malcolm X and Martin Luther

[22] See Dietrich Bonhoeffer, "Christ, Reality, and Good: Christ, Church, and World," *Ethics*, DBW 6: 62-64.

King, Jr., Cone's black liberation theology connects the Jewishness of Jesus with black existence in America. The central question that drives black theology is: How do we speak about God, Jesus, and the human being in a society defined by the legacy of slavery, Jim Crow segregation, lynching, riots, police brutality, and white supremacy? Because blacks in America were oppressed by white supremacy, they clearly understood the oppression of the Jews and the urgency of the Scriptural call to liberation. Sharing a common circumstance of colonial captivity, both Jews and blacks cried out to God the Liberator to break the chains of their colonial oppression.

How might we try to characterize black liberation theology in relation to postcolonial theology? Black liberation theology is the theological trajectory within the black radical movement. The black radical movement was a postcolonial discourse in the 1960s. While a theology student at Northwestern University, Cone read Frantz Fanon's The Wretched of the Earth (1961) and was persuaded by Fanon's analysis of the dehumanizing psychological effect of colonization on the colonized. In A Dying Colonialism (1965) and Black Skin, Whites Masks (1967), Fanon went on to deepen his critique of colonization, offering a global analysis of white supremacy. Fanon heard the cries of poor people in the Third World, who were dominated by the whiteness of colonial regimes, and called for the materialization of anticolonial liberation movements. Fanon offered Cone perspectives and tools to decolonize theology in the United States through a more radical exegesis of Scripture (focusing on themes of oppression and liberation) and a prophetic theology (focusing on the political liberation of black people and the restoration of their dignity). Joining in deep solidarity with activists fighting European and US colonialism in the Third World, Cone sought to fight the principalities and powers of neo-colonization and whites supremacy within the borders of the United States. Interpreting Cone through a post-colonial lens makes sense because black liberation theology is a vector within the black radical movement, which is itself already a postcolonial discourse.

While Fanon offered a clear critique of the colonial logic of whiteness, the Black Arts movement creatively expressed what it meant to be black. While teaching at Adrian College in Detroit in the late 1960s, the Black Arts movement erupted, creating a fertile context for developing a new theopoesis. During this time, Cone devoured the essays of LeRoi Jones (Amiri Baraka) like "*The Revolutionary Theatre*," "*Black Hope*," "*The Legacy of*

Malcolm X," and "*The Coming of the Black Nation*," and "*State/meant.*" Cone's prophetic imagination was ignited by reading Sonia Sanchez's *We a BaddDDD People* (1970), Don Lee L. Lee's (Haki R. Madhubuti) *Think Black!* (1967) and *Black Pride* (1968), Aime Cesaire's *Return to My Native Land* (1960), and even a French existentialist writer Albert Camus's *The Rebel* (1956). The Black Arts movement inspired the African American community to affirm and love their own black selves - skin color, hair texture, bodies, art, music, dance, theatre, history, heroes and heroines. Black was back and it was beautiful.

Transfiguring tragedy into triumph through black self-affirmation, the Black Arts Movement was the aesthetic matrix from which Black Theology would emerge. Bringing together streams of tragedy and liberation, James Baldwin's novel modeled a form of writing that was honest, angry and beautiful. Cone viewed *The Fire Next Time* (1962) as a manifesto of the movement. Baldwin writes, "The only thing white people have that black people need, or should want, is power - and no one holds power forever."[23] Baldwin's dream for black power would begin to break forth into reality through the Black Power movement that was the political matrix for the eruption of James Cone's *Black Theology*.

While Richard Wright wrote a novel titled *Black Power* (1954), it was Stokely Carmichael who would popularize the term during the Meredith March Against Fear. On June 16, 1966, Carmichael addressed the marchers in Greenwood, Mississippi, announcing that the only way to overcome the oppression of white supremacy was through building Black Power. This was a turning point in the Civil Rights Movement, which until that moment had been guided largely by Dr. Martin Luther King, Jr.'s vision of a non-violent love-based activism toward full integration within a white society. In contrast to merely being "integrated" into a white socio-economic system, Carmichael advocated Black autonomy as central to achieving self-determination and black liberation for black people.[24]

[23] James Baldwin, *The Fire Next Time* (New York: Vintage International, 1992), 96.

[24] Stokely Carmichael, "Toward Black Liberation", *Black Fire: An Anthology of Afro-American Writing*. ed. Roi Jones and Larry Neal (Baltimore: Black Classic Press 1968), 119-132.

Inspired by Stokely Carmichael's call for *Black Power*, James Cone forged a black theology of liberation in the fire of the Black Power movement. As a theology professor at Adrian College in Adrian, Michigan, Cone was disturbed by the racial riots in Detroit, seventy miles down the road. He knew in his heart of hearts that Christian theology had to change, becoming relevant to the growing group of black activists who were fighting for justice in cities throughout the United States. When Dr. King was brutally shot dead in while leading a Living Wage movement for sanitation workers in Memphis, Tennessee on April 4, 1968, Cone's revolutionary fire was ignited. Cone sat down in the basement of his brother Cecil's church and wrote Black Theology and Black Power (1969) in five weeks. Cone advocated a black theology that inspired and equipped black people to claim their own power as they worked together to dismantle racist institutions and find their true freedom. A year latter Cone wrote *A Black Theology of Liberation* bringing systematic form to Black Theology.[25]

Jesus Christ was the norm of Cone's theology, but he sought to understand Jesus through black experience. In *The Spirituals and the Blues* (1972) Cone discovered Jesus as cosuffer witnessed to in the soulful music of the black church.[26] Black slaves sang about the suffering of Jesus during the crucifixion in the spiritual "Were you there?"

> Were you there when they crucified my Lord?
>
> were you there when they crucified my Lord?
>
> Oh! Sometimes it causes me to tremble, tremble, tremble;
>
> were you there when they crucified by Lord?

Cone heard in the spirituals the cry of Jesus who was fully human, sharing fully in the suffering of poor people, especially poor black people in America. African Americans oppressed by white supremacy connected deeply with Jesus the Jew in Palestine who was crucified on a Roman Cross. In his book God of the Oppressed (1975), Cone connects the Jewishness of Jesus with

[25] James H. Cone, *Black Theology & Black Power* (New York: Seabury Press, 1969); idem, A Black Theology of Liberation (Maryknoll, NY: Orbis Press, 1970).

[26] James H. Cone, *The Spirituals and the Blues* (New York: Seabury Press, 1972).

black existence in America, developing a sharp critique of racism and a constructive theology of liberation that is relevant to the movement for racial and economic justice. In chapter six, "Who is Jesus Christ for us today?" Cone develops a concrete Christology of blackness in the Americas.[27]

For Cone the problem of racism demands a turn to socio-historical context in order to give a deeper and more pointed analysis of who Jesus Christ is. Cone seeks to achieve this through a dialectical theological method: "Who Jesus is for us today is not decided by focusing our attention exclusively on either the social context alone or the Bible alone but by seeing them in dialectical relation."[28] Frustrated with the theological abstractions of white theologians, Cone demanded that theology come to terms with its multiple contexts, especially the context of oppression as black people sought to mobilize for their own liberation.

Cone's theological call to context took on two forms: a call back to the original context of the biblical story as well as a call to the oppressed in the current context. Examining the concrete Jewish backgrounds of Jesus' context becomes the basis for a contextual theological analysis in the present. While Bonhoeffer affirmed the importance of Jesus' Jewishness, Cone goes further to explain the concrete significance of Jesus' Jewishness for the struggle for racial justice today. Cone writes, "The historical Jesus emphasizes the social context of Christology and thereby establishes the importance of Jesus' racial identity. Jesus was a Jew!"[29]

The particularity of Jesus' person as disclosed in his Jewishness is indispensable for Christological analysis. On the one hand, Jesus' Jewishness pinpoints the importance of his humanity for faith, and on the other, connects God's salvation drama in Jesus with the Exodus-Sinai event."[30] By thinking about Jesus in his concrete particularity - a poor Jew in Palestine - Cone critiques any Christian theology that fails to mention Jesus' ministry to the

[27] James H. Cone, *God of the Oppressed* (New York: Seabury Press, 1975), 108-137.

[28] James H. Cone, *God of the Oppressed*, 113.

[29] James H. Cone, *God of the Oppressed*, 119.

[30] James H. Cone, *God of the Oppressed*, 119.

poor.[31] For Cone the issue was not just that Jesus was poor and ministered to the poor, but that the living Christ continues to minister to the poor, leading the front line struggle for justice today. The provocative claim that "Jesus is black" is how Cone concludes his chapter. By connecting theological method to the history of the black freedom movement, Cone rethinks Christology with an emphasis on Christ's activity in the justice struggles in the here and now.[32]

For Cone, Christ's blackness has twofold significance; it is "both literal and symbolic."[33] At a literal level it means that God revealed as a dark skinned poor Palestinian preacher is in full solidarity with dark skinned poor people in America. Christ's "blackness is literal in the sense that he truly becomes One with the oppressed blacks, taking their suffering as his struggle, the story of our pain, and the rhythm of our bodies," writes Cone.[34] Cone makes a vital theological intervention, by interpreting Israel as an oppressed people and connecting their experience with African American's experience of oppression. The challenge of Black Theology to all Christian theology in the Americas is to reimagine Christianity as a Spirit-led justice movement, ground in the stories of the black freedom struggle from the abolition movement to the civil rights movement, a theological story that is told in Gayraud S. Wilmore's Black Religion and Black Radicalism.[35] On the underside of a white evangelical modernity, prophetic black Christianity disrupts America's racial hierarchy, ushering in a prophetic, intercultural future.

At a symbolic level the blackness of Christ means that God joins the oppressed in every global freedom struggle: "The 'blackness of Christ,' there-

[31] James H. Cone, *God of the Oppressed*, 116.

[32] Cone writes, "The authority of the Bible for Christology, therefore, does not lie in its objective status as the literal Word of God. Rather, it is found in its power to point to the One whom the people have met in the historical struggle of freedom." James H. Cone, *God of the Oppressed*, 112.

[33] James H. Cone, *God of the Oppressed*, 136.

[34] James H. Cone, *God of the Oppressed*, 136.

[35] Gayraud S. Wilmore, *Black Religion and Black Radicalism: An Interpretation of the Religious History of African Americans*. 3rd edition (Maryknoll, NY: Orbis Books, 2010).

fore, is not simply a statement about skin color, but rather, the transcendent affirmation that God has not ever, no not ever, left the oppressed alone in struggle. He was with them in America, Africa and Latin America, and will come in the end of time to consummate fully their freedom."[36] Cone then connects Israel's experience as mediated through the Jewish flesh of Jesus to the experience of black folks and all people of color in the United States and oppressed people throughout the world, critiquing all mainstream white theologies that perpetuate post-Enlightenment abstract discourses: "How can Christian theology truly speak of the hope of Jesus Christ, unless that hope begins and ends with the liberation of the poor in the social existence in which theology takes shape? In America this means that there can be no talk about hope in the Christian sense unless it is a talk about the freedom of black, red, and brown people."[37] While Cone writes theology from black experience, black culture and black history, his theological vision is not exclusively for Afro-Christians, but for all oppressed people, regardless of their race or region. Cone writes, "The God in black theology is the God of and for the oppressed, the God who comes into view in their liberation."[38] Cone's prophetic challenge to Protestant theology is to reclaim Jesus' identity as a revolutionary prophet, give a theological account of race, and construct a prophetic theology that can inspire and equip a new generation of faith leaders in the movement for racial and economic justice.

Cone's most recent book *The Cross and The Lynching Tree* (2011) considers the lynching tree as a cultural site to understand the link between conceptions of Jesus Christ and social world of Jim Crow America.[39] Cone writes, "Theologically speaking, Jesus was the 'first lynchee,' who foreshadowed all the lynched black bodies on American soil. He was crucified by the same principalities and powers that lynched black people in America."[40] As long as black, brown, red, yellow, female and LGBTQ bodies are being crucified

[36] James H. Cone, *God of the Oppressed*, 137.

[37] James H. Cone, *God of the Oppressed*, 128.

[38] James H. Cone, *A Black Theology of Liberation*. Twentieth Anniversary Edition (Maryknoll, N.Y.: Orbis, 1990), 61.

[39] James H. Cone, *The Cross and the Lynching Tree* (Maryknoll, NY: Orbis Books, 2011).

[40] James H. Cone, *The Cross and the Lynching Tree*, 158.

there is no moving beyond Cone's Christological commitment to liberating the oppressed. Prophetic Protestant Christology today must build on Cone's Christology of the oppressed, especially his concern with Jesus' identification with the poor, as the Spirit of Liberation energizes the contemporary struggle for justice.

7. Conclusion

Protestant theology of the future must build a bridge between historical suffering and eschatological hope through a Christ-centered ministry of liberation and reconciliation. Within the Lutheran tradition, Bonhoeffer radicalizes Reformation through his presentation of Jesus the revolutionary, the One for the Other, unto death. Bonhoeffer was the first white western theologian who tried to actively de-center himself from his western worldview and wrestle theologically with a subaltern Christian tradition on its own terms - prophetic black Christianity. In 1930-1931 Bonhoeffer attended Abyssinian Baptist Church in Harlem and encountered a vital, enthusiastic faith with inspiring worship and a profound theology. In Harlem Bonhoeffer was baptized into the depths of black suffering, while also experiencing the promise of the black freedom struggle. What Bonhoeffer encountered in the worship of African Americans in Harlem was the power of revolutionary hope amidst affliction, which he understood theoretically in Karl Barth's Word of God theology, but did not fully existentially grasp until he experienced it first-hand in the black church.

Through his experiences with disaffected African Americans in Harlem and a black social gospel that connected Jesus and black suffering, Bonhoeffer could return to Germany with a deeper sensitivity to Jewish suffering and a stronger commitment to work to end German violence against Jews. While Bonhoeffer was offered a prestigious professorship at Union Theological Seminary in 1939, he turned it down and returned home to Germany to join the Confessing Church's struggle against the fascist regime of Adolf Hitler. When he learned of the mass executions of Jews, Bonhoeffer committed his life to subversive revolutionary action. Bonhoeffer followed his Black Jesus in the path of costly discipleship unto death in Flossenburg, Germany on April 9, 1945. As we celebrate the 500th anniversary of Martin Luther's nailing the 95 Theses to the doors of the Wittenburg Cathedral, Bonhoeffer's

Black Jesus opens up a new trajectory for radicalizing Christology and renewing prophetic Protestant theology today in five ways.

First, through focusing on the particularity of Jesus' Jewish covenantal flesh we can re-root Christianity in its Jewish heritage in order to push ahead toward a truly intercultural and interfaith future. Jesus' Jewishness challenges a Christology that is exclusively western and white to affirm the particularity of the Jewish flesh of Jesus for all people, regardless of their culture, race or religion. Jesus' Jewishness means that all his followers in the World Christian movement are included in the story of the people of Israel. This helps Christians understand that the Christian story is first and foremost a Jewish story, before being a story of the modern western nation state.

Second, Jesus' teaching of the Kingdom renounces the spirit of religious nationalism, an attempt to domesticate Christianity through capitulation to the power of the kingdoms of this world. After Constantine declared Christianity the official religion of the Roman Empire, western Christianity has struggled with this nationalistic tendency. For example, the principle cuius regio eius religio first agreed on at the Diet of Augsburg (1555) and reaffirmed in the Peace of Westphalia (1648) meant that the ruler in German principalities chose the religion of the region. While institutionalizing the divisions of the Reformation and the Counter-Reformation, *cuius regio eius religio*, also squelched religious freedom and the emerging religious pluralism. As Christology became deployed by the nation in the rise of European colonial conquest, Jesus often became a tool of domination and oppression. The creation of a national identity in "America" and "Germany" became increasingly inscribed in colonial hubris, white supremacy, and western hegemony in the 19th and 20th century. Focusing on the Jewishness of Jesus – the one who suffered and died on a Roman Cross - helps us to confess and repent of ways that Christianity has participated in a violent legacy of oppression on behalf of the crown.

Third, radicalizing Christology entails confessing and repenting of anti-Semitism and white supremacy. Christian "replacement theology" - the idea that Christianity replaces Judaism - is a heresy that must be denied and continually struggled against within the church. Likewise, white supremacy should be renounced as a systematic evil that must be dismantled in the church, academy and society. Jennifer M. McBride argues that Bonhoeffer's life and theology challenges North American white Christians to accept guilt

/ take responsibility / repent of the sin of white supremacy as a concrete form of public witness.[41] Reformation theology began as a confession of sin and a confession of faith in Jesus Christ. It is vital that we maintain the confessional spirit of the Reformation today, especially when it comes to renouncing the sins of anti-Semitism and white supremacy.

Fourth, Protestant theology today needs to begin in a spirit of humble listening to the oppressed Other. Following Bonhoeffer, we need to view "the great events of world history from below, from the perspective of the outcast, the suspects, the maltreated, the powerless, the oppressed, the reviled - in short, from the perspective of the suffering."[42] Viewing the world from the prophetic black underside of a white evangelical modernity, James Cone calls us to reimagine how we as Christians relate to historical oppression, interrogating our current complicity in injustice today. Jesus the poor Jew in the Roman empire is the One for the Other, a prophet in solidarity with suffering people around the world, be they Jews in Germany or blacks in America. For theologians of European descent this will require the act of careful, methodological listening to people of African descent, people of Asian descent, and people of Latin American descent. Instead of preaching, western theologians need to become deep listeners, open to transformative encounter with people in the non-western world. White theologians of European descent need to be more intentional in engaging black theologians, liberationist theologians and womanist theologians today, writing theology in a collaborative, conversational, intercultural modality. It is only through honest conversation across racial lines that we can move toward sustainable, collaborative activism for the common good.

[41] Jennifer M. McBride, *The Church for the World: A Theology of Public Witness* (Oxford: Oxford University Press, 2012). Cf. Alexia Salvatierra and I argue that Bonhoeffer's call to confession and repentance are Spirit-led practices of justice and reconciliation, offering concrete examples of the gifts and graces of Christian faith that we as faith-rooted organizers bring to our ministries of public engagement and social transformation. Alexia Salvatierra and Peter Goodwin Heltzel, "Confession and Repentance," *Faith-Rooted Organizing: Mobilizing the Church in Service to the World* (Downers Grove: InterVarsity Press, 2013), 96-98.

[42] Dietrich Bonhoeffer, "After Ten Years: A Reckoning made at New Year 1943", *Letters and Papers from Prison.* ed. Eberhard Bethge (New York: Collier Books, 1953), 17.

Fifth, Jesus' prophetic vision calls us to a ministry of racial and economic justice. Jesus' teaching of the Kingdom is fundamentally an economic teaching, as he started his ministry with an invocation of the Year of Jubilee (Lev 25; Isa 58, 61; Luke 4:18, 19). In the Acts of the Apostles we learn that the early church "devoted themselves to the apostles' teaching and to fellowship, to the breaking of bread and to prayer…they held all things in common, sold their property and gave to anyone who had need" (Acts 2:42-47). Amidst racial division and economic inequity, God's Spirit is energizing a love-based global movement for a "New Economy," a more just, equitable and sustainable economic order for all God's children.

When Martin Luther sent his "Disputation on the Efficacy and Power of Indulgences" to the local archbishop on October 31, 1517, it was more than a theological critique, it was an attack on a hegemonic system of religious, political and economic powers. Martin Luther's economic critique, especially on the practices of the great trading companies and commercial banks, needs to be recovered as we radicalize the theologies of Reformation today.

Reforming the economy is our unfinished agenda. The faith-rooted struggle for racial justice and religious tolerance must press ahead to work for economic democracy. Economic injustice is not only a personal and moral problem; it is a systemic problem that demands a systematic response. A cruciform theology today should work toward building a socio-economic order that offers the opportunity for everyone to make a living wage and return home to a warm hearth where they can love and be loved (1 Cor 1:18). Courageously confronting neo-liberal capitalism requires a comprehensive power analysis, innovative economic alternatives, and an improvisational organizing and advocacy strategy. In the spirit of Kairos Europa and the New Economy Movement in the U.S., we need to convene new spaces to critique capitalism, including analyzing the ownership principles and the growth paradigm that guides it.

If we desire the materialization of the New Economy, we are going to have to organize it. Organizing is the work required to build broad participation and community engagement in public life. Drawing on the deepest wells of our faith, faith-rooted organizing is concerned about both personal and political transformation, forming leaders who do not simply achieve transactional wins, but are transformed in the process of working together such that they come to see the world in new and better ways. Faith-rooted organizing is not about a battle between opposing interests, but about fundamentally transforming our society from the deepest wells of our faith.[43] Our faith traditions bring moral authority, symbolic ritual, and practices of reconciliation that are essential to building a sustainable movement.

Building collective power for the New Economy means that faith leaders need to cross the lines of race and religion, forging new partnerships for the long haul. Building the New Economy demands that faith leaders work to build a multi-sector movement, including active partnership with labor unions, community groups, political clubs, elected officials, and ordinary citizens. Following Jesus the Revolutionary today means saying "Nein!" to an economic system that is oppressing poor people, and actively participating in the poor-led movement for racial and economic justice for all.

As Jesus was the One for the suffering Other, we, too, must courageously continue our struggle for love and justice until all people have their needs met and their suffering has ended. As prophetic Protestants, we celebrate Martin Luther's recovery of the Gospel of Grace received through our faith in Jesus Christ. Yet we renounce the false Gospel of anti-Semitism, colonialism and white supremacy, as we proclaim and embody the love, justice and shalom of God. May we continue to courageously follow in the footsteps of Jesus the Revolutionary! As we descend into the places of suffering and death, may we be the body of Christ, bearing bold witness to the love and life of God hidden in the suffering Jewish flesh of Jesus, hearkening a prophetic, intercultural hope.

43 See Alexia Salvatierra and Peter Goodwin Heltzel, *Faith-Rooted Organizing: Mobilizing the Church in Service to the World* (Downers Grove: InterVarsity Press, 2013).

Prejudice and its Historical Application: A Radical Hermeneutic of Luther's Treatment of the Turks (Muslims) and the Jews

Charles Amjad-Ali

1. Introduction: Re-examining Fundamental "Truths" of Europe

Philosophically and theologically we live in a world in which dialogue (and its various synonyms), as well as an emphasis on multi-religious context, are not only ubiquitous but are regarded as historically unique and epistemologically central. Dialogue is therefore seen as providing novel potential for dealing with the perceived "new phenomenon" of religious and cultural pluralism. This, however, not only ignores the longstanding vibrant and robust experience of such dwelling in Asia and Africa, but also overlooks earlier similar experiences in Europe itself. Underlying this approach is a false and arrogant assumption that this context is incomparable and that the previous centuries had neither such contexts nor experiences and certainly did not have the wherewithal to deal with other religions. Thus Europe is assumed to have been exclusively Christian, in spite of the fact that the Iberian Peninsula (or Roman/Latin Hispania), the most western part of mainland Europe, had been ruled by Muslims for almost 800 years, and also had a huge and highly influential Jewish presence. Added to this was the Turkish imperial expansion starting in the 14th century which resulted in the Islamic control of most of central and eastern Europe. This was the immediate context in which Martin Luther was operating and writing from in the 16th century.

When dealing with Luther's understanding of Islam, it is therefore imperative to take these historical situations and traumas as part of his context. As Bernhard Lohse correctly points out "the history of Luther and the Reformation must always be seen in this larger context."[1] This perhaps provides some justification for the character of his writings about the Turks, even if not always for the content of his sophistry against Muslims, and even worse against the Jews. It must be noted here that while Luther's writings vis-à-vis the Turks and Islam can be somewhat justified, his extreme vitriol against the Jews has no such justification at all. Given this threat there had been many responses: "Catholic writers called for a united crusade to reclaim Constantinople and, occasionally, the Holy Land. Humanists and early Protestants, in addition to approving and urging defensive war strategies, began to study the Ottomans and their religion; some even optimistically hoped to instigate a missionary enterprise among them. And the radical authors of the Reformation urged a pacifist response to Ottoman imperialism with a few expressing hope in a Turkish conquest of Europe."[2] Luther had elements of all these responses but he also has criticisms, some theological, of all of them simultaneously. In this context, Adam Francisco provides a critical clue, stating that "when Luther began his inquiry into the religion of the Turks he would use... [the various earlier writings about Islam] in order to develop his own approach. They provided him information to which he would never be privy, for he never once dialogued with a Muslim or came into contact with Islamic culture. But once he decided that Islam needed to be responded to theologically he had to use what he could obtain in order to begin his own polemical and apologetical writing against the Turks and their religion."[3]

So we must look at Martin Luther as a theologian in this larger context. That he was dealing with other religions like Judaism (Jews) and Islam

[1] Bernhard Lohse, *Martin Luther: An Introduction to His Life and Work,* trans., Robert Schultz (Edinburgh: T & T Clark, 1987), 4.

[2] Adam S. Francisco, *Martin Luther and Islam: A Study in Sixteenth-Century Polemics and Apologetics* (Leiden: Brill, 2007), 31. This paper is deeply indebted for the comprehensive information this groundbreaking work provides. Although I do not always agree with his conclusions, there are few other sources that cover the topic of Luther and the Turks in such comprehensive breadth. For a comprehensive German approach to this issue, see also Johannes Ehmann, *Luther, Türken und Islam: eine Untersuchung zum Türken- und Islambild Martin Luthers (1515 – 1546)* (Gütersloh: Gütersloher Verlagshaus, 2008), which surveys the German scholarship on this subject.

[3] Francisco, 29-30, emphasis added.

(Turks) shows that, though he often wrote as if he was in a mono-religious Christian and mono-cultural milieu (with the heterodoxy of the Roman Catholics and the Anabaptists), he actually did his theology with these other monotheistic faiths in mind. And I would argue that Calvin, as on many other issues, followed him in this tradition also. Both encountered, did polemics, and apologetics vis-à-vis Islam and the Turks and the Jews, though not always in the most irenic, or even Christian way. This assumed mono-religious and, more critically, mono-cultural context is maintained by most Lutheran and Calvinist theologians, even today. Some work has been done on Luther's writings about the Jews, because of the use of those execrable texts by Hitler, and the Lutheran guilt vis-à-vis the holocaust, but his writings on the Turks have been largely ignored, including by most Lutheran theologians. However, I may quickly add that in many respects Luther's encounter and rhetoric vis-à-vis Islam is essentially not so different from some of our contemporary expressions of it, especially since September 11, 2001. Given the fact that what Luther said and wrote about Judaism was used some 400 years later in Germany, this makes me quite apprehensive about how some of Luther's writings vis-à-vis Islam could be utilized for our contemporary anti-Islamic prejudices, biases and victimization, in sum Islamophobia.

2. The Multi-Cultural and Multi-Religious Context of Europe

Europe at the time of Luther and his new theological concerns, was neither mono-religious, nor mono-cultural. It had had a series of historical developments over the last few centuries prior to the Reformation which reflected its highly multi-religious and culturally pluralistic context. These developments were still part of the collective memory, and in fact were the theological and epistemic foundations for the Reformation. Spain was under Muslim rule from 711[4] until the completion of the Reconquista of 1492 (i.e., the fall of Granada, which was the last Islamic state on the Iberian Peninsula). 1492 is now better recognized and famous for Christopher Columbus and the "discovery" (i.e., colonization) of the Americas under the patronage of the most

4 When the Muslim General Tariq ibn Ziyad defeated King Roderic, the last of the Visigoth rulers of Hispania.

Catholic Monarchs, Isabella and Ferdinand. After 1492 these monarchs forcefully converted the Muslims and Jews of Spain to Christianity. The Muslim converts were referred to as Moriscos, i.e., Moorish.[5] The Jewish converts were known as Marranos – meaning pigs or swine, i.e., "filthy-dirty" and "unscrupulous."[6] The expulsion of the Moriscos from Spain began in 1609 and was finally completed in 1614.[7] The Jewish expulsion started earlier, after the genocide of 1391,[8] and is seen as the turning point for the Spanish (Sephardic) Jewish existence in Europe. It was the precursor to the Inquisition some 90 years later and to the expulsion of even the converted Jews which followed. The numbers of those expelled from Spain vary: Juan de Mariana estimates this number to be as high as 800,000;[9] while Rabbi Isidore Loeb estimates it to be as low as 165,000.[10] Loeb also shows that some 90,000 of these refugees migrated to Turkey as they were welcomed by the Sultan.

[5] The term Moriscos was largely applied to the indigenous Spanish Muslim converts and not so much to those of Arab descent.

[6] For Jews to be referred to as pigs or swine, especially in the context of 800 years of Islamic rule (which had similar religious purity laws), was highly derogatory, offensive, and obscene; their descendents, therefore naturally preferred the term *Anusim* - Hebrew for forced.

[7] In 1609 King Philip III issued an Act of Expulsion of the Muslims (*Expulsión de los moriscos*) who were left behind after 1492, because he saw them as having loyalty to the Ottoman Turks and therefore as a subversive fifth column in the Iberian Peninsula. This expulsion was finally completed in 1614. See, esp., Mary E. Perry. *The Handless Maiden: Moriscos and the Politics of Religion in Early Modern Spain* (Princeton: Princeton University Press, 2005).

[8] This genocide took place in different locations all across Spain: Seville, Cordoba, Toledo, Aragon, Catalonia, Majorica, Valencia, Palma, Barcelona, *et al.*

[9] de Mariana was a Spanish Jesuit, regarded highly for his sagacious research and accuracy. See his famous *Historiae de rebus Hispaniae,* a 20 volume work published first in Toledo in 1592 (trans. from Latin into Spanish and even into English by J. Stevens, as *The General History of Spain* in 1699).

[10] Loeb inaugurated and was the first editor of the Jewish journal *Revue des Études Juives*, in Paris, in which he proposes this figure in his article, "Le nombre des juifs de Castille et d'Espagne," in vol. xiv. 1887, 162–183.

Besides this long term presence and influence of Muslims and Jews in western Europe, large portions of central and eastern Europe also lived under similar long term Muslim control, in this case of the Ottoman Turks. This started at least as early as the 1389 battle of Kosovo. With some permutations, this status remained largely unchanged until as late as the First World War, i.e., a period of over 500 years.[11] With the control of Constantinople in 1453, and all of Greece in 1460 (the cradle of the "western civilization"),[12] the Turkish Muslims had a comprehensive and long term presence in this part of Europe as well.

These two long-term multi-religious contexts in the western, central, and eastern parts of Europe, and the presence of the other two monotheistic faiths in "Christian" Europe, belies its mono-religious claim, on the one hand, and forces us to look at the epistemic significance of its multi-religious experiences and dialogical practices on the other. It also demands from us a more critical re-examination of this history and a demythologizing of it for a more honest theological and philosophical task.

Islam has had its own veracity amnesia: it uncritically accepts the "western" claim to the Mediterranean and its contributions. In this way Muslims

[11] This Turkish presence in Europe can be dated to as far back as the Battle of Maritsa in 1371 which the Ottoman Turks won, or to as late as the Turkish victory in the Battle of Kosovo in 1389. The latter has acquired a central role in Serbian folklore and is seen as the epic battle which heralded the beginning of bad luck for Serbia. This folklore played quite a significant role in the Yugoslav and Bosnian wars of the 1990s and the genocide of the Muslims there after some 600 years. It must also be remembered that the Ottoman Empire had taken over the Greek areas of Thrace and much of Macedonia after the Battle of Maritsa in 1371. Sofia fell in 1382, followed by Tarnovgrad in 1393, the state of Romania/Hungary after the Battle of Nicopolis in 1396. The Turkish victory over Hungarian forces in the Battle of Varna, in 1444, expanded their control over the Balkans and was of special concern to Calvin. See my article, "Debilitating Past and Future Hope: Calvin, Calvinism and Islam" in *Reformed World,* Vol. 61, No. 2 (2011), 120-133.

[12] What is now modern Greece was also part of the Ottoman Empire from the mid-15th century until its declaration of independence in 1821, a historical period also known as *Tourkokratia* in Greek (Τουρκοκρατία) or "Turkish rule."

can maintain the complete purity of their absolute Arabian causation and revelation. This is to preserve the myth that the Islamic resources are purely Arab and are neither influenced nor contaminated by the Mediterranean Greco-Roman world, nor by the Indian, Chinese/Mongol, or Zoroastrian worlds, etc. On the other side, when showing a more open approach, these Mediterranean and other sources are not only acknowledged, but the Muslim contribution to them is hyperbolized and exaggerated beyond any factuality and location in truth. The latter position is more for polemical and apologetic sophistry and ends up challenging the veracity of the deep interaction between the Mediterranean and the Muslim world. Some of the recent internal clashes between the different Islamic groups are based on the levels of purity from these Mediterranean and post-Mediterranean sources they wish to maintain and articulate.

3. Christianity as a Western Religion, Luther's Vitriol against Jews and Muslims

Both the amnesia of the West and that of the Muslim world, under even a minimum scrutiny, show that the foundations that each is claiming are not sustainable, even when the necessity of epistemic prejudice is accepted, a la Gadamer.[13] Yet huge epistemological edifices have been erected which take for granted that the West is Christian and the (middle) East is Muslim; this is the fundamental difference between occident (abendland) and orient.[14] This

[13] Hans-Georg Gadamer retrieves the epistemic location of *prejudicum* and sees the Enlightenment itself as having a prejudice against prejudice itself, and thus claiming a transcendent dislocated veracity which is not historically sustainable. See his, *Truth and Method* (New York: Seabury Press, 1975).

[14] See Edward Said, *Orientalism* (New York, Pantheon Books, 1978) and much of the subsequent literature on this theme and the de-privilegization of the taken-for-granted normatives. For a critical early read of this, see Henri Pirenne, *Mohammed and Charlemagne* (London: George Allen & Unwin Ltd., 1954) trans. of *Mohomet et Charlemagne* which was influential on Marc Bloch, among others, in the formation of the critical Annales School of History, from which emerged one of the most significant works on Mediterranean society by Fernand Braudel, *The Mediterranean and the Mediterranean World in the Age of Philip II,* trans. by Siân Reynolds (Berkeley, CA: University of California Press, 1996). For larger implications, see also the

edifice assumes first that Christianity is an exclusively Western religion, thus its non-acknowledgment of the churches in the East. On the other side, Islam makes itself an exclusively Arab religion, even though the majority of Muslims live in the non-Arab world. We have to undo these mythical stereotypifications if we are to live in a just and peaceful world and achieve truth for a righteous society based on common weal and social virtue.

Out of these series of prejudices, untruths, and distortions comes a now almost permanent misunderstanding on both sides. Since we are dealing largely with Luther, the Reformation and Islam in this paper, we must therefore seriously address the issues of centuries-old misunderstandings, and indeed the contrived vilification of the Muslims, their Prophet, their Scriptures, their religion, and their culture, and overcome the ignorance vis-à-vis Islam as a whole. What is even more distressing than this sheer ignorance is the conscious malice, vilification, and calculated distortions of Islam and its contributions, which has been part of the grammar in the west for well over six hundred years. When we give credit to the West and to Christianity for democracy, participatory rights, social justice, equality of genders, and freedom of sexual choice, etc., we conveniently forget that we are borrowing straight from secular sources of the Enlightenment, which actually attacked Christianity and vice versa, it being the only religion that was part of that discourse.

controversial work by Oswald Spengler, *The Decline of the West* (*Der Untergang des Abendlandes*, 1918-1922) which deals with the "oriental mind" and the morphology of cultures, two vols. (New York: Alfred A. Knopf, 1932). In Marxist circles, the concept of Oriental Despotism took on a special significance, see especially Karl A. Wittfogel, *Oriental Despotism: A Comparative Study of Total Power* (New Haven: Yale University Press, 1957).

This sophistry has continued and is now rearticulated in recent years as the clash of civilizations, and "the west versus the rest" (i.e. consumerist capitalism of the west versus the religious and tribal fundamentalism of Islam; and the advanced brilliant technology in the making of Lexus versus the oldest working technology of the Olive grove); in Samuel Huntington, *The Clash of Civilizations and the Remaking of World Order* (New York: Simon and Schuster, 1996); Benjamin Barber, *Jihad vs. McWorld: How Globalism and Tribalism are Reshaping the World* (New York: Random House, 1996); and Thomas Friedman, *Lexus and the Olive Tree: Understanding Globalization* (New York: Picador, 1999), among others.

This vilification was also the case with the Jews, at least until 1945, and from this period on there have emerged new and quite anachronistic readings of Jewish-Christian relations, thus for example the ubiquitousness of the term "Judeo-Christian" for ethics, morality, values, etc., as a retroactive historically permanent fixture,[15] and thus any critique of the state of Israel is perceived as a threat to this newly perpetuated mythology. So when we give credit to the West we locate and give undue credit to Christianity for the achievement of human values without actually paying attention to the religious distortions, challenges, and critiques of these Enlightenment ideologies.

Another social hermeneutical issue we face today is the difficulty of the widely present juxtaposition of incompatible and largely hostile systems of thought, morals, and beliefs. These are embodied in political and economic power(s) of impressive, if not awe-inspiring, presence. We sometimes talk as if this was a new problem – and certainly it is new to the modern world. The Western sense of superiority in every sphere of endeavor has scarcely been challenged for over three hundred years both in its colonial and post-colonial expressions. It has become part of our overall heritage, most painful to abandon as well as to morally adjust to. What is overlooked is the fact that Europe itself went through this painful experience well over a thousand years ago, through the hegemony of the Roman Empire and partly through the hegemonic Muslim expansion after the 7th century. Further, Europe lived with the Muslim challenge more or less permanently, starting at least with the conquest of Spain in 711, through the Crusades starting in 1095, and right up to the 17th century. There was rarely a period of complacency from this challenge throughout the Middle Ages and even well after the Reformation, our mono-religious hermeneutic of this history notwithstanding. The existence of Islam was one of the most far-reaching problems in medieval Christendom. It posed a problem at every level of experience. As a practical problem it called for action and discernment between the competing possibilities of crusade, conversion, coexistence and commercial interchange. As a theological prob-

15 From the previously ubiquitous"Christ-killers" (till around 1939), to the current ubiquitous "Judeo-Christian" label, is a major epistemological shift and is not always a product of high ethical commitment.

lem it called persistently for some answer to the mystery of its existence. What was its providential role in history? Was it a symptom of the world's last days or a stage in Christian development; a heresy, a schism, or a new religion; a work of man or devil; an obscene parody of Christianity, or a system of thought that deserved to be treated with respect? In different places, Luther argued each of these positions, however epistemologically discrete each argument may be in itself. So one finds elements of all these evaluations in various texts of Luther.

4. From Rome to Constantinople (the New *Rum*) and the Founding of Christendom

There are some typical, and clearly incorrect, assertions about the West that need to be examined as part of the larger context of Luther's approach on the issue of the Turks and the Jews. Briefly, the West views itself as being in direct continuity with the Mediterranean culture and civilization and as the successor of the Roman Empire (not simply of the "Western Roman Empire," whatever that term means),[16] without any mediation, much less a primary contribution, from Africa and Asia towards these developments. This historiographical sleight of hand is undertaken in order to emphasize the enduring continuity between "European" history and its "mother" Greco-Roman civilizations of the Mediterranean. Thus at least conceptually locating the Mediterranean[17] exclusively in Europe, even though geographically it is located between Africa, Asia and Europe.

[16] This phrase seems to have been coined in modern historiography to define the Western provinces and courts of the Roman Empire and to give them equal footing with the "Eastern Roman Empire," because of Constantinople. Ostensibly this happened when the capital was shifted from Rome to Byzantium by Constantine in 330, and after his death the former was renamed Constantinople and remained the capital of the Roman Empire till 1204; whatever the status of Charlemagne's Carolingian rule (800-814) with a blessing of the Bishop of Rome (Pope Leo III). For this historiography, see esp. Edward Gibbon, *The History of the Decline and Fall of the Roman Empire* 6 vols. (London: Straham & Cadell, 1776-1789).

[17] The term itself derives from the Latin word *mediterraneus* (*medi-*: "middle" or "between"; + *terra*, "land, earth"): i.e., "in the middle of earth" or "between lands," it

What is critical to understand is the fact that the perception of unbridged Mediterranean continuity and Europe's mono-religious status evolved largely out of a Constantinian Christendom model. What is equally critical to remember, however, is that the location of the capital of this Constantinian Christendom and Empire bordered Asia, if it was not directly in Asia itself, i.e., on the Bosphorus. It had no real contribution from, nor was it ever a direct product as such of, the so-called European "barbarian" tribes: Goths, Visigoths, Huns, Vandals, Franks, Angles, Saxons etc.,[18] who had threatened the Roman Empire. Their aggression and threats led to the move from Rome (Italy) to Byzantium/Constantinople (the New Rome on the Bosphorous) as the new capital of the Empire in the fourth century. It is critical to note that it is here that Christianity becomes the religion of imperial Rome. Constantinople, therefore, is the original location of what came to be called "Christendom," rather than what is now classified as Europe.[19]

Further, it should be remembered that at the beginning of this period there is only one Roman Empire (no such aberrations as the Western and Eastern Roman Empire) which moved its capital from Rome, south into or towards Asia, to a new capital, Constantinople. To the Muslims, this was the *Rum*, the only Rome they knew, having come into being after this shift. The Muslims became the inheritors of this Roman Empire and of most of the Mediterranean, beginning with the initial period of Islamic expansion and conquest, crescendoing finally with the capture of Constantinople in 1453 – the task was complete with *Rum* under the Muslims. With this they inherited the intellec-

being the sea between the then three known continents of Africa, Asia and Europe. The German word for Mediterranean, correctly calls it *Mittelmeer*, i.e., the middle sea.

18 These tribes were variously located in, or were part of, eastern Germany, Pomerania to the Black Sea, Scandinavia, Caucuses to Central Asia, Norman Germanic tribes controlling Portugal and Spain (*Hispania*), Southern Poland, Spain to some parts of North Africa and France, and Britain especially after the Romans left the area in 410 A.D.

19 The first real state to adopt Christianity as its state religion was the Kingdom of Armenia in 301 AD, followed shortly thereafter by the Caucasus Albania (modern-day Azerbaijan), somewhere between 301 and 314. The Armenian and Azerbaijani Orthodox Churches proudly let you know that they were the first Christian kingdoms prior to the establishment of the Christian Imperial power in Constantinople.

tual tradition of the Greco-Roman world, which was then transmitted to the West through Muslim scholars even for as central and pivotal a Christian theologian/philosopher as St. Thomas Aquinas. Sidney Griffiths therefore rightly points out that,

> Al-Farabi (870-950), Ibn Sina/Avicenna (980-1037), and Ibn Rushd/Averroes (1126-1198), are the Muslim philosophers with the most immediate name recognition ... but they are far from being the only ones making major contributions. And, of course, their accomplishments sparked yet another translation movement in the eleventh and twelfth centuries, this time in the Islamo-Christian west, in places like Bologna, Toledo, and Barcelona, where eager minds translated philosophical texts from Arabic into Latin, and provided the impetus for the flowering of scholastic philosophy and theology in the works of Thomas Aquinas, Bonaventure, and Duns Scotus, through the earlier achievements of scholars such as Abelard and Albert the Great.[20]

So it was not by sword that Albert the Great and St. Thomas Aquinas (1224-1274) accepted the Muslim masters for their philosophy (Avicenna and Averroes), and dare I say also for their theology. It was in the light of these masters that Thomas reexamined Christianity and insisted on the perspicuity of the sacred text, as in Islam. This then influenced Luther's *sola*

[20] Sidney H. Griffith, *The Church in the Shadows of the Mosque: Christians and Muslims in the World of Islam* (Princeton: Princeton University Press, 2008), 18. See also Majid Fakhry, *A History of Islamic Philosophy*, 3rd. edition (New York: Columbia University Press, 2004); Fernand van Steenberghen, *Aristotle and the West: The Origins of Latin Aristotelianism*, trans. by Leonard Johnston (New York: Humanities Press, 1970); Charles Burnett, "The Translating Activity in Medieval Spain" in *The Legacy of Muslim Spain* 2 vols., ed. Salma Khadra Jayyusi, vol. 2: 1036-58 (Leiden: E.J. Brill, 1994); Burnett, "Arabic into Latin: The Reception of Arabic Philosophy into Western Europe," in *The Cambridge Companion to Arabic Philosophy,* ed. Peter Adamson and Richard C. Taylor, 370-404 (Cambridge: Cambridge University Press, 2005); John E. Wansborough, *The Sectarian Milieu: Content and Composition of Islamic Salvation History* (Oxford: OUP, 1978). See also, the present author's *Islamophobia: Tearing the Veils of Ignorance* (Johannesburg: Ditshwanelo Car^{2}as, 2005), specifically the first chapter.

scriptura, with had little space for the mediation of *traditio*. On the other hand, it was Thomas' judgment and critique of these, his masters and teachers, and their Aristotelian philosophies, in *summa de veritate* catholique fidei contra gentiles (Treatise on the Truth of the Catholic Faith against Unbelievers),[21] which has determined our position on Islam and Muslims in the West, as well as on Aristotle in the Protestant circles. These were the predecessors and guides to Luther leading up to the Reformation.

The three monotheistic religious traditions certainly borrowed from one another in Muslim-ruled Spain, benefiting especially from the blooming of philosophy and the medieval sciences in the Muslim Middle East. There was more "tolerance" and coexistence than has been imagined or acknowledged. In spite of some recent scholars questioning this notion of peaceful coexistence of Muslims, Jews, and Christians – known as the convivencia – and wondering if it could be defined as "pluralistic,"[22] there was clearly much more interaction, conviviality, acceptance and tolerance for each other in Muslim Spain than in "Christian" Spain after 1492.

5. The Pervasive Fear of Islam and the Crusades

The fear of Islam is not new in Christendom and Christian history. It started with the Islamic conquests as early as the late 7th century, its rapid expansion, and its annexation of almost all the Biblical lands. This early expansion extended to the occupation of three of the five cities of the founding patriarchates (the Pentarchy) of Christianity, viz., Jerusalem, Antioch, and Alexandria; later even Constantinople. Rome was the exception in both cases, though it too came very close to being captured.[23] This was further exacerbated by the fear and awe generated by Muslims during the three centuries of

21 It has traditionally been dated to 1264, though some recent scholarship places it towards the end of Thomas' life, somewhere between 1270 to 1273.

22 See for example Stephen O'Shea, Sea of Faith: Islam and Christianity in the Medieval Mediterranean World (New York: Walker & Company, 2006).

23 Sultan Mehmet II of the Ottoman Empire clearly had his eyes set on Rome, having already captured Otranto in 1480, when he suddenly died and that expansion stopped because of internal Ottoman strife over the question of succession.

the Crusades. The Christian inability to maintain the euphoric success at the capture of the holy land from the Muslims in the First Crusade, and its subsequent failure to sustain this occupation, shook Christianity hard. It generated serious difficulty for Christians, given the ubiquitous religious notion that success and victory shows that God is on our side because of our faith and piety; conversely the same idea provided succor to the Muslims precisely because of their high level of success in these centuries.

The Crusades became a self-justifying cause célèbre for Christianity and played a very significant role in most aspects of European medieval life, be it ecclesial, economic, political, cultural, or social. Having been put on a religious and spiritual footing by the popes starting with Urban II in 1095 at the Council of Clermont, who linked the call for crusade to the wars of independence by Christians taking place on the Iberian peninsula, they were central to the theological development of the Reformation, as I shall show. The Crusades were a series of Christian "holy wars" carried out from 1096 till 1270 against the Muslims in larger Syria and Palestine and subsequently elsewhere in the area. Steven Runciman, one of the major historians of the Crusades, correctly describes them as "a long act of intolerance in the name of God, which is a sin against the Holy Ghost."[24] Others have argued that, "[i]n a broad sense the Crusades were an expression of militant Christianity and European expansion."[25] There were of course the narrower market, economic, and capitalist interests such as those of Venice, and its trade interests with India and China. While Venice did not have a direct role during the crusades themselves, nonetheless it played a significant role in them, restricting this to trade and the political power needed to protect this trade. As the crusades began Venice dominated the Adriatic and eastern Mediterranean trade, especially within the Byzantium empire. With the victory of the first crusade, its merchants quickly established major trading relations with the new Crusader kingdom. Because it was one of the major naval powers of the Mediterranean it became one of the convenient points of departure for many a crusade.

[24] Steven Runciman, *A History of the Crusades* (New York: Harper and Row, 3 volumes, 1967), 480.

[25] See, http://history-world.org/crusades.htm, as accessed on February 9, 2015.

There were at least 8 Crusades, of which the first four are the most relevant. The battle cry of the First Crusade that "God wills it" and "To free the Holy Land of the Infidels" became established as the overt raison d'etre for the subsequent crusades. The first crusade was successful and Jerusalem was taken over in 1099, establishing the crusader Kingdom of Jerusalem, which lasted until 1187. The second was a disaster. The third led to the Treaty of Ramla in 1192 between Saladin and Richard the Lionheart. It was highly favorable for Christians, as it allowed Christians pilgrimage to Jerusalem, despite Muslim control of the city. In the fourth, in 1204, the Crusaders sacked Constantinople (some 250 years prior to its subjugation by the Ottoman Muslims in 1453) desecrating many Orthodox churches including Hagia Sophia (built in 537), one of the most holy ecclesial sites in all of Christianity. As a result a new Latin Kingdom of Byzantium was established there which lasted for 60 years.

What is often forgotten, or not mentioned with any import, is the fact that besides killing an enormous number of non-combatant innocent Muslims, the crusades also killed a massive number of Jews both in Europe as well as in the near east.[26] These genocidal massacres were justified on the grounds that such killings were not sinful because the ones killed were not Christians but infidels (not of the faith). Gustavo Perednik, a scholar of Judeophobia, states "...the first half of this millennium witnessed genocides of Jews as the norm. And this is precisely when the Church reached the zenith of its power... the main genocides were the first three crusades and the four Jew-murdering

[26] This generated a whole series of writings which rework the *Akedah* material (i.e., Abraham's sacrifice of Isaac) in Jewish Rabbinic theological and religious discourses and various art forms including folk songs and folk lore. For a very special treatment of this material during the crusade-based Jewish holocaust, see Shalom Spiegel, *The Last Trial: On the Legends and Lore of the Command to Abraham to Offer Isaac As a Sacrifice: The Akedah,* translated by Judah Goldin (Woodstock, VT: Jewish Lights Publishing, 1993, 3rd edition). For a critical read of the Akedah material for New Testament studies, see, Nils Alstrup Dahl, *Crucified Messiah, and Other Essays* (Minneapolis, MN: Augsburg Press, 1974). For more popular writing see among others Amos Oz's brilliant work, *Unto Death; Crusades and Late Love (Two Novellas)* (New York: Mariner's Books, 1978).

campaigns that followed them."[27] And we can add here that the millennium also ended with a genocide of the Jews in the Holocaust.

6. The Turkish Threat and the Apocalyptic Visions

For Medieval Europe, Islam, now in the guise of the Turk, posed a threat of apocalyptic proportions. Starting with the fourteenth century this threat had become enough of a concern that it was part of various Medieval writings. By the sixteenth century a Turkish victory over Europe seemed palpably immanent: the fall of Constantinople in 1453 (just thirty years before Martin Luther's birth in 1483) was a devastating blow, but the north western expansion of the Ottomans, culminating in the attack on Vienna in 1529, was more existentially debilitating. Though this attack was repulsed by the Habsburgs, at the heavy cost of some 30,000 lives – dead or enslaved, it had not minimized the sense of this imminent threat of the Turks.[28]

The Crusades' anti-Jewish and anti-Islamic sentiments continued into the Reformation period, as is evident in Luther's writings and later even in Calvin. Both seriously polemicized against Islam; however, at the same time what is more significant, is the fact that they both saw Islam as a judgment of God upon a highly corrupt and venal Christianity, especially Roman Catholicism. Therefore, Luther could call Islam "the rod of God." Writing as early

[27] Perednik also rightly points out that: "Pope Urban II called for a campaign 'to free the Holy Land from the Muslim infidel.'... The crusaders decided to start their cleansing on the 'infidels at home,' and pounced upon the Jews all over Lorraine, massacring those who refused baptism. Soon it was rumored that their leader Godfrey had vowed not to set out for the crusade until he had avenged the crucifixion by spilling the blood of the Jews, and that he could not tolerate the continued existence of any man calling himself a Jew. Indeed, one common denominator of the genocides... was the attempt to wipe out the entire Jewish population, children included." So that, "By the end of the 13th century Jews had been expelled from England, France and Germany." See, his "Judeophobia - Anti-Semitism, Jew-Hate and anti-'Zionism'" a series of lectures based on his book *La Judeofobia: Como y Cuando Nace, Donde y Por Que Pervive* (Mexico: Tusquets, 2001), made available online at http://www.zionism-israel.com/his/judeophobia.htm.

[28] Gregory Miller, "Holy War and Holy Terror: View of Islam in German Pamphlet Literature 1520-1545" (Ph.D.: Boston University, 1994), 67-68.

as 1518 Luther says that "To fight against the Turk is the same as resisting God, who visits our sin upon us with this rod."[29] So Luther sees the Turks as God's instrument of punishment against a sinful Christendom, and in response to Pope Leo X's call for a new crusade against the Ottoman Turks, Luther argues, in *Resolutiones disputationum de indulgentiarum virtute* (1518, a copy of which he sent to the Pope), that: "Many, however, even the 'big wheels' in the church, now dream of nothing else than war against the Turk. They want to fight, not against iniquities, but against the lash of iniquity and thus they would oppose God who says that through that lash he himself punishes us for our iniquities because we do not punish ourselves for them."[30] Similarly, as late as 1529, he continues to describe the Turks as the "rod of God's wrath" by which "God is punishing the world."[31]

But these Reformers also saw Islam, along with Catholicism, as "the second horn on the head of the devil." Both these seemingly paradoxical positions vis-à-vis Islam were maintained by Luther and followed by Calvin.[32] For Luther, the Turks were both the rod of God's wrath, and also of Satan. As George Forell argues: "For Luther the devil was always God's devil, i.e., in attempting to counteract God the devil ultimately serves God."[33] So Satan (and thereby the Turks) was being used by God for God's purposes. This was

[29] See, Sarah Henrich and James L. Boyce, "Martin Luther—Translations of Two Prefaces on Islam: Preface to the Libellus de ritu et moribus Turcorum (1530), and Preface to Bibliander's Edition of the Qur'ān (1543)," in *Word & World,* Vol. XVI, No. 2, Spring 1996, 250-266, esp. 252, see their footnote 3 quoting from the *Explanations of the Ninety-Five Theses* in *Luther's Works*, vol. 31:91-92.

[30] See, *Explanations of the Disputation Concerning the Value of Indulgences,* popularly known as the *Explanations of the Ninety-Five Theses* in *Luther's Works*, trans. Harold J. Grimm and Helmut T. Lehmann, vol. 31. (Philadelphia: Muhlenberg Press and Fortress Press, 1957), 79-252, esp. 92.

[31] Henrich and Boyce, 252.

[32] See Amjad-Ali, "Debilitating Past," 120-133.

[33] George Forell, "Luther and the War Against the Turks," in William Russell (ed.), *Martin Luther, Theologian of the Church: Collected Essays* (St. Paul: Luther Seminary, 1994), 127.

further confirmed by an unjust war carried out exclusively for aggressive purposes rather than defensively which is the devil's modus operandi. The Turks were, according to Luther, thus the instrument "with which God is punishing the world as he often does through wicked scoundrels, and sometimes through godly people."[34]

Francisco points out that Luther rarely talks about the Turks without also mentioning the papacy:

> His colleagues recorded him as suggesting that both were the Antichrist. 'The Pope is the spirit of the Antichrist, and the Turk is the flesh of the Antichrist. They both help each other to choke [us], the latter with body and soul, the former with doctrine and spirit.'[35] In his own writings ... he viewed the Pope as the Antichrist whereas the Turks were another sort of demonic aberration. Along with the rest of the Muslim world, they were followers of the beast of Apocalypse 20:10, which was Muhammad. The situation, according to Luther's exegesis of the passage was thus: Muhammad's kingdom (the beast) reigned in the East and the papacy (the false prophet of Antichrist) reigned in the West. Both were poised under the command of Satan waiting for orders to commence the final assault upon the church. 'Because the end of the world is at hand,' he wrote 'the Devil must attack Christendom with both of his forces.' Yet, interestingly, and probably due to proximity, Luther almost always viewed the papacy as the bigger threat than Muhammad and the Turks. He often remarked that compared to the Pope, 'Muhammad appears before the world as a pure saint.' Nevertheless, both played an integral role in his eschatological view of history and his assessment of the nature of the Turkish threat.[36]

7. Medieval Christendom's Approach to Islam and the Jews

Norman Daniel, a philosopher, political theorist, and ethicist at Harvard University, writing about the western 'scientific' approach towards Islam,

[34] *On War Against the Turks,* LW 46:170. See Francisco, 80.

[35] *D. Martin Luthers Werke: Tischreden*, 6 vols. (Weimar: Bohlau, 1912–1921).1:135.15–17: 'Papa est spiritus Antichristi, et Turca est caro Antichristi. Sie helffen beyde einander wurgen, hic corpore et gladio, ille doctrina et spiritu'; cf. also 3:158.31–35.

[36] Francisco, 83-4.

rightly advises us that, "… even when we read the more detached scholars, we need to keep in mind how medieval Christendom argued, because it has always been and still is part of the make-up of every western mind brought to bear on the subject."[37] From a very different perspective, Colin Chapman, an evangelical missionary who had spent time in the Near East School of Theology, London Bible College and at various academic institutions in the UK, writes that, "At the time of the Reformation, Protestants saw Islam alongside Roman Catholicism as embodiments of the Antichrist, while Catholics saw in Islam many of the features they hated most in the Protestants. Then, with the coming of the Enlightenment, the rationalists took their turn to denigrate Islam and pour scorn on the Prophet."[38] What is consistent in these two critical quotes from highly divergent sources is the ubiquitous anti-Islamic attitude and judgment in Western history which has been the epistemic normative over quite a few centuries, even when the discourse involves interlocutors of very different, antagonistic, and hostile ideological starting points. The modern-day expressions of Islamophobia have roots in Christian faith history and they have long term consistency even when the various social, ideological and structural permutations have changed, and even when our vocabulary of prejudice has undergone quite a few euphemistic alterations.

There are a significant number of publications covering the history of Christian-Muslim encounters (which have proliferated especially since 9/11). The quality varies widely, though some (mostly dating back a few decades prior to 9/11) are of a high quality. Most of the Christian theologians referenced in these texts, who had significant interactions with Islam prior to, and even during, the crusades, lived under Islamic rule. These theologians were religious minorities dwelling under Islamic control and the overall Islamic cultural milieu, and were therefore defined by it, their polemics against Islam notwithstanding. Albert Hourani rightly points out that "by the tenth century … men and women in the Near East and the Maghreb lived in a universe which was defined in terms of Islam. … Time was marked by the five daily

[37] Norman Daniel, *Islam and the West: The Making of an Image* (Edinburgh: Edinburgh University Press, 1960; revised edition 1993), 326.

[38] Colin Chapman, *Islam and the West: Conflict, Coexistence or Conversion?* (London: Paternoster Press, 1998), 11.

prayers, the weekly sermon in the Mosque, the annual fast in the month of Ramadan and the pilgrimage to Mecca, and the Muslim calendar."[39] That they were for the most part able to carry out their apologetic and polemical work (especially against the Prophet Muhammad) whilst under exacting Muslim rule (in the larger Syria, Maghreb, Spain, and Turkey), shows the level of intellectual space that these societies must have had, despite the propaganda to the contrary.[40]

Though the Jews were theologically the closest and oldest neighbor to Christianity (the concepts of *praeparatio evangelica*, Messiah, etc.), they were a vulnerable victim to an aggressive Christianity immediately following Constantine's "conversion" in the early 4th century. Islam, on the other hand, being a major post-Christian religion, posed a serious challenge to the sufficiency and efficaciousness of Christianity. Just as Christianity saw Judaism as *praeparatio evangelica*, Islam saw both Judaism and Christianity (its monotheistic predecessors) as *praeparatio Islamica*, to coin a phrase. Its rapid phenomenal growth and conquests immediately following its founding were perceived by Islam as clear indications of the validity and efficaciousness of its cause. Therefore Islam was a challenge for Christians theologically, geographically, numerically, politically and economically. Located so

[39] See his, *A History of Arab Peoples* (New York: Warner Books, 1992), 54-57. This, by the way, is the experience of all Christians living in Islamic contexts even today, though the level of tolerance has decreased significantly in the recent years. Unfortunately these Christians are not fully a part of the contemporary ecumenical discussion vis-à-vis Christian-Muslim relations which is supervised by "Christian concern" in the Western context and by their "objective" approach.

[40] The most significant names are: John Sedra, a Monophysitic Jacobite patriarch of Antioch from 631-48; John of Damascus, a Malkite (d.749/764), arguably the author of the very first *Summa Theologica*; Theodore bar Koni, a Syriac Christian, (d. 792), author of *Scholian,* a commentary on the Old and New Testament; Patriarch Timothy I, of the Church of the East, (727/8-823); Theodore Abu Kurrah, a Malachite from Edessa who was the Bishop of Harran also in Syria (c. 755-830), who actually did his Christian theology in Arabic and wrote in both Syriac and Arabic; Hunayn ibn Ishaq (808-873) Nestorian physician, philosopher and translator, known for his translation into Arabic of Greek philosophical and scientific texts; Elyas of Nisibis, a Nestorian (975-1046); and Paul of Antioch (ca. 1180) Malachite bishop. Cf. Griffith, *op. cit.*; and Wansborough, *op. cit.*

close, it posed a threatening and confrontational challenge, a neighbor to be vilified and where possible rooted out. Philip Hitti, the great Lebanese Christian Arab historian, formerly at Princeton University, speaks of this relationship as: "The two communities have been yoked together through cooperation and conflict, tolerance and hatred, dialogue and diatribe, personal friendship and communal strife."[41] Hourani, formerly of Oxford University, also a great historian with a Christian Lebanese background, describes it as a "long and intimate, an ambiguous and usually painful relationship."[42] So in spite of the high theological claim and the great divine imperative of "loving our neighbors as ourselves," we Christians have hated to love and have loved to hate our closest neighbor, the Muslims.

Both Hitti and Hourani are correct in giving their respective evaluations of the paradoxical history of the Christian-Muslim relationship, especially vis-à-vis Western Christianity and Islam. Luther represents this ambiguity, and the seeming contradiction, in his attitude towards the Muslims. Over time he shows the same contradictory attitude towards the Jews, but there his negativity is much more vitriolic. This is clear in his total volte-face vis-à-vis the Jews. In his earlier writings, he has a relatively positive evaluation, especially given the overall negative attitude towards Jews prevalent at the time. His first statement about the Jews comes from his letter of 1514, addressed to Pastor Georg Spalatin, the secretary/advisor to imperial Elector Frederick the Wise: "Conversion of the Jews will be the work of God alone operating from within, and not of man working — or rather playing — from without. If these offences be taken away, worse will follow. For they are thus given over by the wrath of God to reprobation, that they may become incorrigible, as Ecclesiastes says, for every one who is incorrigible is rendered worse rather than better by correction."[43]

41 Philip Hitti, *Islam and the West* (Princeton, NJ.: Van Nostrand, 1962), 6.

42 Albert Hourani, *Europe and the Middle East* (London: Macmillan Press, 1980), 71-2.

43 Martin Luther, "Luther to George Spalatin," in *Luther's Correspondence and Other Contemporaneous Letters*, trans. Henry Preserved Smith (Philadelphia: Lutheran Publication Society, 1913), 1:29.

Then in 1519 Luther challenges the doctrine of *Servitus Judaeorum* (Servitude of the Jews) established by Justinian I in *Corpus Juris Civilis* (Body of Civil Law) between 529-34 and the theologians defending it: "Absurd theologians defend hatred for the Jews... What Jew would consent to enter our ranks when he sees the cruelty and enmity we wreak on them – that in our behavior towards them we less resemble Christians than beasts?"[44] Luther makes the most comprehensive statement for the Jews in That Jesus Christ was Born a Jew written in 1523, again with a very heavy critique of those theologians who support an anti-Jewish position:

> If I had been a Jew and had seen such dolts and blockheads govern and teach the Christian faith, I would sooner have become a hog than a Christian. They have dealt with the Jews as if they were dogs rather than human beings; they have done little else than deride them and seize their property. When they baptize them they show them nothing of Christian doctrine or life, but only subject them to popishness and mockery... If the apostles, who also were Jews, had dealt with us Gentiles as we Gentiles deal with the Jews, there would never have been a Christian among the Gentiles... When we are inclined to boast of our position [as Christians] we should remember that we are but Gentiles, while the Jews are of the lineage of Christ. We are aliens and in-laws; they are blood relatives, cousins, and brothers of our Lord. Therefore, if one is to boast of flesh and blood the Jews are actually nearer to Christ than we are... If we really want to help them, we must be guided in our dealings with them not by papal law but by the law of Christian love. We must receive them cordially, and permit them to trade and work with us, that they may have occasion and opportunity to associate with us, hear our Christian teaching, and witness our Christian life. If some of them should prove stiff-necked, what of it? After all, we ourselves are not all good Christians either.[45]

By 1543, however, with the publication of On the Jews and their Lies, Luther himself has become one of those "absurd" "dolts" and "blockhead" theologians, making highly immoral if not totally sinful, and scurrilous claims

[44] Luther quoted in Elliott Rosenberg, *But Were They Good for the Jews?* (New York: Birch Lane Press, 1997), 65.

[45] Martin Luther, "That Jesus Christ was Born a Jew," Trans. Walter I. Brandt, in *Luther's Works* (Philadelphia: Fortress Press, 1962), 200–201, 229, emphasis added.

about the Jews. He says that they are a "base, whoring people, that is, no people of God, and their boast of lineage, circumcision, and law must be accounted as filth,"[46] in direct contradiction of what he said earlier.

> What shall we Christians do with this rejected and condemned people, the Jews?... we dare not tolerate their conduct, now that we are aware of their lying and reviling and blaspheming... I shall give you my sincere advice: First, to set fire to their synagogues or schools and to bury and cover with dirt whatever will not burn, so that no man will ever again see a stone or cinder of them... Second,... that their houses also be razed and destroyed... Instead they might be lodged under a roof or in a barn, like the gypsies... Third,... that all their prayer books and Talmudic writings, in which such idolatry, lies, cursing, and blasphemy are taught, be taken from them. Fourth,... that their rabbis be forbidden to teach henceforth on pain of loss of life and limb... Fifth,... that safe-conduct on the highways be abolished completely for the Jews... Sixth,... that usury be prohibited to them, and that all cash and treasure of silver and gold be taken from them and put aside for safekeeping... by it [usury] they have stolen and robbed from us all they possess. Seventh, I recommend putting a flail, an ax, a hoe, a spade, a distaff, or a spindle into the hands of young, strong Jews and Jewesses and letting them earn their bread in the sweat of their brow... we suffer as much as we do from these base children of the devil, this brood of vipers... these venomous serpents and devil's children.[47]

Several months later still in 1543, Luther wrote *Vom Schem Hamphoras* und *Vom Geschlecht Christi* (Of the Unknowable Name and the Generations of Christ):

> Here in Wittenburg, in our parish church, there is a sow carved into the stone under which lie young pigs and Jews who are sucking; behind the sow stands a rabbi who is lifting up the right leg of the sow, raises behind the sow, bows down and looks with great effort into the Talmud under the sow, as if he wanted to read and see something most difficult

[46] Martin Luther, "On the Jews and Their Lies," in *Luther's Works,* vol. 47: *The Christian in Society IV*, trans. by Martin H. Bertram (Philadelphia: Fortress Press: 1971), 268-293, emphasis added; see also Robert Michael, *Holy Hatred: Christianity, Antisemitism, and the Holocaust* (New York; Palgrave Macmillan, 2006), 111.

[47] Ibid., section 11, emphasis added.

and exceptional; no doubt they gained their Shem Hamphoras from that place.[48]

So Luther goes from giving the Jews a special significance, associating them with Christ, to a complete vilification, bile and calling them the Devil's progeny within a twenty year period. The reasons for this change of attitude are nowhere articulated in Luther and the suggested reasons by some scholars make little or no sense. He advised an almost bodily, material, and spiritual eradication of the Jews, in a litany eerily reminiscent of Hitler's Nazi regime – as they put into practice what Luther proscribed.

8. Luther's Seeming Contradictory Views of Islam and the Turks

So it is clear that Luther sits well within the tradition of negatively evaluating both Judaism and Islam. Nonetheless, he is one of the earliest of the major Western theologians to acknowledge the critical role of Islam, in spite of facing its threat and imminent conquest of Europe. This is present in many of his writings and not, as is so often portrayed, exclusively in his *On the War Against the Turks*. Luther advised that "in whatever way possible the religion and customs of 'Muhammadanism' be published and spread abroad."[49] It is particularly fascinating to recall that Luther towards the end of his life in 1543 was critically instrumental in the publication of a new translation of the Qur'an into Latin by Theodore Bibliander.[50] This, for whatever reason is not given much publicity, perhaps because of the much more infamous publication of *On the Jews and their Lies* in the same year.

[48] *Schem Hamphoras* is the Hebrew rabbinic name for the ineffable name of God, the *tetragrammaton*. Luther's use of the term was in itself a taunt and insult to Jewish sensitivities. See Gerhard Falk, *The Jew in Christian Theology: Martin Luther's Anti-jewish Vom Schem Hamphoras, Previously Unpublished in English, and Other Milestones in Church Doctrine Concerning Judaism* (Jefferson, NC: McFarland & Company, Inc., 2013).

[49] op. cit. Henrich & Boyce, 255.

[50] Born in Bischofszell, Switzerland, *Theodor Buchmann* is known by his Greek name of *Theodore Bibliander,* a common practice (along with Latin) to raise the status of the person in middle Europe.

Bibliander had studied Arabic, and upon Luther's request he published a reworked version of the Latin Qur'an based on Robert Ketton's seminal, though not always accurate, translation (Lex Mahumet pseudoprophete, "The Law of Muhammad, the False Prophet") of 1143.[51] In 1542, Luther used his influence on the Council of Basel which had banned and confiscated Bibliander's Qur'an. Persuaded by Luther's letter, the Council lifted the ban and released the text on the condition that both Luther and Melanchthon wrote prefaces to it. The Qur'an was finally published in 1543 along with these prefaces. Henrich and Boyce summarize that,

> The main burden of Luther's preface ...was to argue once again for the clear presentation of the teachings of Muhammad so that by contrast they might be more readily refuted by the clear teachings of the church about Christ, the incarnation, his death for our sins, and the resurrection, and so that Christians might thereby be armed in conflict with the enemy by a sure and certain knowledge of the central tenets of their own faith.[52]

Besides these warnings and critiques, Luther at the very end of his preface writes,

> In this age of ours how many varied enemies have we already seen? Papist defenders of idolatry, the Jews, the multifarious monstrosities of the Anabaptists, Servetus, and others. Let us now prepare ourselves against Muhammad. But what can we say about matters that are still outside our knowledge? Therefore, it is of value for the learned to read the writings of the enemy in order to refute them more keenly, to cut them to pieces and to overturn them, in order that they might be able to bring some to safety, or certainly to fortify our people with more sturdy arguments.[53]

So Luther's approach was to attempt to overcome the existing lacuna of knowledge vis-à-vis the religion of the Turks. According to Southern, this

51 It is worth mentioning, to quote Francisco, that, "There is certainly no reason to deny that Robert's translation is best described as a paraphrase and, likewise, that it served to fuel the majority of medieval anti-Muslim polemics," Francisco, 12.

52 Henrich & Boyce, 256.

53 Ibid., 266.

was because "he looked forward to the probability that Christendom would be engulfed in Islam."[54]

It is important to remember here that one of the most significant contributions of the Reformation was the de-priviligization of the *lingua sacra or religiosis* of Latin, and making the vernacular *lingua popularis* German operational both for the reading and hermeneutics of the sacred texts and religious rituals. This made religion more egalitarian, less sacerdotal, and more cognitive rather than superstitious and mysterious. Reformation Christianity, including the Anabaptists, at that juncture was the originary expression of this change, while other Christian expression continued in this distinction even in the West.[55] While epistemologically one may put down those religions (including many Christian communities) which maintain the distinction between the sacred value of the *lingua sacra/religiosis* and the comprehensive value of a vernacular language, many scholars continue to give Arabic Muslims a privileged position when dealing with Islam because of the sacred value of Arabic. Their numbers do not demand this privilege as at least 80% of Muslims are non-Arabic speaking.[56]

Luther did not have either of these problems and therefore when he looked at Islam he recognized the Arabic language as a lingua sacra and gave it a central place. He insisted on a new translation of the Qur'an into Latin and not German (still holding to the distinction between *lingua sacra* and *lingua popularis* in spite of his own theological emphasis on the latter as being valuable for both tasks – perhaps this was his way of maintaining the distinction between the *lingua intelligentia/academia* and the *lingua popularis*). But it is important to remember that he was not looking at Arabic Islam; rather his understanding of Islam was based on equating it with the Turks, the contem-

[54] R.W. Southern, *Western Views of Islam in the Middle Ages* (Cambridge, MA: Harvard University Press, 1962, 3rd printing 1982), 105-106.

[55] It took the Roman Catholics some 450 years to reach this position at the end of Vatican II (1963-65).

[56] One wonders whether this emphasis on Arabs and Arabic is not based on some self-interested understanding of the Islamic world and its geo-political and economic value – both for oil and for the state of Israel.

porary imperial enemy. So he uses "Mohammedans" and "Turks" interchangeably when discussing Islam and Muslims.

Assessing the nature of the Muslim faith and culture and the threat that it posed to Christians, Luther argued, in his preface to *Libellus de ritu et moribus Turcorum* (1530), that it was critical for Christians to know the Islamic scripture and Muslim culture and to study it:

> Since we now have the Turk and his religion at our very doorstep our people must be warned lest, either moved by the splendor of the Turkish religion and the external appearances of their customs or displeased by the meager display of our own faith or the deformity of our customs, they deny their Christ and follow Muhammad."[57]

Earlier in the text he argued,

> ... we see that the religion of the Turks or Muhammad is far more splendid in ceremonies – and, I might almost say, in customs – than ours, even including that of the religious or all the clerics. The modesty and simplicity of their food, clothing, dwellings, and everything else, as well as the fasts, prayers, and common gatherings of the people that this book reveals are nowhere seen among us ... which of our monks, be it a Carthusian (they who wish to appear the best) or a Benedictine, is not put to shame by the miraculous and wondrous abstinence and discipline among their religious? Our religious are mere shadows when compared to them, and our people clearly profane when compared to theirs. Not even true Christians, not Christ himself, not the apostles or prophets ever exhibited so great a display. This is the reason why many persons so easily depart from faith in Christ for Muhammadanism and adhere to it so tenaciously. I sincerely believe that no papist, monk, cleric, or their equal in faith would be able to remain in their faith if they should spend three days among the Turks. ... Indeed, in all these things the Turks are by far superior.[58]

Very high praise indeed! Though clearly for a negative telos.

[57] op. cit. Henrich & Boyce, 260.

[58] op. cit. Henrich & Boyce, 259, emphasis added.

9. Contra-Catholic Crusade and Anabaptist Pacifism, Luther on Christian Vocation and the Two Kingdom Theory

In his earlier writings Luther did not explicitly endorse or condemn the various military measures taken against the Turks, but he did completely reject the idea of a new crusade. In 1518 when his opinion was solicited by George Spalatin vis-à-vis the papal plans for another crusade against the Turks, he responded

> If I rightly understand you, you ask whether an expedition against the Turks can be defended by me on biblical grounds. Even supposing the war should be undertaken for pious reasons rather than for gain, I confess that I cannot promise what you ask, but rather the opposite... It seems to me if we must have any Turkish war, we ought to begin with ourselves. In vain we wage carnal wars without, while at home we are conquered by spiritual battles... Now that the Roman Curia is more tyrannical than any Turk, fighting with such portentous deeds against Christ and against his Church, and now that the clergy is sunk in the depth of avarice, ambition and luxury, and now that the face of the Church is everywhere most wretched, there is no hope of a successful war or of victory. As far as I can see, God fights against us; first, we must conquer him with tears, pure prayers, holy life and pure faith.[59]

Thus for Luther the real threat to Christianity was not so much from the Turks but rather from the "papacy's subjugation of the church to false doctrine."[60] We have already mentioned above Luther's response to Pope Leo X's call for a new crusade against the Ottoman Turks. And again, in *Von den guten Werken*, "Christendom is being destroyed not by the Turks, but by those who are supposed to defend it."[61] Luther's overall denouncement of the papacy, and particularly against the demand for a quite popular crusade/holy war in the face of an imminent Turkish invasion, had already angered the Roman Church. Luther's apparent lack of direct attack on the Turks further exacerbated the matter, so now with popular support the Roman Church sought his excommunication with a little more gusto. Luther in his personal

[59] *Luther's Correspondence,* 1:140-141, as quoted in Francisco, 68.

[60] Francisco, 68.

[61] *Von den guten Werken, Luther's Works*, Vol. 44:72, as quoted in Francisco, 69.

correspondence had been very negative vis-à-vis the Pope since as early as 1518, arguing that Rome was more tyrannical than the Turk.[62] Luther went further in 1518 and "publicly declared that the Pope was not only a 'tyrant' of Christianity but also the 'Antichrist'."[63] He made matters worse when, in 1520, he hyperbolized that the true "Turks" were the Pope's servants, his "lackeys and whores."[64] The Pope's response to this sustained attack was to threaten to excommunicate Luther in 1520. Among Luther's many alleged heretical and scandalous teachings denounced by the papacy in the bull, *Exsurge Domine* (1520), was a summary of an early statement he had made with regards to the Turks: "to fight against the Turks is to fight against God's visitation upon our iniquities."[65]

Luther's response to the Papal bull of excommunication was to maintain:

> This article does not mean that we are not to fight against the Turk, as that holy manufacturer of heresies, the pope charges. It means, rather, that we should mend our ways and cause God to be gracious to us. We should not plunge into war, relying on the pope's indulgence with which he has deceived Christians in the past and is deceiving them still... All the pope accomplishes with his crusading indulgences and his promises of heaven is to lead Christians with their lives into death and with their souls into hell. This is, of course, the proper work of the Antichrist. God does not demand crusades, indulgences, and wars. He wants us to live good lives. But the pope and his followers run from goodness faster than from anything else, yet he wants to devour the Turks... This is the reason why our war against the Turks is so successful – so that where he formerly held one mile of land he now holds a hundred. But we still do

[62] Cf. his letter to George Spalatin cited above, also see his letter to Wenzel Link (1483-1547), Johann Staupitz's successor as vicar general of the Augustinian order, in *D. Martin Luthers Werke: Briefwechsel*, 18 vols. (Weimar: Böhlau, 1930–1985) 1:270.13-14, as cited in Francisco, 69.

[63] Francisco, 69, quoting "Eyn Sermon von den newen Testament," in *Luther's Works*, Vol. 35:107.

[64] *Luther's Works*, Vol. 35:90.

[65] 'Exsurge Domine', in Carl Mirbt (ed.), *Quellen zur Geschichte des Papsttums und das römische Katholizismus*, 2nd. edn. (Tübingen: J.C.B. Mohr, 1901), 184. Pope Leo X also sent a letter to Elector Frederick accompanying the bull, claiming that Luther 'favors Turks'. See Francisco, 70, footnote 11.

> not see it so completely have we been taken by this Roman leader of the blind.[66]

This does not mean that Luther was a pacifist, something for which he strongly condemned the Anabaptists. Rather, he endorsed a military response against the Turks. See for example, the *Türkenbüchlein* – the so called Turkish writings, the most well known of which is *Vom Kriege wider die Türken* (On War Against the Turks) (1529). He writes the latter in order to counter those "stupid preachers amongst us Germans … who are making us believe that we ought not and must not fight. Some are even so foolish to say that it is not proper for Christians to bear the temporal sword or to be rulers... some actually want the Turk to come and rule because they think our German people are wild and uncivilized."[67] With the Ottoman Turks beginning to seriously encroach on Europe with Suleyman I's conquest of Belgrade in 1521, the Kingdom of Hungary in 1526, and the (repelled) Ottoman attack on Vienna in 1529, the threat of Ottoman occupation of Europe began to seem very realistic indeed. It was not so much a question of a crusade against the Turks (i.e., an offensive attack on Turkish territory outside of Europe), but rather now a very real possibility of having to defend western European territory against Ottoman occupation.

In On War Against the Turks, Luther argues that although in his earlier writings he had argued that Christians must fight their wars by spiritual means, i.e., through repentance and reform, and indeed this was still valid, he had maintained a non-fighting position vis-à-vis the Turks because the Pope had been pushing for this war as a Holy War to be undertaken in the name of Christ, something which Luther found extremely offensive. But he wanted to maintain that they must fight the Turks as part of their secular vocation. This was not to be a crusade, a holy war against the Turkish religion, but rather a secular war, led by secular not religious leaders, against an invader. If one were going to go to war against heresy, one would have to start with Roman Catholicism. "Let the Turk believe and live as he will, just as one lets the

[66] *Luther's Works*, vol. 32:89-91, as quoted in Francisco, 70. The Pope officially excommunicated Luther in 1521 via the bull *Decet Romanum Pontificem.*

[67] *Luther's Works*, 46:161–162, emphasis added.

papacy and other false Christians live."[68] Now, he urged everyone to take up arms against the Turks, not as a religious issue but yet as an issue of vocation, theologically expanding that concept beyond the exclusivity of the priestly calling. In *Eine Heerpredigt wider den Türken* (1530), he encourages Christians to embrace the vocation of soldiery, because "Such a person should know that they were merely defending themselves 'against the Turks in a war started by them,' which they were entitled and even obliged to do so... for in battling the Turks one was 'fighting against an enemy of God and a blasphemer of Christ, indeed, the Devil himself.'"[69]

Two of the central tenets of Luther's theology – the Two Kingdoms, and the concept of *vocatio dei* – were, I believe, deeply influenced by the context of the Turkish presence and the responses it generated from the Roman Catholic Church, invoking the crusade or, conversely, the pacifism of the Anabaptists. The latter, while agreeing with Luther that Islam was the Rod of God to purge Christianity from its sin and calumny, saw his resistance against the Turks as un-Christian, and against God's ordination and design. Unlike the pacifism of the Anabaptists, who were not worried about how they were perceived in society, Luther still needed the support of the people, especially his princely friends, and thus his correspondence with the Reverend Spalatin mentioned above. Therefore he develops a very novel and creative idea of seeing a broader notion of *vocatio dei*, rather than the already existing narrow understanding of restricting it exclusively to the sacramental and priestly duties. It is through this notion of soldiery as a vocation, and the vocation of a soldier, that he can counter both the crusading holy war Roman Catholic mindset, on the one hand, and the pacifist Anabaptist mindset, on the other. In this way Luther reconfigures the notion of a just war theory away from the Catholic notion of a religious war, and refutes the Anabaptist position of total pacifism with no place for warring of any kind. For Luther, therefore, at issue is not so much a definition of warring itself, but of two sets of governance – civil and religious –, as well as the notion of the Christian vocation being larger than residing exclusively in the priesthood. Warring is

68 *Luther's Works*, 46:185–186.

69 Francisco, 77, quoting „Eine Heerpredigt wider den Türken." in *Luther's Works* 30/2:173.4–5, 9.

thus in the domain of the civil governance and to be initiated and conducted by this side of the two kingdoms and not to be undertaken as a holy war or crusade initiated by the Church where it had no place to be undertaking this vocation.

10. The Anachronism of *Cuius Regio Eius Religio* and the de facto Exclusion of the Other

It must be remembered that Luther's approach towards the Muslims, especially the Turks, was based on fear, dread and vulnerability and therefore had a profound apocalyptic dimension. His position vis-à-vis the Jews, on the other hand, is towards a highly vulnerable, weak, and constantly threatened minority. The Jews had lived with the Sword of Damocles hanging over their head throughout Europe, escalating especially after the Spanish massacre of 1391 and the beginning of the Jewish genocide and final expulsion from Spain a century later. The question in the western European context, which by the mid-nineteenth century was framed as the Jewish Question or Judenfrage, was whether Jews could be citizens: first, of the Holy Roman Empire, and then, post-Reformation, this was further expanded vis-à-vis the recently emerging independent autonomous princely states/fiefdoms, which Luther, for good or bad, had supported and been affiliated with. This was especially critical after the Peace of Augsburg between the Holy Roman Emperor, Charles V, and the forces of the Schmalkaldic League, the alliance of Lutheran princes, in September 1555. The agreement acknowledged the status of Lutheran Princes and the Augsburg Confession of 1530 and ratified a critical clause: "*cuius regio, eius religio*" (whose realm, his religion). This among other issues becomes one of the central clauses codified in the much more secular Treaty of Westphalia of 1648, which is seen as the founding of the modern nation state system.[70] The centrality of this concept even in the secular Treaty of Westphalia by default excluded the Jews and those Christians who had no such prince with a controlling realm, such as the Anabaptists. The Jews and the Anabaptists had to either convert or adopt the religion of

[70] Some form of "*cuius regio, eius religio,*" is *de jure* still present and applicable in many of the European nation-states which were not occupied by the Communists, even though *de facto* they may not see themselves as Christian states.

their local princes, giving up their respective faith positions or face persecution even unto death. A fate which both groups had to face on a number of occasions.[71]

11. The Essentialization of Islam, from *Judenfrage* to *Muslimfrage* and the Turkish Minorities in Germany

To search for the contemporaneous application and relevancy of Luther's discussions of the Turks and the Jews, especially in light of the horrific appropriation of Luther's anti-Jewish sentiments in Nazi Germany, a critical but brief examination of the situation of the Turks in contemporary Germany is vital. Much of what we see in Germany is equally applicable to the rest of Europe. With the overcoming of old nationalist identities generated after Westphalia in 1648 in mainland Europe, and the consolidation of a "united European identity," with similar transcendent nationalism as in the USA, the question of "the Other" acquires a critical importance. This applies especially to non-European immigrants (nationalised or otherwise), especially the Muslims, and in Germany, specifically the Turks. This has become even more crucial since September 11 and the growth of Islamophobic rhetoric. The contemporary presence of Islam, and its growing radicalization, has posed a whole series of questions, and challenges some of the fundamental assumptions behind liberal democracy and the rights regimes that have been in place in Europe. Issues such as freedom of speech versus hate speech; the character of religious freedom in a post-Christian secular context; the derogatory images of the Prophet Muhammad and the associated terroristic essentialization of Islam; the scare-mongering rhetoric of the imposition of Shariah law by Islam in secular Europe; the freedom of religion and expression embodied in the right to wear the veil versus the state imposition of a dress-code; the issue of Charlie Hebdo's freedom of press and speech, and the parameters of hate

[71] A critical and highly scandalous example of this intolerance is the German Peasants' War of 1524-25 where a third of the peasants, approximately 100,000, were killed by the armies of the feudal princes, supported by Luther. The worst example of this is that just in the one-day battle of Frankenhausen, approximately 6,000 peasants were massacred. So in 1525 Luther pens, "*Wider die räuberischen und mörderischen Rotten der Bauern*" (*Against the Murderous, Thieving Hordes of Peasants*).

speech against foreigners; the rise of (neo-Nazi) organizations like PEGIDA[72] and its xenophobic politics; nationalist political parties and their extreme xenophobia like Geert Wilders' Partij voor de Vrijheid, and Marine Le Pen's Front National; etc., all demand a serious reevaluation of democracy, the accepted human rights regimes, and the recognition of the reconstructive role of immigrants in European history after the second World War, and the role of compensatory justice.

Given the horrific history of the Holocaust, with some level of cooperation by most of Europe, or at least acquiescence through silence, (though there were clearly exceptional cases), it is rightly no longer acceptable to make anti-Jewish and "anti-Semitic" statements or to deny the Holocaust;[73] these are justly perceived as hate crimes. The same status however is not given to the Muslim minorities which now actually reside in Europe. Thus the anti-semitic language, imagery, political and military rhetoric once applied towards the Jews can now be used with impunity or little restriction against the Muslims and Islam, clearly with appropriate adjustments.

Our examination of the contemporary German context after the Second World War must begin with the critical reconstruction of a war-ravaged Germany destroyed by six years of devastation. The Germans at the time had no

[72] *Patriotische Europäer gegen die Islamisierung des Abendlandes*, or Patriotic Europeans Against the Islamization of the West.

[73] Though when this valid restriction against the vilification of a people or individuals is expanded to cover the state, moral or otherwise, it entails taking away the right of ethical discourse itself, which is a *sine qua non* for modern democracy and transparent and accountable governance. So if any critique of the state, even for its most immoral acts, is seen as a pejorative judgment against a particular people, there is a serious confusion of categories. If this is not challenged then the issue of restorative justice which is supposed to be behind this position is itself seriously damaged, if not totally nullified, and the idea of critical virtuous thought and citizenship itself is put into serious question. The lack of these rights were central in generating the crimes against a people in the first place. So when a critique of this state is seen as anti-semitic and all critical conversation is shut down then we have a major confusion between the people (*demos*) and the state (*basileia*). This curtails the core value of the ability of moral discourse against the state and its coercive overreach.

major colonies,[74] and a large number of their own young men had been killed or seriously injured in the two World Wars (from 1914-1945). Germany therefore had to recruit foreign labor for their reconstruction and re-industrialization after the second world war.[75] The demands of the American Marshall Plan had already met some challenges with the loss of half of Germany to the Soviet Union (and later the building of the Berlin Wall in 1961), which seriously restricted the flow of labor for industrialization purposes and the ever expanding demands generated by the *Wirtschaftswunder* (economic miracle) of the 1950s. All this expanded the demand for labor with few indigenous resources to draw upon, so Germany entered into several bilateral labor agreements with different countries.[76] The largest portion of these laborers were from Muslim societies, most significantly from Turkey.[77] In

[74] The division of Africa among the European states had taken place during the Berlin Conference of 1884-85, with representatives of: Austria-Hungary, Belgium, Denmark, France, Germany, Great Britain, Italy, the Netherlands, Portugal, Russia, Spain, Sweden-Norway, *Turkey,* and *USA*, (emphasis added) and by 1914, Africa had been fully divided into fifty new states. After 1885 Germany was the third largest colonial presence in Africa, controlling Tanganyika (now part of Tanzania), Ruanda-Urundi (now Rwanda and Burundi), Wituland (part of Kenya) and Kionga Triangle (part of Mozambique) together they were called German East Africa; Namibia and part of present Botswana, were the German South-West Africa; and Togoland and Kamerun (which included besides Cameroon, the northern part of Gabon and Congo, western part of Central African Republic, southwestern Chad and the far eastern part of Nigeria). However, within thirty years, these colonies were occupied by its enemies during World War I and were completely confiscated in the Treaty of Versailles in 1919.

[75] Euphemistically referred to as *Gastarbeiter* (guest workers) as compared to the contextually more negative *Fremdarbeiter* (foreign or alien workers), which had referred to the forced labor conscripted from German-occupied Europe to work in agriculture and industry during the Second World War.

[76] The bilateral agreements which Germany entered for importing labor were with Italy (1955), Spain (1960), Greece (1960) (all three had been fascist societies; respectively under Mussolini, Franco, and Ioannis Metaxa), Turkey (1961), Morocco (1963), Portugal (1964), Tunisia (1965) and finally Yugoslavia (1968), while still under Tito's communist rule.

[77] See the highly critical study by Sonja Haug, Stephanie Müssig & Anja Stichs, *Muslimisches Leben in Deutschland im Auftrag der Deutschen Islam Konferenz*,

2009 it was estimated by Germany's Federal Office for Migration and Refugees that there were 4.3 million Muslims in Germany, i.e., 5.2% of the overall population. Around 63% of these were of Turkish descent (i.e., 2.7 million, constituting 3.0% the total population). About 65% of these Muslims were fully German citizens. This gives some sense of the contemporary numerical context of religious minorities in Germany which becomes especially critical when compared to the Jewish population in the pre-WWII Germany: "In prewar central Europe, the largest Jewish community was in Germany, with about 500,000 members (0.75% of the total German population)."[78] If this small number of Jews was found unacceptable from 1933 onwards, and therefore there was widespread acceptance of the concentration camps and even genocide,[79] one wonders where the current much larger Turkish and Muslim presence could lead to if some trigger is set into motion. We have been facing the *Muslimfrage*, in various forms, now the worry is that it could be converted to a more violent structured removal of the contemporary Others like that exercised vis-à-vis the Jews during the Second World War.

In the contemporary context, the Turks in Germany are, on the one hand, a vulnerable, weak, and dependent ethnic and religious minority, like the Jews of Luther's time. They can be and are at times treated with capricious disregard and high moral and social coercion. Because of the causal link of being initially a "lower/laboring class" vulnerable ethnic minority, what Luther wrote about the Ottoman Turks does not apply directly to the contemporary

(Berlin: Bundesamt für Migration und Flüchtlinge, 2009) [Muslim Life in Germany, published on behalf of the German Islam Conference by the Federal Office for Migration and Refugees], available at: http://www.bmi.bund.de/cae/servlet/contentblob/566008/publicationFile/31710/vollversion_studie_muslim_leben_deutschland_.pdf.

78 See, "Jewish Population of Europe in 1933: Population Data by Country" in the United States Holocaust Memorial Museum's *Holocaust Encyclopedia*, at http://www.ushmm.org/wlc/en/article.php?ModuleId=10005161.

79 For the comprehensive involvement of the German populace in this morally dark period in German history, see, Daniel J. Goldhagen, *Hitler's Willing Executioners: Ordinary Germans and the Holocaust* (New York: Alfred A. Knopf, 1996).

German Turks. However, what he wrote about the Jews could be quite easily applied to them.

On the other hand, they are Muslims and thus are the new binary enemy after the Cold War and the collapse of the Soviet Union. They are therefore essentialized and stereotyped as part of the "War against Terror." The status of the Turks in Germany has undergone a major shift since September 11, 2001 (as was the case for all Muslim immigrants across Europe). From being a vulnerable blue-collar labor force, and therefore somewhat tolerated for economic and social convenience, the Muslims have now come to represent the new *Inbegriff der Feindschaft* (enemy-ness) with almost apocalyptic implications for what Western social values stand for, and therefore are a threat and challenge to this "normative virtuous life." Here therefore, Luther's texts on the Ottoman Turks can be applied rather directly. This entailed a major shift, and with it new sets of prejudices: Islam and Muslims are no longer seen as a weak and vulnerable minority living in Europe in culturally and socially specific ghettos, but rather a highly hyperbolized threatening and very powerful enemy, both inside and outside, which could take over Europe at very short notice and impose its law (Shariah) on the local citizens and the European values and achievements. So vis-à-vis the current European Islamic presence, both of Luther's approaches towards the Jews and the Turks have application and possibilities.

12. The Use of Hermeneutical *Subtilitas* (*Intelligendi*, *Explicandi*, and *Applicandi*): Towards the Role of the Other in Human History

Hans-Georg Gadamer defines application as the integral part of the hermeneutical task, and he argues that this application entails the understanding of the text in the contemporary situation of the interpreter itself.[80] This is what completes the hermeneutical circle for him because it recognizes the location

[80] See his *Truth and Method* (New York: Seabury Press, 1975), 274, see also Haoming Liu, "Subtilitas Applicandi as Self-Knowledge: A Critique of the Concept of Application in Hans-Georg Gadamer's Truth and Method," in *The Journal of Speculative Philosophy, New Series*, Vol. 10, No. 2 (1996), 128-147.

of the interpreter with all her/his existing pre-judgments (*prejudicium*, *prejudices*) as the arche and telos of the hermeneutical task. In this paper, I have tried to achieve such a hermeneutical task on Luther's texts vis-à-vis the Muslims (Turks) and the Jews, the historical events in which his writings emerged, and the overall the context of his work, in order to radicalize the Reformation in light of pre-judgments present against the "Other." Behind this hermeneutical task was a special concern for the development of Reformation theology with the focus on the religious Other(ness) of the Muslims (Turks) and the Jews during that period. It demanded a radical hermeneutic of Luther's texts, both their larger and narrower contexts, and an assessment of the tradition of their interpretation within the European prejudicium.

If we take the triadic unity, or the three moments of the hermeneutical task (viz., *subtilitas intelligendi, subtilitas explicandi* and *subtilitas applicandi*), as being theologically and historically valid and essential, I hope I have achieved these three moments in this paper through a critical demythologizing of the taken-for-granted interpretation of certain ossified dogmas and positions. I have also tried to place different interpretations of the historical context in which Luther's texts emerged. *Subtilitas intelligendi* requires a sound understanding, a discernment whether we really understand a passage or the events surrounding it, and to pay attention to the difficulties that lie in the way of understanding it. The search for a proper approach and way of investigating the historical events or epochs lead to a radicalizing moment of understanding Luther's texts and biography. *Subtilitas explicandi* required a look at those historical events or epochs as having perspicuous argument and illustration, which I have tried to demonstrate and thus achieve some level of clarity. It also requires a demythologizing of the taken-for-granted fixed interpretation so that we may move beyond the ossified traditions and dogmas which have cast a veil on this self-explanatory perspicuity. At the same time I have placed the original events and texts themselves under the hermeneutical scrutiny of reason and struggle in order to overcome the obscureness which some of these events and epochs have generated. This then has its own radicalizing moment on the Reformation.

The *subtilitas intelligendi* and *subtilitas explicandi* though critical for the hermeneutical task are, however, incomplete without the *subtilitas applicandi*. The last not only demands the validity of the first two *subtilitas* in light of the ethical and moral application of ideas, but also as to what are the ethical and moral values of Luther's texts vis-à-vis the Other, and the surrounding events, for us today. In the context of this paper, it demanded an application of a critical hermeneutic to explain the spoken and unspoken contents and contours, so that we attempt and project their application vis-à-vis the contemporary "Other(s)." This was especially critical because of the horrendous effective history of the previous hermeneutic and (im)moral practice of the dominant "Christian" majority on a religious and cultural Jewish minority. The acknowledged, and even perhaps unconscious application of Luther's text, and moral standing and voice, to achieve these immoral acts left behind a history of their interpretation and debilitating "effective (or effectual) history" (*Wirkungsgeschichte*). This is to say that to understand the "effective/effectual history" of these texts, is also a study of their *subtilitas applicandi.* More than this it also defines the self-knowledge/prejudices which also lie behind this *subtilitas applicandi* and which makes it so poignant for the hermeneutical task and its radicalizing vocation.

The application of these texts, epochs, or events, have to be of value and must therefore be understood as being applicable to the present situation as well. For according to Gadamer "... if the heart of the hermeneutical problem is that the same tradition must always be understood in a different way, the problem, logically speaking, is that of the relationship between the universal and the particular."[81] This has a direct bearing on the task behind this project, namely, a way of radicalizing the Reformation. We must go beyond both the sanctification of the Reformation texts and events for generating doctrinal and dogmatic material and certitude, and also the self-justificational attitude we develop towards these Reformation texts. Rather the task should be to provide radical and critical clues for our own self-understanding in our situation and in our time for a more virtuous approach to the contemporary "Other;" so that justice and peace prevails and that with Aimè Cèsaire we can say:

> for it is not true that the work of man is done
>
> that we have no business being on earth
>
> that we parasite the world

[81] *Truth and Method*, 278.

that it is enough for us to heel to the world whereas the work of man (sic) has only began
and man (sic) still must overcome all the interdictions wedged in the recesses of his fervor
and no race has a monopoly on beauty, on intelligence, on strength
and there is room for everyone at the convocation of conquest.[82]

[82] Aimé Césaire, *Notebook of a Return to the Native Land*, trans. Clayton Eshleman and Annette Smith (Middletown, CT: Wesleyan University Press, 2001), 44. This long poem was originally published in Paris in 1939 and again in 1947 as *Cahier d'un retour au pays natal*.

MIGRATIONS OF ENCHANTMENT IN THE RADICAL REFORMATION: THE UNDOING OF A MATERIAL AND NATURAL WORLD

Karl Koop

The idea that the modern world has become disenchanted probably took its most enduring form in Max Weber's *The Protestant Ethic and the Spirit of Capitalism*, first published in 1904-05.[1] Weber believed that in the modern period the world had lost some of its allure and had become lifeless.[2] He saw this as a part of a great historic secularizing process tied to capitalism, the industrial revolution, the rise in science and technology, and the rationalistic world view of the Enlightenment.[3] He also linked the notion of disenchantment with the sixteenth-century Reformation, particularly the way in which Protestants rejected the sacramental world as a means of salvation and upheld a more intellectualized religion, in which mystical and spiritual forces were removed from common life.[4]

Weber was neither the first nor the last to draw connections between the Reformation and secularism. In the nineteenth century the Spanish philosopher, Jaime Balmes linked Protestant perspectives to the ascendant secular-

[1] Max Weber, *The Protestant Ethic and the Spirit of Capitalism*, trans. Talcott Parsons (London: Unwin Hyman, 1989).

[2] Patrick Sherry, "Disenchantment, Re-enchantment, and Enchantment," *Modern Theology* 25 (July 2009): 369. Sherry notes that the term had been used in various grammatical forms by writers before Weber, such as Wieland and Schiller, the latter using the verb "*entzaubern*" to mean something like "losing its magic."

[3] Sherry, "Disenchantment, Re-enchantment, and Enchantment," 370.

[4] Alexandra Walsham, "The Reformation and 'The Disenchantment of the World' Reassessed," *The Historical Journal* 51 (June 2008): 498.

ism of his day,[5] while Weber's contemporary, Ernst Troeltsch, viewed the Reformation as a catalyst of modernity, although in an indirect fashion. More recently these perspectives on the Reformation have proven to be remarkably resilient and have re-emerged in revised iterations in works such as Charles Taylor's *A Secular Age* and Brad Gregory's *The Unintended Reformation*.[6]

Nevertheless, Weber's views have also come under serious critique. In her review essay examining the relationship between the Reformation and the process of "disenchantment," Alexandra Walsheim attributes much of the recent criticism to the late Robert Scribner, who argued that the Reformation played a rather marginal role in the process of desacralization. Attending to the sensibilities of popular culture, Scribner found significant continuities between various medieval and Protestant mentalities, concluding that Protestantism "did not entirely dispense with holy persons, places, times, or objects; it engendered rituals and even a magic of its own."[7] Walsham's perspectives have been influenced by Scribner but also take into account the notion of a "Long Reformation," where religious reform and renewal extends over several centuries. Walsham sees dynamic processes evolving over a lengthy period of time whereby "the early Reformation (both Catholic and Protestant) grew out of and embodied a moment of scepticism and "rationalism" that slowly faded, giving way in later generations to a fresh receptiveness to the supernatural and sacred."[8] She contends that theories of history that privilege linear and mono-directional historical trajectories need to be rejected in favour of reciprocal and dialectical patterns, which also may be found in other periods of history, not just the Reformation era.[9]

This chapter begins with the assumption that dialectical patterns of enchantment are observable throughout Christian history, with the late medie-

[5] Ephraim Radner, "The Reformation Wrongly Blamed," *First Things* (June/July, 2012): 47-48.

[6] Charles Taylor, *A Secular Age* (Cambridge, MA: The Belknap Press , 2007); Brad S. Gregory, *The Unintended Reformation: How a Relgious Revolution Secularized Society* (Cambridge, MA: The Belknap Press, 2012).

[7] Walsheim, "The Reformation and `The Disenchantment of the World' Reassessed," 500.

[8] Ibid., 527.

[9] Ibid., 527-28.

val and Reformation eras demonstrating an inward turn. I use the term "enchantment" to refer to the sacred and to the way in which the divine is present in the world. In focussing on Anabaptism in the Radical Reformation, I argue that the Anabaptists did not disregard the idea of the sacred but tended to shift its location away from the realm of nature and materiality to the realm of anthropology and ecclesiology. There were certain gains that were achieved in this shift. Nevertheless, I contend that there was a certain kind of undoing in that the Anabaptists, together with the other Reformers, lost the conceptual framework for thinking positively about the material and natural world. Modern day inheritors of the Reformation do well to retrieve theological frameworks that undergird the material and natural world, particularly in light of the challenges facing our modern civilization—the desecration of land, water, and air, and the over-consumption of resources. Such retrieval would be in keeping with certain theological traditions of the early Christian era and with the spirit of the Reformation, which initially called for faithfulness to the biblical witness and the importance of addressing the pressing issues of the times.

1. Dialectical Patterns of Enchantment

Already in the first centuries of Christian experience, the sacred was subjected to dialectical patterns of enchantment. Christianity was birthed in the context of the Greco-Roman world, influenced by Neo-Platonism, which tended to negate the natural and material world. In such an intellectual environment, influenced by their Jewish heritage, Christians advocated a distinctive world-affirming view that their neighbors found shocking and offensive. Christians believed that all temporal materiality, all nature, while not yet perfected, was the ground of God's self-revelation, worthy of reverence and redemption. "The world was not an evil imprisonment, not a dispensable illusion, but the bearer of God's glory."[10] The "Word made flesh" at Christ's incarnation was "an unparalleled development" in world history, representing

[10] Richard Tarnas, *The Passion of the Western Mind: Understanding the Ideas that have Shaped our World View* (New York: Ballantine Books, 1991), 127.

"not nature's antithesis, but its fulfillment."[11] The Christian theme of resurrection held forth the promise that all of humankind, all materiality and all physical reality would be swept up in a final consummation. Nothing would be left out of God's perfecting salvation.

Yet this affirmation of the natural and material world was not embraced by all Christians. Under the influence of Neo-Platonism, many believers viewed the body as the residence of sin and evil, while the human soul was the exclusive recipient of divine redemption. The attention to trans-worldly reality reinforced a metaphysical dualism that in turn gave way to a moral asceticism, which augmented the mystical and the interior dimension of Christian experience.[12] The most radical expression of this metaphysical dualism was probably held by Gnostic thinkers who refused to embrace both the created order and its creator. So the followers of Marcion rejected the notion of the incarnation of the divine logos and posited a deep gulf between "between the beneficent Father of Jesus Christ and the malignant demiurge of creation."[13]

Gnostic tendencies were found especially among Christian communities of asceticism, but they were also met with strong opposition by Christian apologists such as Irenaeus (c. 130-202) who fiercely argued that the material world was a direct product of God's creation, and that the body was the essential link between the material and the immaterial world.[14] In the writings of Athanasius (c. 296-373) and Cyril of Alexandria (c. 376-444) the im-

[11] Tarnas, *The Passion of the Western Mind*, 139.

[12] Ibid., 140-148. Of course not all forms of asceticism accentuate this metaphysical dualism. For a discussion on this, see Philip LeMasters, "Incarnation, Sacrament, and the Environment in Orthodox Thought," *Worship* 81 (May 2007): 219-221.

[13] Jan Milic Lochman, *The Faith We Confess: An Ecumenical Dogmatics*, trans. David Lewis (Philadelphia: Fortress Press, 1984), 59.

[14] John D. Zizoulas, "The Early Christian Community," in Bernard McGinn, John Meyendorff, and Jean Leclercq, eds., *Christian Spirituality: Origins to the Twelfth Century* (New York: The Crossroad, 1997), 1:36. See, for example, selections of Irenaeus's work *Against Heresies* in Cyril C. Richardson, ed. and trans., *Early Christian Fathers*, The Library of Christian Classics (Philadelphia: The Westminster Press, 1953), 1: 358-397.

portance of the incarnation as the means of salvation was likewise upheld,[15] while early Rules of Faith and creedal expressions, along with the Christological formulas articulated at Nicaea, Constantinople, and Chalcedon, all affirmed the created order together with the human nature of Christ as the means of salvation.

Further, most of these confessional statements reflected an eschatological hope that rested upon the conviction that the body would experience resurrection.[16] In these various ways a major element within Christianity brought a "materialistic" world view to the Greco-Roman world through which the material acquired decisive significance while seeking to maintain a healthy distance from pantheism. In reaction to the rhetoric of the iconoclasts who sought to eradicate the visual dimension of liturgical experience, John of Damascus (c. 676-749) defended the use of icons and linked their presence with the incarnation: "I do not worship matter. I worship the Creator of matter who became matter for my sake, who willed to take his abode in matter, and who through matter wrought my salvation."[17]

This movement that valued the material and the natural world was not linear or mono-directional. Some very influential thinkers of the classical period tended to polarize spirit and matter, body and soul, and the propensity to view all of nature as corrupt, lived on.[18] Within the Alexandrian School, particularly in the thought of Origen, the distinction between spirit and matter persisted as it also did in the "uplifting" mystical spirituality of Pseudo-

[15] Athanasius, "The Incarnation of the Word" in Philip Schaff and Henry Wallace eds, *Nicene and Post-Nicene Fathers of the Christian Church* (Grand Rapids, MI: Wm. B. Eerdmans, 1953), 4: 36-67. Alexander Schmemann refers to Cyril of Alexandria as a central teacher of the incarnation as well. See Alexander Schmemann, *Historical Road to Orthodoxy*, translated by Lydia W. Kesich (Crestwood, NY: St. Vladimir's Seminary Press, 1977), 124-136.

[16] Zizioulous, "The Early Christian Community," 36.

[17] John of Damascus, *On the Divine* Images 1.16, trans. by David Anderson (Crestwood, NY: St. Vladimir's Seminary Press, 1980), 23, quoted in Leonid Ouspensky, "Icon and Art," *Christian Spirituality*, 384.

[18] Tarnas, *The Passion of the Western Mind*, 139.

Dionysius.[19] Under the lingering influence of Neo-Platonism and Manichaean dualism, the distinction between spirit and matter continued with Augustine, who clearly exemplified an interior otherworldly religiosity, even while affirming God's gracious fecundity in bringing forth creation.[20] Augustine's more inward and otherworldly spirituality dominated much of the Middle Ages and would only be seriously challenged after the West came under Aristotelian influence. In the thirteenth century Thomas Aquinas asserted that nature itself could reflect divine wisdom and that it had "inherent religious value"; it was "not just as a dim reflection of the supernatural."[21] This "worldliness" came about through a deep reverence of the incarnate Word.[22] While not forsaking the transcendent in Augustine's theology, Thomas Aquinas reminded Christians of the intrinsic worth and dynamism of this world and that everything should be viewed as good in so far as it existed.[23]

Thomas' "worldly" influence continued beyond the high Middle Ages, but it was also met by counter forces that would come to dominate late medieval and Reformation thinking. One of those forces was a return of Platonism, ushered in by Petrarch's renaissance, and humanist desire to re-educate Europe.[24] Another force was a wave of mystical fervor that swept the Rhineland environs involving thousands of women and men, both lay persons and spiritual elites. The mystics were intensely devotional, Christ-centred, and ultimately concerned about achieving inner union with God.[25]

The fountainhead of German mysticism was Meister Eckhardt, whose metaphysical vision involved partaking of the divine nature, experiencing divini-

[19] See Paul Rorem, "The Uplifting Spirituality of Pseudo-Dionysius" in *Christian Spirituality*, 132-149

[20] Tarnas, *The Passion of the Western Mind*, 148, 154. For a further discussion on Augustine's inward turn, see Jürgen Moltmann, *The Spirit of Life: a Universal Affirmation*, trans. by Margaret Kohl (Minneapolis: Fortress Press, 1992), 89-93.

[21] Tarnas, *The Passion of the Western Mind*, 180.

[22] Josef Pieper, "Of the Goodness of the World," *Orate Fratres* 25 (September 1951): 435.

[23] Ibid., 434.

[24] Tarnas, *The Passion of the Western Mind*, 209-219.

[25] Ibid., 197.

zation, and leading a sanctified life involving love and service.[26] Werner Packull has observed that Eckhardt's mystical Christianity transcended ordinary sense perception, in which all externals, including the body, were to be subordinated to the soul. "For only in total detachment (Gelassenheit) from all creatureliness could the `inner Word' be apprehended."[27] Eckhardt warned believers not to be dependent on the outer and the sensual. Those who displayed false confidence in the mediating power of the sacraments, for example, would never know Christ in truth. Salvation, according to Ekhardt's theologia mystica, involved a gradual disengagement from externals climaxing in union with the Divine.[28] Since mystical union included a unity of wills, following after Christ meant that the Christian life included strong ascetic and moralistic overtones.[29] Meister Eckhardt gave the mystical tradition distinct definition but later mystics, such as Johannes Tauler and the author of the *Theologia Germanica*, were clearly influenced by Eckhardt, establishing his mysticism as the devotional lingua franca in the late medieval period. Treading the same path was the *devotio moderna* of the Brethren of the Common Life, whose best known leader was Thomas a Kempis, the likely author of *The Imitation of Christ*. In this devotion, great emphasis was put on private prayer, introspection, the practice of journaling, and contempt for the world (*contemptus mundi*).[30]

In the sixteenth century Martin Luther's reforming interests in many ways countered the inward turn of the *via mystica*. Luther believed that Christians were called into worldly vocations and were meant to engage social, economic, and political realities. Nevertheless, Luther had a well-informed in-

[26] Ibid.

[27] Werner O. Packull, *Mysticism and the Early South German-Austrian Anabaptist Movement 1525-1531* (Scottsdale, PA: Herald Press, 1977), 22.

[28] Packull, *Mysticism*, 23. Martha Kirkpatrick takes a somewhat different view of Eckhart as well as the mystic, Hildegard of Bingen. See "`For God so loved the World'": An Incarnational Theology," *Anglican Theological Review* 91 (2009): 197 and 211.

[29] Packull, *Mysticism*, 24.

[30] Taylor, *A Secular Age*, 70.

terest in German and Latin mysticism and even published versions of the *Theologia Germanica*.[31] The internalizing and individualizing emphasis in mysticism would find an echo in Luther's emphasis on personal faith and the individual conscience.[32] Moreover, while Luther sought to retain the corporeal reality of the divine presence in the Eucharistic ritual, his confidence that material elements might themselves have saving power, by comparison with the established Roman Catholic doctrine, was diminished. This shifting away from viewing material reality as a means of grace was accentuated further by Ulrich Zwingli, who viewed the Eucharist as a memorial meal, and who understood spiritual baptism, not water baptism, as the primary "means by which individuals were drawn into the orbit of divine salvation."[33]

These desacralizing tendencies in Luther and Zwingli found wide-spread approval among sixteenth century reformers who not only questioned medieval understandings of baptism and Eucharist but also took critical aim of the entire sacramental world view that had assumed that the material world was holy and divinely infused. Material culture became suspect such that "altars, priestly vestments, church music, paintings, and sculptures were stripped down in a surge of iconoclasm that took these `signs and wonders' of God for idols."[34] In this way, the Protestant Reformers chipped away at the sacred as it had been experienced for centuries, and moved in the direction of favoring a spirituality more subjective than what had been experienced in the Thomistic era that counted on the natural and material world to convey divine grace. With the Reformer's increased distinction between the Creator and creature, between divine transcendence and the world's contingency, the early moderns of the Reformation era increasingly viewed nature's character as mundane. In these developments, according to Richard Tarnas, there was also

[31] On Luther's relation to mysticism see Steven Ozment, *The Age of Reform 1250-1550: An Intellectual and Religious History of Late Medieval and Reformation Europe* (New Haven: Yale University Press, 1980), especially 239-244.

[32] See Ulrich Duchrow, "Hat Luther den Individualismus der Moderne mitverursacht?" in this series.

[33] Timothy George, *Theology of the Reformers* (Nashville: Broadman Press, 1988), 139.

[34] Regina Mara Schwartz, *Sacramental Poetics at the Dawn of Secularism: When God Left the World* (Stanford: Stanford University Press, 2008), 11.

increasing emphasis given to humanity's dominion over creation contributing to humanity's sense of superiority over the natural and material world.[35]

2. Anabaptists and the Sacred

The Anabaptists embraced the Protestant Reformation program with its message of salvation by grace through faith but were critical of the notion that grace could be received through the church's sacraments. Influenced by the late medieval mystical traditions, they also incorporated in their theology an inward and other-worldly orientation, which was accentuated in times of persecution. In their reforming efforts they did not desacralize the world, but re-imagined the sacred, for the most part shifting its location away from a natural and material jurisdiction to the realm of the anthropological and the ecclesiological. In some of their commentaries on the Creed, the Anabaptists interpreted the theology of the first article in personal and subjectivist

[35] Tarnas, *The Passion of the Western Mind*, 241. Jan Milic Lochman suggests that in Luther's interpretation of the Creed in his Small Catechism of 1529, there was a noticeable shift in emphasis from affirming the Creator of heaven and earth to focussing attention on the confessing subject. He states that "by transferring the main weight of the confession from faith in the Creator to the vital interests of the confessing Christian, characteristic tendencies in Protestantism were reinforced that led in the direction of a privatization of the faith in creation. It also lent credence to the assumption that the world had been created exclusively for humanity's sake, as our object, our domain" (Lochmann, *The Faith We Confess*, 67). Lochman's perspective needs further analysis in light of Luther's other writings, and perhaps does not sufficiently take into account the genre of catechetical writing that by nature will be more personal and individualistic in tone. I wish to thank Ulrich Duchrow for drawing my attention to this observation.

terms.[36] Among others, a two-kingdom theology encouraged dualistic thinking leading some to associate natural creation with the fallen world.[37]

To be fair, there were Anabaptists from the South German environs who believed that the divine was at work through the natural order, particularly in their teaching on "The Gospel of All Creatures." The teaching "incorporated the medieval assumption of a hierarchical chain of being. God had structured creation so that the lower orders found their fulfillment in submission to the rule of the higher."[38] Thus animals were ordained to serve humanity, while humanity was created to serve God. Hans Hut, a key proponent of this "Gospel" likely drew his ideas from Thomas Müntzer, as well as conclusions drawn from Genesis 1:28, where humankind was instructed to subdue and have dominion over creation. Hut examined the world of nature, convinced that it was a source of revelation, and that "the principle of fulfillment through suffering [was] revealed in every creature."[39] As Werner Packull has

[36] See, for example, Anabaptist interpretations of the creed, such as Hubmaier's "Twelve Articles in Prayer Form," in H. Wayne Pipkin and John Howard Yoder, trans. and eds., *Balthasar Hubmaier: Theologian of Anabaptism* (Scottsdale, PA: Herald Press, 1989), 235; Leonard Schiemer, "The Apostles Creed: An Interpretation," in Cornelius J. Dyck, ed., *Spiritual Life in Anabaptism* (Scottsdale, PA: Herald Press, 1995), 31-32; "A Confession of Faith by Jörg Maler," in Karl Koop, ed., *Confessions of Faith in the Anabaptist Tradition 1527-1660* (Kitchener, ON: Pandora Press, 2006), 38-39.

[37] Thomas Finger, "An Anabaptist/Mennonite Theology of Creation," in *Creation and the Environment: An Anabaptist Perspective on a Sustainable World*, ed. Calvin Redekop (Baltimore: Johns Hopkins University Press, 2000), 154. For other perspectives on Anabaptism and creation, see other essays in the volume by Redekop as well as Calvin Redekop, "Mennonites, Creation and Work," *Christian Scholar's Review* 22 (June 1993): 348-66; Calvin Redekop, "Toward a Mennonite Theology and Ethic of Creation," *Mennonite Quarterly Review* 60 (July 1986): 387-403; Royden Loewen, "The Quiet on the Land: The Environment in Mennonite Historiography," *Journal of Mennonite Studies* 23 (2005), 151-64; Dan Epp-Tiessen, ed., *Vision: A Journal for Church and Theology,* vol. 9 (Spring 2008), entire issue. I wish to thank Kathy McCamis, a student at Canadian Mennonite University, for making me aware of this literature.

[38] Packull, *Mysticism*, 69.

[39] Rollin Stely Armour, *Anabaptist Baptism: A Representative Study* (Scottsdale, PA: Herald Press, 1966), 81. For an extended discussion on "The Gospel of All Creatures,"

noted, "it was Hut's achievement that he gave the external witness of the creatures a greater autonomous role."[40] The divine order that was infused in nature revealed "the principle of redemptive and restorative suffering" whereby creation "not only mirrored the omnipotence of the Creator, but revealed His redemptive activity."[41] For a time Hut even emphasized that the witness in nature was a reflection "of the crucified Son and of the cathartic quality of suffering."[42] Followers of Hut, such as Leonhard Schiemer and Hans Schlaffer, assimilated some of Hut's ideas, as did Pilgram Marpeck who linked "the suffering of the creatures to the suffering of Christ and the believer."[43]

For most Anabaptists, however, the divine was not to be found in nature, but in the realm of anthropology and ecclesiology. Hans Denck, for instance, maintained that the sacred was lodged within humanity that contained a divine spark, presupposing divine immanence, leading to cooperation between the human and divine in the process of salvation.[44] Denck could not accept the Lutheran teaching of salvation *via iustitia aliena* of Christ, nor the formula *simul iustus et peccator* which conflicted with his understanding of gradual deification or divinization. Denck's internalizing religion also challenged sacramentalism, which insisted on grace being transmitted to the believer by external means. Grace, according to Denck, "was the divine Word itself ef-

see Armour, *Anabaptist Baptism*, 64-68, 71-74, 80-83. For a rendition of Hut's teaching see his "The Mystery of Baptism," in Walter Klaassen, ed., *Anabaptism in Outline: Selected Primary Sources* (Scottsdale, PA: Herald Press, 1981), 48-53.

40 Packull, *Mysticism*, 70.

41 Packull, *Mysticism*, 70.

42 Packull, *Mysticism*, 70.

43 Neal Blough, *Christ in Our Midst: Incarnation, Church and Discipleship in the Theology of Pilgram Marpeck* (Kitchener, ON: Pandora Press, 2007), 32. The teaching on "The Gospel of All Creatures" probably extended to the Marpeck circle, although in a reduced form. For example, see in "A Confession of Faith by Jörg Maler (1554) according to the Treasures of the Holy Scriptures," in Koop, *Confessions of Faith in the Anabaptist Tradition*, 38-39.

44 Discussion on the divine spark, for example, can be seen in Denck's essay, "Concerning True Love," in *The Spiritual Legacy of Hans Denck: Interpretation and Translation of Key Texts*, by Clarence Bauman (New York: E. J. Brill, 1991), 182-203.

fecting a transformation in the sinner and enabling him to imitate Christ's holy example."[45] The divine Word, which Denck located within the believer, was the logical corollary leading to outward action. Not some outer reality, but the inner Word was the ontological basis for holiness and a life of discipleship, which mirrored actual righteousness, rather than imputed righteousness of a Lutheran kind. As the inner reality of the believer was being transformed in union with Christ, so the outward expression of the Christian life was placed in conformity with the life of Christ through the power of the Holy Spirit.[46]

A similar theological trajectory existed among first generation Anabaptists in the Low Countries. A starting presupposition among these radical reformers, however, was not the belief in the presence of a divine spark within every human being, but the conviction that earthly flesh was thoroughly corrupted due to the fall that took place in the Garden of Eden when Adam and Eve disobeyed God. With this belief and consequences of the fall, these Anabaptists questioned how a Savior with an earthly body could be an adequate sacrifice, strong enough to overcome the powers of evil that now dominated the world and all flesh.[47] Melchior Hoffman, who brought Anabaptists ideas to the Low Countries in the first place, concluded that Jesus Christ had indeed become incarnate in bodily form but his flesh must have had heavenly origins. The Word had indeed become flesh but could not have received his flesh from Mary, since all human flesh must have been corrupted through the fall. Only heavenly flesh, Hoffman reasoned, was sufficiently strong enough to overcome the powers of evil.[48]

These ideas were picked up by second generation leaders in the north, Menno Simons and Dirk Philips, even as they attempted to maintain a Chalcedonian Christology, affirming both Christ's deity and humanity. Like Hoffman, Menno Simons and Dirk Philips asserted that the flesh of Jesus

[45] Packull, *Mysticism,* 52.

[46] For a summary of Denck's thought, see Packull, *Mysticism*, 35-61.

[47] Karl Koop, *Anabaptist-Mennonite Confessions of Faith: The Development of a Tradition* (Kitchener, ON: Pandora Press, 2004), 92.

[48] See Melchior Hoffman's "Truthful Witness," in Klaassen, *Anabaptism in Outline*, 27-28.

could not be associated with Mary's flesh in any way because of its earthly association. Jesus was conceived in Mary, not of Mary.[49] This had implications for believers and their transformed status. Through the experience of the new birth, believers became partakers of Christ's nature, experiencing a form of divinization and regeneration. The regenerated life of the Christian had its ontological basis in the heavenly flesh of Christ; for this flesh indeed had the power to be truly transformative. While human beings were born with a corruptible nature, the rebirth provided the basis for outward holiness and faith active in love. With God becoming human, through the power of the Holy Spirit, humanity could become divine, receive eternal life and become clothed with divine moral characteristics.[50] The corporate expression of this new humanity was the community of saints, the church, a regenerated body "without spot or wrinkle," maintaining Christ-like ethical standards guaranteed through the practice of church discipline. Salvation was experienced through participation in this community with its liturgy, ceremonies, and discipline. But here the sacramental dimension was not as much present in the specific elements of bread, wine, liturgy, and discipline. Far more, Menno Simons and Dirk Philips viewed the church itself as sacrament.

On the question of the individual sacraments, such as the Eucharistic meal, Anabaptists everywhere were in essential agreement with Zwingli in their denial that the elements mediated grace. Ostensibly, the meal was seen a memorial of Christ's death, and a sign of fellowship and Christian unity. Commonly citing the Creed, they noted that Christ had ascended into heaven and that he presently sits at the right hand of the Father. Thus, Christ's flesh and blood were not actually present in the elements themselves. Against the backdrop of the Roman Catholic Church espousing a doctrine of transubstan-

[49] See, for example, Menno Simons, "The Incarnation of our Lord," in *The Complete Writings of Menno Simons,* trans. Leonard Verduin, ed J. C. Wenger (Scottsdale, PA: Herald Press, 1984), 785-834; Dirk Philips, "The Incarnation of our Lord," in *The Writings of Dirk Philips 1504-1568*, trans. Cornelius J. Dyck, William E. Keeney, and Alvin J. Beachy (Scottsdale, PA: Herald Press, 1992), 134-151. Although this view deviated from classical formulations, it was consistent with the common wisdom of the day that assumed that women did not contribute anything biologically of themselves to their offspring.

[50] Koop, *Anabaptist-Mennonite Confessions of Faith*, 100.

tiation, the Anabaptists stated in countless court records that the bread was only bread, the wine only wine.[51] But in practice and beyond the reaches of courtroom rhetoric, most Anabaptists did not view the elements lightly. They wrote extensively about the profound meaning of the Supper and they participated in the meal with reverence and deep devotion.

Pilgram Marpeck stood out as an Anabaptist who actually came very close to Roman Catholic teaching, articulating a view that the sacraments themselves involved mediating grace. Marpeck believed that the elements of water, bread, and wine were physical windows and doors which participated in the divine and through which the divine could be known. They were "physical means of growth into divine love and the mature spiritual life.[52] Yet, among the Anabaptists, Marpeck's perspective was unique. Anabaptists were far more likely to view the elements as subordinate to the more important experience of the believer that takes place inwardly. Conrad Grebel, writing within a Swiss context, referred to outer baptism as that which signifies the Christian walk more deeply rooted in inner baptism.[53] Other Anabaptists inferred that the elements were sacred in a spiritual sense. Menno Simons, for instance, stated that the Supper was a "holy sacramental sign," "an emblem of Christian love," and "a communion of the flesh and blood of Christ," which brought about a spiritual communion with Christ.[54] Likewise, Dirk Philips referred to the eating in the communion meal as a spiritual activity, not of the body but of the "mouth of the soul."[55] What these Anabaptists had in common was not a belief that the body of Christ was physically present in water, bread, and wine, but that Christ was in fact truly present in the believ-

[51] C. Arnold Snyder, "Was the Bread only Bread, and the Wine only Wine? Sacramental Theology in Five Anabaptist Hymns," *Conrad Grebel Review* 24 (Fall 2006): 26.

[52] C. Arnold Snyder, *Anabaptist History and Theology: An Introduction* (Kitchener, ON: Pandora Press, 1995), 362. See Pilgram Marpeck, "A Clear and Useful Instruction," in *The Writings of Pilgram Marpeck*, trans and ed. William Klassen and Walter Klaassen (Scottsdale, PA: Herald Press, 1978), 69-106.

[53] See Klaassen, *Anabaptism in Outline*, 164-65; 191-92.

[54] Ibid., 208-210.

[55] Ibid., 206.

er. This supposition became the basis of a further understanding of the corporate body of Christ, the church, as the primary locus of Christ's presence.

In the Roman Catholic Church, the sacraments were viewed in the elements of the Mass, in physical images, in the juridical structures of the church, in the priesthood, and in the magisterium. This, together with other Protestants, the Anabaptists repudiated. Nevertheless, they believed that the people of God, the visible community gathered locally, were members of Christ's body. Far from being a metaphor for the church, the language concerning the body of Christ was intended as a literal description.[56] Christ was indeed present through the church together with its words and good deeds with the relation to Christ being one of incorporation.[57]

This idea of incorporation and living as members of Christ's body was especially prominent in the theology of Pilgram Marpeck, who grounded his ecclesiology in the incarnation. Marpeck believed that "not only did a good God bring a good creation into being, the centrality of the physical side of creation in the saving process was revealed, confirmed, and cemented by the incarnation."[58] Accordingly, salvation came through the humanity of Christ with the clearest expression of divine love taking place within the community of love, the church, which was understood as the "primary place of God's presence and action."[59] The church as the body of Christ was "a sacramental offer of God's grace, mercy, and salvation for all."[60] As in the incarnation, Marpeck believed that God's presence would continue to be offered "through the physical Body of Christ to individuals and to the world by means of external and visible testimonies, ceremonies, and acts of love."[61] Marpeck's logic was further drawn from the writings of the Gospel of John that included

[56] Snyder, *Anabaptist History and Theology*, 355.

[57] Brian Hamilton, "The Ground of Perfection: Michael Sattler on `the Body of Christ,'" in Abe Dueck, Helmut Harder, and Karl Koop, *New Perspectives in Believers Church Ecclesiology* (Winnipeg, MB: CMU Press, 2010), 143.

[58] Snyder, *Anabaptist History and Theology*, 361.

[59] Blough, *Christ in our Midst*, 246.

[60] Snyder, *Anabaptist History and Theology*, 362.

[61] Ibid..

Trinitarian dimensions. In the same way that the Word had become flesh, in Jesus the Word was "prolonged throughout history in the concrete life of the believing community through the power of the Holy Spirit."[62] As the Father had sent Jesus into the world, Marpeck reasoned, so also the church was now being sent into the world to be a witness to the world (John 20: 21-22) through worship, love, and service.[63]

This emphasis of the church as a sacramental body was also a part of the ecclesiology of Michael Sattler, a leader among the Swiss Anabaptists. Scholars in the past have tended to emphasize the voluntary aspect of willing disciples that constituted Swiss Anabaptism.[64] But as Brian Hamilton has noted, this definition of the Christian community fails to fully explain the essential necessity of the church for the Anabaptists. For Sattler, the church was essential because she was the body of Christ, "and because unity with Christ's body [was] itself the essence of salvation."[65] In this way reconciliation and the atoning work of Christ could not be separated from the life of the church. Sattler insisted on the union between Christ and the Christian community, what Augustine had referred to as "the *totus Christus, caput et membra*, the whole Jesus Christ, head and members."[66] For this reason, ethical issues, such as taking up the sword, or swearing oaths, could also not be set aside merely on the grounds that they were contrary to the teachings of Christ. More fundamentally, disobedience to Christ's teachings and example was problematic because such action destroyed the ontological and sacramental unity that was presumed when the believer was incorporated into Christ's body.

[62] Blough, *Christ in our Midst*, 246.

[63] Ibid., 245-46.

[64] Hamilton, "The Ground of Perfection," 143.

[65] Hamilton, "The Ground of Perfection," 143-144. For a compendium of Sattler's writings, see John Howard Yoder, ed. and trans., *The Legacy of Michael Sattler* (Scottsdale, PA: Herald Press, 1973).

[66] Hamilton, "The Ground of Perfection," 149. Hamilton is drawing on Augustine's "In Johannis Evangelium Tractatus", XXVIII.1, in *Corpus Christianorum Series Latina* 36, ed. R. Willems (New York: Brepols, 1954).

These teachings on the church illustrate the extent to which Anabaptists were willing to maintain a belief in the divine presence existent in the church, and they are yet another illustration of how they found ways of envisioning the sacred outside of the natural and the material world. Whether Anabaptists emphasized the holy presence of the divine in the individual, in ethical action, or in corporate expression, they did not disenchant the world as Weber might have it, but facilitated migrations of enchantment so as to re-enchant their world in a new format. In Marpeck's theology and in some other South German expressions of "The Gospel of All Creatures," we see glimpses of a theology affirming the natural and material world. Far more conspicuous in Anabaptist thought, however, was a heightened awareness of the sacred located in the realm of anthropology and ecclesiology. The sacred was not denied but present within the divinized new humanity, within the believer who had experienced the new birth, and within the body of Christ, the community of saints. If we were to take the time to contemplate the longer view, the "Long Reformation" of Anabaptism, we would most certainly see a continuation of this tradition, less attentive to the natural and the material world, and more deeply invested in anthropological and ecclesiological concerns. If we were to examine two of the most significant movements in which Mennonites were engaged from the seventeenth to the nineteenth centuries—the Dutch Collegiant and Pietist movements—we would see this ongoing attention to the anthropological and the ecclesiological; we would not see much emphasis on the natural and material world.[67]

The Protestant radicals brought a new sense of the divine presence in the realm of the individual and the communal. But their contributions raise questions as to what may have been lost in these migrations of the sacred. Could it be that the Anabaptists, along with other Protestants, lost the ability to speak constructively about the material and the natural world—a language

[67] See Andrew Fix, *Prophecy and Reason: The Dutch Collegiants in the Early Enlightenment* (Princeton: Princeton University Press, 1991); Robert Friedmann, *Mennonite Piety through the Centuries: Its Genius and its Literature* (Goshen, IN: The Mennonite Historical Society, 1949). The question of the extent to which Mennonites of the early enlightenment would have been attuned to aesthetics, or the extent to which later Pietists were influenced by German Romanticism, where nature becomes divinely infused, requires further examination.

that we desperately need in view of the environmental challenges facing us in our time (Thesis 35)?

3. Retrieving other Imaginaries

Our judgements of the Reformation era need to be measured with care. We must recall that the late middle ages and Reformation eras were periods in which Europeans were living with much anxiety. The anxiety was linked to a preoccupation with suffering and death that was brought on by the twin experiences of famine and plague. The agrarian crisis was so severe in the early fourteenth century that in some regions people resorted to cannibalism. The pandemics that swept Europe reached their climax with the bubonic plague of 1349 that brought death to about one third of Europe's population. Added to these calamities were economic and politic instabilities, and the savageries of warfare with the introduction of the gunpowder canon—all of which contributed to a morbid preoccupation with death.[68]

Because death brought every individual before the terrifying judgement seat of a holy and wrathful God, it was particularly moral anxiety that became the preoccupation of late medieval and early modern Christians. Luther's struggle to find a gracious God was thus clearly paradigmatic for his time. As Timothy George has put it, Luther was "just like everybody else, only more so."[69] His doctrine of justification by grace through faith was a direct response to the issues and concerns of his age. In addition to moral anxieties, Europe longed for alternative forms of community, the sharing of economic resources, and new social patterns of interaction as the emerging capitalist economy was calling into question older patterns of relationship. All of these concerns were at the forefront as both magisterial and radical reformers discussed the importance of personal justification by grace through faith, the divinization or rebirth of the individual, and the holy nature of the church.

[68] See Karl Georg Zinn, *Kanonen und Pest: Über die Ursprünge der Neuzeit im 14. und 15. Jahrhundert* (Opladen: Westdeutscher Verlag, 1989).

[69] George, *The Theology of the Reformers*, 23.

But our age is a different one. To be sure we long for a gracious God, and the questions about what it means to be authentically human or what it means to be authentically in community persist. But these longings and questions have changed in complexity in light of the challenges of globalization, growing economic disparities, and technological advances which appear to be beyond our control. At present we are also facing human engineered environmental devastation of unprecedented proportions. From the loss of glacier fields and the visible contamination of air and water to waste dumps and species extinction, "the planet is facing assaults from human activity as never before."[70] As Martha Kirkpatrick has put it, "the decline in the natural systems that sustain life and the rising aggregated social demand due to population and consumption increases are on a collision course. This makes the environmental crisis one of the most pressing and immediate problems of our age."[71]

We have recognized this crisis of our planet for decades, but many Christians have resisted the seriousness of the situation, either questioning the science of global warming, or perhaps dismissing environmental concerns because they appear to be politicized. Yet the preoccupation with science or politics is wrongly placed. Christians should not, in the first instance, be solely preoccupied in affirming or denying the science of global warming--as important as the science surely is. Nor should Christians, in the first instance, solely concern themselves with whether the environmental discussion is ideologically driven—as surely as it is driven from both the left and the right. It is far more important, in the first instance, that Christians begin to seriously ask what it means when the Bible tells them that "the earth is the Lord's and all that is in it" (Ps. 24:1). It is far more urgent for them to contemplate the importance of the stewardship of creation (Gen. 1: 26-28) and fully come to terms with the fundamental Christian conviction that God so loved the world that the "Word became flesh and lived among us" (Jn. 1:14). It is also imperative that they began to ask what it means when Scripture reveals that all of

[70] Martha Kirkpatrick, "`For God so Loved the World": An Incarnational Ecology," *Anglican Theological Review* 91 (2009): 191.

[71] Kirkpatrick, "`For God so Loved the World,'" 192.

creation longs for the redemption that is to come (Rom. 8; see Thesis 33 and 34).

Some pre-modern traditions seem to be in a better position than the Reformation traditions in addressing environmental concerns. In antiquity and in the middle ages we see a posture attentive to the natural and the material world that is less apparent in modern times. This is particularly the case when we consider the incarnational theology of Irenaeus, the embrace of the material and iconic in John of Damascus, or the appropriation of a natural theology in Thomas Aquinas, who sees all of reality as divinely infused. These ancient and medieval thinkers, along with their associates, had a profound sense of the divine in all of reality. It is therefore not surprising that contemporary theologians rooted in the pre-modern era continue to reflect positively on the material and natural world.

Philip LeMasters notes that "the incarnation of Jesus Christ is the lynchpin of Orthodoxy's view of the place of matter in our life before God."[72] Writing from the perspective of the Eastern Orthodox tradition, Alexander Schmemann has argued for the importance of seeing "the world as sacrament," and that now in modern times "the world must be recovered."[73] He maintains that everything that exists is a divine gift to humanity and everything that exists is intended to make God known and to bring about communion with God: "God blesses everything he creates, and, in biblical language, this means that he makes all creation the sign and means of his presence and wisdom, love and revelation. `O taste and see how gracious the Lord is.'"[74] After centuries of denominational absolutism, surely the Reformation traditions would be enriched if they would open themselves to learning from the Orthodox and Roman Catholic traditions, which have a better sense of God's presence in the natural and material world.

[72] LeMasters, "Incarnation, Sacrament, and the Environment in Orthodox Thought," 212.

[73] Alexander Schmemann, *The World as Sacrament* (London: Darton Longman & Todd, 1966), 12.

[74] Ibid., 14. For another eastern perspective, especially in light of the views of Gregory of Nazianzus see Sigurd Bergmann, *Creation Set Free: The Spirit as Liberator of Nature* (Grand Rapids: Eerdmans, 2005).

Yet perhaps there is also a constructive potential within the Reformation itself. In the sixteenth century, confidence in the Apostles Creed as a foundation for Christian understanding was an almost universal conviction among the varying proponents of reform.[75] Especially a re-reading of this text in light of its polemic against Gnostic tendencies in early Christianity might shed new light on the inherent value of God's creation, the affirmation of the humanity of Christ, the presence of the Spirit in the world, and the resurrection of the body. A further resource from the Reformation is the emphasis on peace, which was an important theme of a number of Anabaptist Reformers. If peace and reconciliation is at the heart of the message of Jesus,[76] the church will not only need to consider how the neighbor and enemy are to be treated as a faithful response to the cross, but they will also need to consider what it means to be reconciled and at peace with the whole of God's creation.

Finally, the theme of grace, which was a central motif for both magisterial and radical reformers, needs deeper consideration.[77] Norman Wirzba has observed that the language of grace is important because it points to our being called into intimacy with God, who is also intimately in communion with the world.[78] When we acknowledge this grace and live out our unique calling in God's image, "we learn to highlight, promote, and make concrete God's loving, life-giving intentions for the whole world."[79] Because "Christ is the one through whom all things are created (cf. John 1:3; Col 1:15-20), we should

[75] See Russel Snyder-Penner, "The Ten Commandments, the Lord's Prayer, and the Apostles' Creed as Early Anabaptist Texts," *Mennonite Quarterly Review* 68 (July 1994): 318. For Luther's view on the Creed, along with the Ten Commandments and the Lord's Prayer, see Martin Luther, "A Short Exposition on the Decalogue, the Apostles' Creed and the Lord's Prayer," in Bertram Lee Woolf, trans, and ed., *Reformation Writings of Martin Luther*, The Basis of the Protestant Reformation (New York: Philosophical Library Inc., 1953), 1:71.

[76] See, for instance, John Howard Yoder, *The Politics of Jesus: Vicit Agnus Noster*, 2nd edition (Grand Rapids: Eerdmans, 1994).

[77] For a study on grace in the radical reformation see Alvin J. Beachy, *The Concept of Grace in the Radical Reformation* (Nieuwkoop: B. De Graaf, 1977).

[78] Wirzba, "Agrarianism," 246.

[79] Ibid., 247.

not be surprised to learn that in Christ `all things' will also be redeemed."[80] If Wirzba is correct, then true faith is not about migrating into an otherworldly orientation. The language of grace is an invitation to draw nearer to the heart of the world "and there discover the life of God at work"[81] (Thesis 36). If the Reformers—both mainline and radical--were living in the present age, they would call for nothing less.

[80] Wirzba, "*Agrarianism*," 247-48. Jürgen Moltmann develops a cosmic Christology along these lines. See especially *The Way of Jesus Christ: Christology in Messianic Dimensions* (San Francisco: Harper SanFrancisco, 1990), 274-291.

[81] Wirzba, "*Agrarianism*," 250.

Heterotopic Citizenship: Luther's Two Kingdoms Theory in a Globalized Age

Wanda Deifelt

Martin Luther never developed a political theory, but his theology does inform the way Christians live in society, making it both public and political. Luther's "two kingdom theory" has often been misinterpreted to justify passivity and obedience toward civil authorities. At closer look, however, his theology applies to the everyday practices of politics, economics, and religious affairs. In the context of globalization, a Lutheran theology not only fosters citizenship as individual rights and responsibilities directed toward one's own nation, but it encourages heterotopic citizenship, that is, active participation in civil society that does not seek selfish interests but the common good, particularly the wellbeing of those considered "others" in society.

A limited understanding of citizenship as individual rights reduces the potential citizenship has in fostering civic responsibility, accountability, advocacy, and full participation in civil society. A Lutheran theology invites us to understand citizenship from a different angle: the Christian as a participant of the body politic, one who looks out not only for his or her own interests but for the wellbeing of all, on both local and global perspectives.

1. Martin Luther's Distinction of the Two Kingdoms

When Lutheran theologians talk about public theology (or the role of theology in the political arena), they usually refer to Martin Luther's "two kingdom theory."[1] Luther himself never employed the language of "kingdoms" (Reich) as a systematic or doctrinal topic. Rather, it served as a framework for viewing human life as it witnesses God's rule in conflict with the devil.[2]

[1] Luther, Martin, "Secular authority: to what extent it should be obeyed," in *Martin Luther: Selections from His Writings*, ed. John Dillenberger (New York: Random House, 1962), 363-402.

[2] For an ethical reflection on the consequences of Luther's views on the demonic as applied to the economy, see, for instance, Guillermo Hansen, "Money, Religion, and

Luther describes two realms or reigns in which God rules and the devil tries to subvert human faithfulness. One is the kingdom of the world, which is for those who are not Christians and therefore are governed by the law. The other is the kingdom of God, for those who are true believers and subjects to Christ. Although Christians belong to both realms, Luther states that unbelievers belong only to the world, while the kingdom of God is reserved only for true believers.

This description can be misconstrued to enforce the notion that there are two mutually exclusive types of citizenship, one heavenly (for Christians) and the other one earthly (for unbelievers). Luther employs a dualistic language to describe his theory, sometimes labelled as governments (Regiment), right-hand and left-hand, or heavenly and earthly. This binary language can create the false assumption that human beings are divided into two categories: those who are concerned with heavenly matters and those who are concerned with worldly affairs. A misunderstanding of the two kingdom theory might also lead to a hierarchical view of earth and heaven, with Christians paying little attention to the present reality as they hurry toward eternal bliss. Nothing could be further from Luther's theology.[3]

Luther says that the spiritual and earthly governments constitute two realms: one is guided by the law and the other is guided by the gospel, but both belong to God. They are not in opposition to one another, since both contend against the devil. God rules over both kingdoms (heaven and earth) and instituted two kinds of government. One is spiritual, through which humans become devout and righteous. This authority acts through the Word and without the sword, and righteousness is given through the gospel. The other is earthly government, through which humans are compelled to be righteous

Tyranny: God and the Demonic in Luther's Antifragile Theology." In Wanda Deifelt (ed.), *Market and Margins: Lutheran Perspectives (*Minneapolis: Lutheran University Press, 2014), 31-68.

[3] The superimposition of a dualistic model of an autonomous public order and a privatized religious devotion upon Luther's two kingdoms has been widely criticized. See, for instance, Ulrich Duchrow, *Global Economy: A Confessional Issue for the Churches?* Trans. David Lewis (Geneva: WCC Publications, 1987), 9-15; Karl H. Hertz, ed. *Two Kingdoms and One World: A Sourcebook in Christian Social* Ethics (Minneapolis: Augsbug, 1976); Craig L. Nessan, "Lutheran Social Ministriy: Reclaiming Luther's Two Kingdoms." *Missio Apostolica* vol. 11, issue n. 2, 2003, p. 91-98; James Arne Nestingen, "The Two Kingdom Distinction: An Analysis with Suggestion." *Word & World* vol. XIX, number 3, summer 1999, 268-275.

before the world. This transitory righteousness is accomplished through the sword, which makes sure that believers and unbelievers alike comply with the law, living in justice and peace.

These two realms, however, are interdependent. They testify that God rules over the whole world and does so in two ways. While the worldly kingdom is governed by secular authority and is made up of the law, lawmakers, and those who enforce the law, the spiritual kingdom is concerned with making true Christians. In his treatise Secular Authority: to what extent it should be obeyed, Luther states that every kingdom must have its own laws and regulations, but the worldly government has laws that extend no farther than to life and property and what is external upon earth.[4] The earthly government is supposed to regulate on issues that are secular, bodily, pertaining to the outer human being. Luther defends that "we must firmly establish secular law and the sword, and that no one may doubt that it is in the world by God's will and ordinance."[5] Furthermore, secular authorities cannot coerce people's spiritual belief. The sword is used to punish, keep order, and protect those that are of the kingdom of God, but it can never be used to impose religion and regulate matters of faith.

Here it is important to be reminded of Luther's distinction between law and gospel and active and passive righteousness. While the fulfillment of the law plays no role in terms of salvation, it still is necessary in the temporal kingdom. Through grace (passive righteousness), in an eschatological perspective, Christians are citizens of heaven. However, they are also citizens of this world, responsible for the questions and challenges of this age (active righteousness).

> Passive righteousness constitutes this relationship, but the active righteousness obeys the law that defines humanity… The believer's passive righteousness and the gospel provide motivation for living in proper relationship with God's creatures (Luther's earthly realm), and

[4] Civil righteousness (*iustitia civilis*) is promoted by the law and pertains only to the earthly realm (does not lead to salvation). Righteousness in Christ (*iustitia christiana*) is a given righteousness, consists of the forgiveness of sins, and is enduring.

[5] Luther, Martin, "Secular authority: to what extent it should be obeyed," in *Martin Luther: Selections from His Writings*, ed. Dillenberger, John (New York: Random House, 1962), 366.

the law guides the actions produced by that motivation, directing decisions on how to be righteous towards other creatures actively.[6]

Good governance is instituted by God as part of God's care for the entire creation. Of course, if the world were composed of real Christians, there would be no need for government or for the law because, as Luther saw it, the righteous do more than all that the law demands. Since, however, such true Christians are hard to find, all citizens are subject to the sword because they need the law to instruct, constrain, and compel them to do what is good. In the earthly realm, the law is not only good and necessary, but it is also God-given.

Although not always evident, Luther's distinction of the two kingdoms was a critique of the Christendom model prevalent during his day, when church and state were so entangled that there was almost no distinction of competences and attributes between them. The Christendom model held by European Catholicism followed the idea of Corpus Christianum – a society guided by Christian values in its social, political, and economic life. This notion united the Western Christian world under the Roman Catholic Church and its endeavors were supposed to lead to a religiously uniform community. In fact, however, it created a theocracy with Catholic clergy wielding political authority. The crusades, the fight against the Moors in Spain, the discovery of the Americas, and the Inquisition gave Christendom a new impetus.

The separation between church and state cannot be legitimately ascribed to Luther, but he draws a distinction of competences between the two. He does not, however, separate or define them as autonomous entities, since both are expressions of God's care and "neither is sufficient in the world without the other."[7] Luther establishes a comprehensive system which allocates specific roles and attributes to each realm. In doing so, he distinguishes each kingdom, its authority, and how they are to serve God. Luther claims that it is the responsibility of the political authorities to achieve economic, political, and social reforms that also affect the church; and it is the task of the church to

[6] Robert Kolb, "Luther's Hermeneutics of Distinctions: Law and Gospel, Two Kinds of Righteousness, Two Realms, Freedom and Bondage" in Robert Kolb, Irene Dingel and L'ubomír Batka, eds. *The Oxford Handbook of Martin Luther's Theology* (Oxford: Oxford University Press, 2014), 178-179.

[7] Luther, "Secular Authority," 371.

confront the political authorities of God's will.[8] Both kingdoms have a common foundation (God is the Lord) and a common goal (human wellbeing). "The church must be a watchdog in the world, called to discern whether churchly and worldly orders support or neglect the divine intention of maintaining a good creation."[9]

However, if one were to rule the world according to the gospel, putting aside secular law because all are baptized and Christian, society would turn into savage beasts. Luther does not envision the possibility of a truly Christian society or nation: "Therefore, it is out of the question that there should be a common Christian government over the whole world, nay even over one land or company of people."[10] For Luther, the idea that human beings join together to promote the common good out of their own volition is absurd. The paradox of human existence – a reality of already and not yet, of being sinner and saint at the same time – prevents humanity from doing good works solely out of human concern. The good done to others is done by God, who acts in and through us. Because human affairs are tainted by selfish interests, there is need for laws and government to assure the administration of justice. Ultimately, everything that belongs to the earthly realm, to our bodies, comes from the goodness of God.

> Every creature of God is good, and nothing to be rejected by the believing and those who know the truth. Among 'every creature of God' you must reckon not simply food and drink, clothes and shoes, but also government, citizenship, protection and administration of justice.[11]

Martin Luther's ethic is that Christians live not in themselves, but in Christ and in their neighbor.[12] It is an opening to the other. Our way of looking at the world expands to go beyond the interests of individuals, groups, or humanity in general, but to be concerned for the wellbeing of the entire creation. Christians live in Christ through faith and in their neighbor through love. By faith Christians are caught up beyond themselves into God. By love

[8] Altmann, Walter, *Luther and Liberation: a Latin American Perspective* (Minneapolis: Fortress Press, 1992).

[9] Gritsch, Eric, *A History of Lutheranism* (Minneapolis: Fortress Press, 2002), 105.

[10] Luther, "Secular Authority," 371.

[11] Luther, "Secular Authority," 378.

[12] Luther, Martin, "The freedom of a Christian," in *Martin Luther: Selections from His Writings*, ed. Dillenberger, John (New York: Random House, 1962), 79.

they descend beneath themselves into their neighbor. Although good works have no place when it comes to the merit of salvation, they are an intrinsic part of Christian life. While Christians are citizens of heaven, they are also citizens on earth and in this capacity they advocate for their neighbor and strive to promote the common good.

2. Citizenship

Commonly understood, a citizen is a native-born or naturalized person who owes allegiance to a particular country and is entitled to its protection. Citizenship can be both the relationships between a State and an individual citizen and the political relationship between the citizens themselves. To be vested with rights and privileges also includes having duties and meeting obligations. The actions, opinions, and virtues of citizens allow them to be viewed as members of society. Political theorists affirm that human beings are essentially social and political animals who join efforts and deliberate on how to live together. Ideally, the goal of citizens is to promote the common good by establishing justice in community, based on the fulfillment of those who share in this just arrangement.[13] In a democratic system, citizens are the free and equal participants of the body politic.

Historically, however, citizenship did not always imply full participation of all individuals in the social, economic or political decision-making processes.[14] Rather, going back to its Greek root, only free, propertied males who benefited from the patriarchal rules could be citizens. All others were subjects.

> In Aristotle, citizenship was viewed primarily in terms of duties – citizens were legally obliged to take their turn in public office, and sacrificed part of their private life to do so. In the modern world, influenced by liberalism, citizenship is increasingly viewed as a matter

[13] "Common good" *The Oxford Dictionary of Philosophy*. Simon Blackburn (Oxford University Press, 1996). *Oxford Reference Online*. Oxford University ress. <http://www.oxfordreference.com/views/ENTRY.html?subview=Main&entry=t98.e2728>

[14] Nash, Kate, "Between citizenship and human rights," *Sociology* (Dec 2009, Vol. 43, Issue 6), 1067-1083.

of rights – citizens have the right to participate in public life, but also the right to place private commitments ahead of political involvement.[15]

The tension between rights and responsibilities shows that citizenship refers not only to a legal status, but to the role one is expected to play in a particular society and the amount of agency that entails. If our modern notion of democracy implies that all citizens can be full and equal participants in the political process, that is not necessarily the case in other times and places. The French Revolution was instrumental in revisiting the notion of citizenship, showing that people who are governed by monarchs or military dictators cannot be called citizens, but rather subjects. Yet, not even the French revolution achieved the enfranchisement of all: women, for instance, were not given the same rights. The Declaration of the Rights of Man and the Citizen, which defined French citizenship after the revolution of 1789, pointedly failed to address the legal status of women.

The main argument for this exclusion was that the natural order of creation leads to natural rights.[16] Since Aristotle's civic-republican thought, it was presumed that political virtues and qualities were inherent only to men, who shared the same nature and capacity to think rationally. Because women were considered by nature inferior to men, they were excluded from such rights and responsibilities. The basis for this arrangement was that nature allocates specific traits to men and women, equipping males for the public world and females for childrearing and household chores. Jean-Jacques Rousseau's The Social Contract (1762), for instance, envisions a democracy where all citizens are presumed to be equal by nature (and invites them to draw a social contract to define how the state should be run).[17] Only men, however, are allowed to participate in this social contract. In his magnum opus on education, Rousseau similarly reduces women to the household: "she is made to please and to be subjugated, she ought to make herself agreeable to man in-

[15] Will Kymlicka "Citizenship" *The Oxford Companion to Philosophy* (Oxford University Press 2005). *Oxford Reference Online*. Oxford University Press. <http://www.oxford-reference.com/views/ENTRY.html?subview=Main&entry=t116.e400>

[16] Gabriella Bonacchi and Angela Groppi. *O dilema da cidadania: direitos e deveres das mulheres* (São Paulo: UNESP, 1995).

[17] Rousseau, Jean-Jacques. *Political writings*. Translated and edited by Frederick Watkins (New York: Thomas Nelson, 1953).

stead of arousing him."[18] Women are given the task of educating children in the virtues of citizenship, but while Emile serves the State, Sophie serves Emile.

In 1791, Olympe de Gouges used the Declaration of the Rights of Man and the Citizen as a blueprint to argue for equal rights, equal obligations, equal participation, and an equal share in wealth between both sexes. Her Déclaration des droits de la femme et de la citoyenne (Declaration of the Rights of Woman and Female Citizen) advocates that liberty and justice should be guaranteed in the public and private spheres. She invoked the argument of "natural rights," so popular in the eighteenth century, to refute the notion that women were by nature apolitical beings, belonging to the private sphere of the family household. Her plea for democracy was met with the guillotine.

> Liberty and justice consist of rendering to persons those things that belong to them; thus, the exercise of woman's natural rights is limited only by the perpetual tyranny with which man opposes her; these limits must be changed according to the laws of nature and reason.[19]

The main problem with the classic republican tradition of political thought, whether Aristotle, Machiavelli or Rousseau, is that the models of society they envision do not allow for the participation and representation of all. The principles of exclusion, usually based on the natural order, presume that some are better equipped for leadership than others. Throughout history, similar principles were invoked to create "others" who were kept at bay from the decision-making processes. This was the basis for keeping slaves, indigenous populations, and those who have been colonized as legal minors. To be "othered" is to be deemed socially, politically, or morally inferior. The social principles that justify the enfranchisement of some do not lead to dismantle the arguments that support the disenfranchisement of others.

[18] Rousseau, Jean-Jacques. *Emile, or On Education*. Translation by Allan Bloom (New York: Basic Books, 1979), 358. In this work, Rousseau dedicates four books to the education of Emile. Book five, the last in the sequence, addresses women's education by creating the character "Sophie" as Emile's companion.

[19] Olympe de Gouge's quote found in Rian VOET, *Feminism and citizenship* (London: Sage, 1998), 20.

3. Heterotopia

Michel Foucault developed the idea of heterotopia in contrast to the notion of utopia.[20] Whereas utopia presents society either in its perfected form or turned upside down, it nevertheless refers to unreal places. Utopias are never a mere escape of reality because they describe the qualities necessary to build desirable of near perfect communities or societies. Their role is to look forward and to give incentives to a better future. The current expectations, for a better life, take shape in the future, elsewhere. While it can function as a mental and spiritual engagement that makes the ideal society or community a concrete reality, it can also serve as an analogy for current yet never actualized expectations. Utopia, therefore, is a no-place and describes something that does not exist.

Heterotopia, on the other hand, describes places and spaces that function in non-hegemonic conditions. It is a real place that stands outside of known space – a space of otherness. While utopia is an unreal, idealized representation of an idea or image, heterotopia is the parallel space that contains the undesirable, that which is not here nor there. It has layers of meaning and relates to other places. Heterotopia is the parallel space that contains the unwanted bodies which make the utopia possible. Heterotopia is a physical approximation of utopia, a place that is not a place, existing on its own and in itself, and still open. Like a prison or cemetery, it is a parallel space that contains undesirable bodies to make a real utopian space possible.

If the early modern notion of space was one of emplacement, our current reality, according to Foucault, is marked by juxtaposition and simultaneity in which the near and far coexist side-by-side with the dispersed. In the words of Deleuze and Guattari, it is a time of "de-territorialization," when social, political, or cultural practices are severed from their native places and populations. For Foucault, "our experience of the world is less that of a long life developing through time than that of a network that connects points and intersects with its own skein."[21] While being, at the same time, bound to time

[20] Michel Foucault's article "Des Espace Autres," presented originally as a lecture in 1967, was published by the French journal *Architecture/Mouvement/Continuité* in 1984. See the translation in English at http://web.mit.edu/allanmc/www/foucault1.pdf.

[21] Foucault, 1.

and space, the very notion of territory or space has changed with globalization. The local community becomes part of the global culture, and vice-versa.

These cross-boundaries are experienced with more fluidity between sacred and profane places, personal and private space, social and professional arenas, cultural and useful areas, or leisure and work. "[W]e live inside a set of relations that delineate sites which are irreducible to one another and absolutely not superimposed on one another."[22] Our time is one in which space takes the form of relations among sites. Heterotopia describes the place and space that is simultaneously physical and mental, and that opens dimensions of perception or relationship to other places that are not always obvious. It can allow for escape, transformation, or revelation.

Foucault uses the example of one's reflection in the mirror for the duality and contradiction of the no-place and the real place. As a placeless place, the mirror is a metaphor for utopia because the image one sees does not exist (it is a virtual, unreal space that opens up behind the surface). But it is also heterotopia because the mirror is a real object that exerts a counteraction on the position one occupies (it shapes the way we see our own image). "Starting from this gaze that is, as it were, directed toward me, from the ground of this virtual space that is on the other side of the glass, I come back toward myself; I begin again to direct my eyes toward myself and to reconstitute myself there where I am."[23]

Through heterotopia, it is possible to understand the place of the other. It contains both the affirmation and the negation in an ongoing process of correlation. All binary systems that characterize Western civilization no longer exist in a hierarchical manner, but they coexist. If the one is in the other, they are not absolute but are interconnected. The other is not an isolated reality, rather a present and absent, real and unreal, close and distant being who challenges me and demands a response.

4. The role of the other

The argument for social exclusion is best articulated through a rhetoric that cannot be contested. Political theorists often employ the language of divine

[22] Foucault, 3.

[23] Foucault, 4.

will or the natural order of creation to explain social arrangements. The name of God – or Supreme Being and Author of all things – is invoked to justify why certain groups are superior to others (even when the language of superiority is only insinuated). Rousseau, for instance, argued that "The Supreme Being wanted to do honor to the human species in everything… While abandoning man to immoderate passions, He joins reason to these passions in order to govern them. While abandoning woman to unlimited desires, He joins modesty to these desires in order to constrain them."[24] Thus, while men receive reason from God, women are given modesty, and this places them differently in the world.

If the name of God is so easily invoked to justify discrimination, it is not surprising that Christianity itself plays a role in creating social "others." Because Christianity establishes a tension between the present reality and the world to come (eschaton), the church has often perceived itself as a gatekeeper for "celestial citizenship." In particular the motto "extra ecclesiam nulla salus" (outside the church there is no salvation), in the Christendom model, led to the presumption that salvation in the future leads to privileges already in the here and now ("earthly citizenship"). In addition, other Christian sectors overlook disenfranchisement in the present reality or brush oppression and discrimination aside in light of a future bliss. Such teachings do not support participatory citizenship and need to be placed under critique because they contradict the tenets of Christianity itself. As we will see in what follows, Christian teachings can foster a sense of collective responsibility and accountability that broaden the notion of citizenship itself.

If citizenship rights are used to articulate the social, political and economic exclusion of a significant portion of society, should the concept of citizenship be revisited? For instance, we know that what kept the Greek city-state in place were not only its rules and government, but also an ideology that assured the superiority of some over others. It is said that Greek citizens thanked the gods daily for being humans, not beasts; male, not female; Greeks, and not barbarians. The same is true for the Roman Empire. Representation was a privilege of the elite, the patricians and high court officials. The dichotomy and hierarchy of male over female, free over slave, culture over nature, public over private, production over reproduction, and mind over body ascertained privileges depending on which side of the spectrum one was located. So, if citizens self-identify as superiors, then citizenship

[24] Rousseau, *Emile,* 359.

exists so that others may be kept out or at bay. If, however, citizenship is not reduced to representation, but includes participation in the social and cultural fabric, then the notion of citizenship needs to address those who have historically been outcast.

Enrique Dussel develops an ethical system that takes otherness as a starting point.[25] Speaking from a liberationist approach, he envisions symmetric participation and transformative praxis as counter-models to the colonial, capitalist, and globalized ideologies that deem most peoples as "others." There is no ethics unless the cultural, social, and economic "others" are taken into consideration. For Dussel, ethics is the concern and the concrete actions carried out for the dignity and freedom of all the members of the community, and not only those who have been granted certain rights and privileges. Societies should be judged particularly for what is done to those who are not representatives of normative discourse or beneficiaries of structures of political and economic power.

Will Kymlicka approaches this debate from a liberal perspective, starting with the value of freedom, and defends group specified rights for ethnic minorities. Freedom implies not only free choice but also a context of choice, which is provided by cultural membership. Cultures determine how people view each other, which also determines how individuals view themselves. A proponent of diversity, Kymlicka contends that "in multi-nation states, some people's cultural membership can only be recognized and protected by endorsing group-differentiated rights within the state."[26] He does not argue for a universalistic theory of citizenship but for differentiated citizenship (apart from equal individual rights there are also group-specified rights), since certain rights can only be given to certain groups for the protection of their group membership.

> But it is increasingly recognized that the sorts of civic virtues required for a large pluralistic modern society, and the appropriate means to promote them, may differ from those required from those required from a small, homogeneous city-state. The goals of citizenship, and the means of promoting it, must take into account the levels and forms of ethnic and religious pluralism.[27]

[25] Enrique Dussel, *Ethics and Community* (Maryknoll: Orbis, 1988).

[26] Will Kymlicka, *Multicultural citizenship: A liberal theory of minority rights* (Oxford: Clarendon, 1995), 125.

[27] Will Kymlikca and Wayne Norman (ed.). "Introduction," *Citizenship in diverse societies* (New York: Oxford University Press, 2000), 8.

The fact that we live in ever changing pluralistic societies requires a broader understanding of citizenship. Dussel and Kymlicka offer different approaches on how citizenship rights can include those who have been excluded and made "others" in society. Although the language of rights and responsibilities serves this to a great extent, the issues of participation and advocacy cannot be addressed solely from this perspective. Here is where religious discourse and care might have an additional contribution to offer to the ongoing debate. By drawing from religious teachings that foment citizenship participation, the debate is not restricted to virtues, but includes the responsibility of citizens to advocate for each other.[28]

5. Heterotopic citizenship as political participation and advocacy

If Christianity sees its contribution as one among many, and the church (regardless of denomination) perceives itself as part of civil society, then it can contribute towards a view of citizenship that goes beyond the language of rights and duties, and allows for transformative participation. To accomplish that, we need to move from an analysis of citizenship and otherness to the Christian theological teachings that foster social responsibility and accountability for the wellbeing of all.

The tension between rights and duties shows that citizenship is not only a legal status, but reflects a normative ideal. Creating normative ideals requires participation in decision-making processes. Here, also religious identity plays a role, since this participation is informed by the values and traditions of particular communities. The language of rights and duties serves this to a great extent, but it does not explain what motivates people to seek the greater good, to ac-

[28] There is a large body of literature dealing with citizen virtues, as exemplified by William Galston's typology of four virtues: 1) General virtues: courage, law-abidingness, loyalty; 2) Social virtues: independence, open-mindedness; 3) Economic virtues: work ethic, capacity to delay self-gratification, adaptability to economic and technological change; 4) Political virtues: capacity to discern and respect the rights of others, willingness to demand only what they can pay for, ability to evaluate the performance of those in office, willingness to engage in public discourse. William Galston, *Liberal purposes: Gods, Virtues, and Duties in the Liberal State* (Cambridge: Cambridge University Press, 1991), 221-224.

tively participate in social service and to advocate on behalf of others. This is where Lutheran theology can contribute to the ongoing debate on citizenship.

By focusing not solely on the rights and duties of citizens vis-à-vis the state, but addressing the principles that guide individuals and communities to be responsible, there is an epistemological shift. For instance, in comparing duty-based versus engaged citizenship, recent studies concluded that engaged citizens are more participatory, global, and committed to social justice than their duty-based counterparts.[29] Engagement and participation in the social and democratic processes stem from the perception individuals and communities have of their role in the world. Such perception is influenced by religious beliefs.

Lutheran theology might have less to offer if the language of citizenship is reduced to rights and duties. Luther's views are shaped by a medieval mentality that did not contemplate civil liberties and rights, and it would be anachronistic to expect his theology to address changes engendered much later (such as through the French Revolution, the independence of former colonies, and the plea of native populations, African Americans, and women for their civil rights). Although the language of personal gain is employed, Luther's notion of justice benefitting oneself comes only in light of its effect on the neighbor, when advocating for the wellbeing of others:

> In what concerns you and yours, you govern yourself by the Gospel and suffer injustice for yourself as a true Christian; in what concerns others and belongs to them, you govern yourself according to love and suffer no injustice for your neighbor's sake; this the Gospel does not forbid, but rather commands in another place.[30]

The political vocation of a Christian is to pursue neighborly love fashioned by relationships of justice. Christians are devout and righteous before the world not because they want to be rewarded with eternal life. They do, how-

[29] Mark K. McBeth, Donna Lybecker. Kacee A. Garner, "The story of good citizenship: framing public policy in the context of duty-based versus engaged citizenship," in *Politics & Policy* (Feb 2010, Vol. 38, Issue 1), 1-23.

[30] Luther, "Secular Authority," 375.

ever, fulfill their vocation and carry on with their responsibilities. Christians are not to escape this world nor defer responsibility to others. To the contrary, Christians are called to serve the world, the earthly kingdom, in whichever capacity is needed. That calling, vocation (or Beruf) takes shape in different offices, ranging from the tasks of educator, public servant, or parent. Our vocation locates us in our social relationships in family, work, church, country, and as global citizens, allowing us to specify the neighbor to whom Jesus is actually referring today.

> As a [person] can serve God in the state of matrimony, in husbandry, or at a trade, for the benefit of his fellow [human beings], and must serve [God] if necessity demand; just so he can also serve God in the State and should serve [God] there, if the necessities of his neighbor demand it; for the State is God's servant and workman to punish the evil and protect the good.[31]

For Luther, citizenship refers not only to the individual, but also how individuals live in community. Citizens are the inhabitants of the polis, the city. If we are to translate this to our own context, citizenship cannot be reduced to the ballot a citizen casts every so often (which still can defer the responsibility of decision-making to others) or to be elected for public office, but to which extent one is a participant in the decision-making processes. For instance, to measure the political participation of Lutherans simply by asking how many officials elected to office are Lutherans is an oversimplification of Luther's public theology. Although election to public office is one dimension of citizenship, it is not all. A deeper understanding of political participation must name the strategies and levels of involvement Lutherans have encountered to further the rights of others, assure the wellbeing of those who are marginalized, or address the needs of neighbors.

In this sense, Lutherans are expected to exercise their citizenship without seeking personal gain or fame, but out of concern for the wellbeing of others. This move away from single-issue politics onto a broader agenda that contemplates particularly the displaced and less powerful in society has been

[31] Luther, "Secular Authority," 378.

articulated under the rubric of heterotopic citizenship.[32] Citizenship includes advocacy on behalf of social groups, communal causes, or collective efforts for the promotion of the common good. This requires a prophetic voice in denouncing the effects of greed and the nefarious consequences of material accumulation.[33] When advocacy is not seen as citizenship it is reduced to charity. The role of the Christian citizen is to advocate on behalf of others:

> Since, however, a true Christian lives and labors on earth not for himself but for his neighbor, therefore the whole spirit of his life impels him to do even that which he need not do, but which is profitable and necessary for his neighbor. Because the sword is a very great benefit and necessary to the whole world, to preserve peace, to punish sin and to prevent evil, he submits most willingly to the rule of the sword, pays tax, honors those in authority, serves, helps, and does all he can to further the government…Although he needs none of these things for himself and it is not necessary for him to do them, yet he considers what is for the good and profit of others...[34]

The right of the citizen to be a citizen – not in terms of privileges but in terms of participation in the earthly realm and living out Christian responsibility – is enabled through the different spheres that bear God's promises. In the political sphere (politia), God promises to govern with justice and calls leaders to serve in that capacity. In the economic sphere (oeconomia), God promises to care for the needs of all God's creatures and creates different instances, from household to marketplace, to assure wellbeing. In the eccle-

[32] A recent publication addressing the role of citizenship and its relationship to otherness is Wyller, Trygve (ed.) *Heterotopic Citizen: New Research on religious Work for the Disadvantaged* (Göttingen: Vandenhoeck & Ruprecht, 2009).

[33] Several statements have been issued addressing economic justice. See, for instance, the *Public Statement on "Daily Bread" instead of Greed: an LWF Call for Economic and Climate Justice,* adopted at the Lutheran World Federation eleventh Assembly in Stuttgart, 2010 (https://www.lutheranworld.org/sites/default/files/LWF-Eleventh-Assembly-Report-EN.pdf); a *Public Statement on Illegitimate Debt* was adopted at the tenth assembly in Winnipeg, 2003 (http://lwf-assembly2003.org/lwf-assembly/htdocs/ PDFs/ LWF_Assembly_Resolutions-EN.pdf); and the Evangelical Lutheran Church in America's Social Statement *Sufficient, Sustainable Livelihood for All*, adopted at the sixth Churchwide Assembly of the ELCA in 1999 (http://www.elca.org/Faith/Faith-and-Society/Social-Statements/Economic-Life).

[34] Luther, "Secular Authority," 373.

sial sphere (ecclesia), God promises to communicate God's Word to our hearts and minds and calls believers to life in community to witness and learn about their faith.

Christians are called to advocate on behalf of others and, in doing so, live out the love of the neighbor, as instilled by Christ, while also promoting changes in society at large.[35] As Luther points out, citizenship involves a component of responsibility for and accountability to the neighbor who requires a response. When Luther unfolds the consequences of neighborly love, he establishes that this love is more than a virtue one possesses (as moral excellence or goodness) or an obligation (as fulfillment of the law). It is a way of life, an ability to interact, engage, and genuinely care. It is a responsibility in the sense that we respond to God's call, voiced though the needs of our neighbor.

> For, as we said, love of neighbor seeks not its own, considers not how great or how small, but how profitable and how needful for neighbor or community the works are (1 Cor. 13:5).[36]

It is easier to join efforts to promote self-interests than it is to advocate for others. It is easier to be self-involved than it is to be attentive to the needs of the neighbor. And yet, that is the challenge of the Christian life. It takes intentionality to move beyond citizenship solely as individual rights and duties and willingly engage in sustained debates on how we organize ourselves as society, how we employ natural resources, how we care for the environment, what entails fair wages, or how we educate the younger generations. The desire for justice needs to be instilled. It is not a given reality. A Lutheran contribution to citizenship is to reclaim the role of service and calling, informing us about the needs of the neighbor and compelling us to think about our role in the world in light of the gospel.

To care for the neighbor is to assure dignity and life in abundance, act for justice and peace, and enable that another may flourish as a full human being created in the image of God. It implies a genuine concern for the neighbor's needs and the willingness to promote the free and equal participation of all in

[35] An interesting example of the involvement of the church in citizenship formation can be found in Brazil. See Rudolf Von Sinner, "Towards a theology of citizenship as public theology in Brazil," *Religion & Theology* (Vol. 16, 2009), 181-206.

[36] Luther, Secular Authority, p. 381.

the body politic. The neighbor is not a mere receiver of one's favor or charity. The neighbor is the other with whom I engage as an equal, the one who brings me closer to Christ, and the one for whom I am Christ.

Lutherans know that holiness is achieved not through good deeds, but through Christ, whom we follow. We are saved not because we serve, but we serve because we are saved. This model of social participation based on neighborly love fosters citizenship not only as individual rights and responsibilities, but as active participation in civil society. Christians will seek the wellbeing of their neighbor not because it is the law, but because such good works are committed in freedom, out of love. This includes an active role in political affairs, in works of advocacy, and genuine concern for the wellbeing of others. Citizenship is not reduced to individual rights or obligation, but it is a Christian service. By serving the other, the neighbor, we are also serving Christ.

THE PRIESTHOOD OF ALL BELIEVERS: MARTIN LUTHER AND THE CHURCH OF ADAM

Vítor Westhelle

"Be still, my heart, the great trees are prayers"
Tagore

1. Introduction

Days are among us, and they have been around with a decisive penchant for almost a century in which church-talk has been held captive again, yet not specifically to the church in Rome. This most recent installment of the "Babylonian captivity," is double-sided, entrapping all conversation about church either to its inner institutional formation or to its assimilation into the politico-cultural order of the day.

Most denominations – Roman Catholicism with its robust magisterium, Eastern Orthodox with their elaborate liturgy, Pentecostalism with its charismatic spontaneity, financial and organizational strength, and mainline Protestants with its congregationalism and ecumenical endeavors – articulate their teachings about the church and its ministry either out of their own resources, their own "public," or else draw from the public arena in which they find themselves immersed and adjusted. With few protests, church-talk has been a territorial dispute shifting from fighting over borders to signing truce treatises.

The challenge to the church calls for liberation from this double captivity: either being obsessed by its own home economics and keeping its house in order and its books solvent, or adjusting itself to the whims of the regime of the day. The two options may appear alternatively but occasionally they assail the church simultaneously. While "home economics" is necessary for the church, the political order also needs to be a critical companion. But if the church loses its identity to either or both of these, the church displays its captivity either as idolatry or as demonry. Idolatry results from being obsessively preoccupied with its own house, whereas not having a public voice is a manifestation of the symptoms of demonic possession, being rendered mute, incapable of having an authentic public voice. The litmus test for discerning if the church's own integrity is being maintained and its calling fulfilled is through a distinct practice that ensures its authenticity and freedom.

2. Priesthood of All Believers: The Reformatory Signature

In his "Open Letter to the Christian Nobility" of 1520 Luther writes this passage, revealing "the priesthood of all believers" as the signature of a major Reformation teaching of the Reformation:

> If a little group of pious Christian laymen were taken captive and set down in a wilderness, and had among them no priest consecrated by a bishop, and if there in the wilderness they were to agree in choosing one of themselves, married or unmarried, and were to charge him with the office of baptizing, saying mass, absolving and preaching, such a man would be as truly a priest as though all bishops and popes had consecrated him.[1]

The implications of this for ecclesiology are immense and recognized; the political impact has not been so obvious. Even though as it had been known for almost a century, since the Italian humanist Lorenzo Valla revealed the fraud of the "Donation of Constantine" (of which Luther was not only aware but helped to disseminate), the Roman Church still amassed enormous political and economic power. An attack on the chain of power in the church was nothing short of a revolutionary political gesture, which was at the origin of modern democracy. To attack the most organized and hierarchical estate in medieval Europe had a trickle-down effect with extraordinary consequences for the political realm, but also for the household and emerging financial capitalism.

Luther was more radical than what today is conveyed by the idea of "reforming" the church. First, he was dealing with the institution whose power could not be rivaled by any other institution. Second, because the universalized the institution, its truth was made contingent upon a subjective experience without a necessary causal relationship to the institution. "Church" meant for Luther something like what could be called "religion," arguably a universal phenomenon, but also designating the singularity of an event whose truthfulness precedes any demonstration. This is the succeeding character of church as event, its singularity and non-reproducibility, while as an

[1] *Luther's Works* [hereafter, LW] (St. Louis: Concordia and Minneapolis: Fortress), vol. 44: 128.

institution, as ecclesia it endures, has some permanence, and is always relative and relational.

In his Lectures on Genesis he explains the establishment of the Sabbath day as "intended for the worship of God. … [in] which God speaks with us through His Word and we, in turn, speak with Him through prayer and faith." The human, says Luther, "was specially created for the knowledge and worship of God." "This is the real purpose of the seventh day: that the Word of God be preached and heard."[2]

In addition, God built for Adam, "as it were, a temple: … the tree of the knowledge of good and evil was Adam's church, altar and pulpit … somewhat like a chapel in which there were many trees of the same variety, namely, the trees of the knowledge of good and evil."[3] In Luther's view the "church was established first."[4] This is indeed a radically catholic view of the church, it includes all humans insofar as all are descendents of Adam "who would have gathered on the Sabbath day … where trees were planted in large number."[5]

The Reformer's interpretation that there were several trees of life and also of the knowledge of good and evil "does not appear at all preposterous," as he insists, it is indeed intriguing and very revealing. Hence, we also can postulate that this multiplicity portends, consciously or not in Luther's mind, the diversity of religions and their different forms of worship and the diversity of their organizations. This at least is consistent with Luther's and the Reformation's conception of the multi-center character of the church. This is quite a radical view of what "catholic" means: every tree of life offers sustenance and a vital space for different communities. Every tree of the knowledge of good and evil, which for Luther was also the tree of life, is a place of worship and discernment, and there are many of them: to each tree its creed; to each creed its prayer, its piety.

The tree or trees as the figure of the church that Luther dwells on for so many pages of his Lectures on Genesis is exceedingly rich in imagery. Nevertheless, we can only understand the role it plays in Luther's theology and the suggestive plays with the metaphor by looking at the way he places it in

[2] LW 1:80f.

[3] LW 1: 95.

[4] LW 1: 104; but see LW 1, 94f.

[5] LW 1: 105.

relation to two other institutions mandated by God, which flank the church. Here Luther is not talking about the church-community as event, but as ecclesia, church as institution that entails endurance and guards as its treasures the traces of the event that occasioned it. Being the first institution established by divine mandate, it stands in proximity to the household, which for Luther's medieval mind encompassed all that pertained to the *oeconomia*, the rule of the house, from biological reproduction to the production of the means for the sustenance of life (i.e., sex and labor). This sphere covered all domestic affairs as well as the economy in the modern sense of the word; only with the industrial revolution did economy move out of the domain of the household.

The other sphere is politics (*politia*) that included everything from the state administration to courts, guilds and associations (*societates*) which would roughly correspond to what we would call the state and civil society. The church, or to keep with Luther's symbolic metaphor, the tree in the garden, is what provides for respite. It is where people can gather between the space of the house, where nourishment is produced and provided (nehren), and the public space of the city, where the practice of governance is exercised for protection (wehren). Here relations with each other are kept in check, laws are legislated, framed, and enforced. To use another set of metaphors, the church's location is the space between the "house" and the "street."[6]

3. The Church between Economics and Politics

Luther was working with the popular tripartite division of estates in the Middle Ages, that finds its roots in classical antiquity, specifically in Plato and Aristotle. It is impossible to simply translate these social strata or estates to a modern society as ours. For example, the American and the French revolutions did away with the nobility's entitlement of being the guardian of civil affairs. The economy, since the emergence of industrial capitalism and the industrial revolution, is no longer lodged primarily in the space of the household.

Nevertheless, there is a fundamental core procedure that distinguishes each of these instituted mandates, an operational principle at the nucleus of each that still remains the same. These operational principles can be recognized as

[6] Roberto DaMatta, A casa e a Rua: espaço, cidadania, mulher e a morte no Brasil (Rio de Janeiro: Rocco, 1997).

discrete human faculties. In the case of the church, it is the audible and visible word of God that addresses humans in their vita passiva and elicits human response in form of doxological praise or lament. In the case of the household or the economy, it is human biological reproduction and labor, the production of the means for the sustenance of life and its reproduction. Finally, civil government is concerned with human intercommunication for the sake of building a reasonable, equitable and peaceful order in the earthly city, with positive laws to foster and regulate it.

The church is this reality that stands squarely in the in-between spaces where life is produced and reproduced, and the space of political life or of human communication, policy making and activities that form mores and legislation. Between these two spaces stands the church, as a tree in the garden between the house and the public space of streets and buildings where civil life is lived out, negotiated and administered. While we are active in the *oeconomia* and in the *politia*, we are totally passive as the church event takes place.

This "third space" is the space between spaces (Homi Bhabha). It distinguishes itself from the other two, not as a demarcated territory; it is not the result of the human active drives, creating an institution sui generis and non-representable.[7] The church borrows its institutional life from the economic realm, and its legitimacy as an institution from the political régime. It is a hybrid space, or rather hybrid territory. In one sense it is an ordinary space: a grounded space (*terra*). But, in another sense, it is also that which evokes what Rudolph Otto called the *tremendum et fascinans*. This territory is the one that also frightens (*terrere*). In the first sense of its hybrid character, territory as terra, the church borrows from its earthly institutional neighbors sustenance and legitimacy. In the words of Luther: "The home must produce, whereas the city must guard, protect and defend. Then follows the third, God's own home and city, that is the church, which must obtain people from the home and protection and defense from the city."[8] Yet often it loses itself in these neighboring fields, thus falling into idolatry or being possessed, unable to find its voice.

The one sphere, the space of the *oikos*, is represented by human interaction with nature, providing for the sustenance of life and reproduction of the species. The other space of the polis is represented by human interactions that

[7] Homi Bhabha, *The Location of Culture* (London: Routledge, 1994), 37-39.

[8] LW 41: 177f.

result in what is normative, legal, or governance that make it possible to live together. In distinguishing between these two spaces in Bondage of the Will, Luther insists that in and through these spaces God "does not work without us."[9] In politics and economy, even if God has the efficient and final agency it is the human who is the subject of the relation to its object. In case of the economy, it is the relationship to nature; in case of politics it is the relationship to the other as a subject with whom we interact. In the case of the economy and politics, the human achieves a representation of herself through which she constructs an identity. In one case the representation is a material object extracted from nature through labor or present in an offspring being generated biologically. In the other case the representation is done by one recognizing oneself in the encounter with the other.

In the "third space" of the church, God works through our preaching, consoling, admonishing, but there is something distinct. Strictly speaking, we cannot define the church as such. As long as we define it, however, we can only do it by pointing to external characteristics, vestiges of the event that founds it. Essentially, however, it is not left up to us. We can only refer to it as this elusive "third space" determined by God's enunciation of the Word and the promise to be present materially in the elements of the sacraments. What we "do" is not our action, but only our re-action. This is why properly speaking we can say that the church happens as God speaks; Luther called it *creatura evangelii*,[10] the creature not of our doing and making, but of God's good word, even as it comes through our mouth. Church happens![11]

Already in the Hebrew Scriptures the Tent of the Tabernacle provides such an image for the church – a "house" on the way. It was a tent; neither the intimate and stable space of the household, nor utterly exposed to the world outside, but the presence of the divine in dynamic transition. According to its earthly nature, the church is always relative, never absolute. It is always in this tension between the politics and homestead, being "in" and "out" at the same time. Whenever one says "church" a conjunction must follow to indicate where the church finds itself in this polarity that comprises its hybrid identity, constituted by its interface with politics and the economy.

[9] LW 33:243

[10] WA 2, 43, 6f.

[11] In the lecture on Galatians where Luther called the church creature of the gospel he refers to Paul's letter to the Corinthians (1 Cor 4:15) in which Paul claims to have generated the community through the gospel.

Thus, here on earth there are these three overlapping spheres with distinct functions. This is why the Reformer was so adamant in keeping the relative character of the church. Now we need to protect its relativity from falling into either idolatry and demonry, whereas in Luther's time, the church was attempting to subsume all under itself: "Now why should we have the blasphemous, bogus law or government of the pope over and above these three high divine governments … of God? It presumes to be everything, yet is nothing."[12]

In the book of Acts, Luke often refers to the Christian community in a paradoxical way – as those of the "Way" (*hodos*: road, way, street, path; cf. Acts 9:2; 19:23; 22:4; 24:22). But then he refers to the church in the "house (*oikos*) of …," suggesting a place of refuge and safety. With regard to a speech of Paul in Ephesus, he refers to the double, asymmetrical tasks of the church's public and domestic roles. "I did not shrink from doing anything helpful, proclaiming the message to you and teaching you in public [*demosía*] and from house to house [*kat' oíkous*]."[13] Refuge and displacement are complementary images that suggest simultaneously movement and exposure as well as a sense of security, of calm and ease. Exposure and also haven, solace and risk, ease and dis-ease, wanderlust and refuge are often the biblical notions attached to the church. As opposite as they are, they also complement each other, and together suggest an unstable sense of happening.

Already in 1522 this was how Luther characterized the earthly church: "The necessary signs of the church we have are baptism, the bread [Lord's Supper] and the all-powerful Gospel."[14] But it was Melanchthon in the 1530 Augsburg Confession (art. VII) who provided the classical wording: "The church is the assembly of saints in which the gospel is taught purely and the sacraments are administered rightly."[15] These external signs, also called symbols by Luther, point to the two secular realities adjacent to the church. The sacraments symbolize the church as a place of nourishment and sustenance, which are the "house" function of the church, while the proclaimed word points to its public character or "street" function where public an-

[12] LW 41: 177.

[13] Acts 20: 20.

[14] WA 7: 720, 34-36: Signum necessarium est, quod habemus, Baptisma scilicet, panem et omnium potissimum Evangelium: tria haec sunt Christianorum symbola, tesserae et caracteres.

[15] Calvin followed this literally. *Institutes*, Book Four, I, 10.

nouncements are made. But when either *oeconomia* or *politia* ensnares the church into their domains, the church falls prey to idolatry and to demonry, respectively.

This is why late in *The Councils and the Church* of 1539 Luther lists seven external signs of the church, apparently parting company with the traditional marks of administrating the sacraments and proclaiming the word. Actually the first six marks only unfold the classic definition, entailing word and sacrament in a gathered assembly (1.Word, 2. Baptism, 3. Eucharist, 4. Absolution (return to baptism), 5. Ministry, 6. Worship). However, Luther adds another external sign: the cross, as the endurance of suffering in the midst of trial (Anfechtung). What this addition infers is that if the church seeks safety by aligning itself with the dominant politics, or guarantees its sustenance by amassing economic resources, it cannot proclaim the word that disturbs the political order and legality, nor administer the sacrament that nourishes and renews the life of faith. The cross is the mark of the earthly church, its ordeal faced in faithfulness to the gospel that brought it into being.

4. Adjacency: Exposure and Shelter

The reality of the "third space" is best explained by the Greek word *chōra*. *Chōra* designates a liminal space, a boundary space which is a space between spaces. An example of such space is Golgotha. It is located outside of the walls of the city of Jerusalem; hence it is not in Jerusalem as such. But neither is it in another village or in the country side; it is in the adjacency of Jerusalem. The word "adjacency" comes from the Latin (*ad-iacere*) and means "lying by," lying by what is considered home, as well as by the political world of the other.

This notion of adjacency that designates the limit of the familiar and the exposure to the outer spaces, infused with danger and promises, is a way to approach the reality of the church. The church finds its existence in this limit between what is ours (our language, culture, and values) and that which is foreign to us, the strange world out there of danger and promises. As such it is the space of belonging and of transit and displacement. Adjacency is the threshold and gateway through which we are sent out to become guests of others as well as the opening through which we host those who are strangers and unlike us.

In sermon XLV of the "Homilies on the Acts"[16] Chrysostom, the great preacher of the 5th century raises his voice against his fellow Christians who have accommodated themselves to what had become the rich Constantinian church with plenty of "money and revenues." Institutions for the care of the poor and strangers were created as the church tried to address its diaconal task. *Xenodoxeion*, as they were called, were places for the care of the foreigner, the homeless, the sick and the poor. It seems strange that this great preacher would attack what apparently was a good effort of stewardship. With his thundering golden mouth, Chrysostom launches an attack on them for they were being used by the now well-off Christians to avoid the face of the poor themselves. They were protecting themselves from being exposed directly to the reality nearby now that the church was wealthy enough to shield itself from the unpleasant reality of the other. The incisiveness of Chrysostom's argument reveals someone who was ashamed of his fellow Christians for he knew that the church should be adjacent to the pain and the wounds of the world, instead of protecting itself from it.

The church as adjacency happens by allowing the other, the poor, and the stranger to emerge, to have a voice, to have a face. Luther's words convey the same sentiment as the church of his day looked for glory and power by gazing at the heavenly splendor of doctrine and of power. He said: "The world is full of God. In every alley, at your door you find Christ; stare not at heavens."[17]

However, adjacency is not only about exposure. Paradoxically it is also about sheltering, refuge and protection. In situations of minority communities when losing their self-identity is threatened, the sheltering function of the church in its sanctuary character needs to be lifted up. In dominant or hegemonic communities, exposure needs to be preached and practiced, as Chrysostom did. But the end result is quite different if the church either offers shelter or practices exposure.

Exposure without sheltering leads to despair. It is the "despair of weakness" that Kierkegaard talks about, which is the loss of the defused self, described by demonry, or demonic possession in which we are lost in the polis, incapable of being ourselves or having a voice of our own. This is the sin of

[16] *The Nicene and Post-Nicene Fathers*. Vol. 11, Philip Schaff, ed. (Peabody, MA: Hendrickson, 1995), 272-277.

[17] Also ist die welt vol von Gott. In allen gassen, für deiner thur findest du Christum. Gaff nicht ynn himel. WA 20: 514, 27f.

politics when the church is assimilated and acculturated, muting the word that calls for another world. On the other hand, refuge without vulnerability and exposure is idolatrous segregation. It is idolatrous because it is navel gazing as Luther defined idolatry in his famous expression incurvatus in se ipso (bent onto oneself). This is the sin of the economy, or of the household into which the church is tempted to insulate itself, caring only for its own institutional self-preservation. These two ailments are indicative of the church's double captivity.

5. Blessed Difference

What in Luther's mind grants the freedom of the Christian and its simultaneous dutifulness in the three spheres, which he sees as necessary and sufficient? In referring to these spheres, which he also refers to as hierarchies, orders, estates, Luther writes: "These three hierarchies ordained by God, and we need no more, indeed we have enough and more than enough … in these three."[18] In and through them we are sanctified. The household or *oeconomia* must provide for nourishment, sustenance and procreation. Civil life, secular government or *politia* must protect and enforce equity. The church must be the time and space of Shabbat for the word of God to be proclaimed and dispensed.

Church "happens" in the conjunctive, simultaneous reality of shelter and exposure. It finds itself called upon by the establishment of the Shabbat, rather than an existence defined by either the chores of home-keeping or the political demands. It exists by the unilateral Word of God, but as an institutional reality it speaks with its own particularity in dialectic with these other spheres. It also does not subsist apart from the adjacency of politics and economy, but it is a word that calls for another world and a balm for the weary soul of all of us who find ourselves so often homeless. All this pertains to the church in its earthly and secular calling. The church event, however, is something else as well. It points to another reality that is not controlled by the coordinates of time and space, yet it manifests itself in these coordinates, leaving traces and vestiges that the ecclesia is called to administer and celebrate. The church universal, the, *ecclesia catholica*, emanates from a singular event.

Christians are not excused from participating in any of the divinely instituted orders, as Luther states in the Confession of 1528: "But the wholly or-

[18] LW 41: 177.

ders and true religious institutions established by God are these three: the office of priest, the estate of marriage, the civil government. All … are engaged in works which are all together holy in God's sight."[19] However, Luther insists on another distinction for discriminating among the orders.[20] The earthly and spiritual regimes are not symmetrical alternatives. "For to be holy [*heilig*] and to be saved [blessed/*selig*] are two entirely different things. We are saved [*selig*] through Christ alone; but we become holy both through this faith and through these divine foundations and orders."[21]

All that makes us holy is accomplished through these three spheres. Luther maintained that even the Turks (i.e. Muslims) have much holiness about them and constitute ecclesiae.[22] What is meant by the difference between being holy and blessed are not stages in an axiological scale. Their difference does not entail comparison even if they affect each other. Their relation is more akin to the difference between falling in love and getting married, between being healthy and feeling great. They belong to different orders of discourse irreducible to each other but coexist with each other like the finite and the infinite.

The priesthood of all saints is to practice this holiness with particular reference to the ecclesial sphere. This attribution of holiness to every member of the church focuses on the church, but applies in equal measure to the *oeconomia* and *politia*. This holiness is an attribute of every person; each is entitled to decide, delegate, dispute and legislate in matters political. Every man and woman is equally entitled to participate and make appropriate decisions for nourishing and sustaining the household and the economy. The criteria of reasonableness and equity supply the underlying principle, which is democratic to its core.

While this is good and salutary, it is not the same as blessedness. We receive that by the event of Christ alone in our midst, the presence among us, adjacent to us in its infinitude, neither dogmatically nor confessionally controlled. A suggestive hint is offered by Luther in introducing the seventh holy possession of the church: cross and suffering. This is the only mark of the church that is not only a sanctifying mark, as were the others in yielding

[19] LW 37: 365.

[20] Vult Deus esse discrimina ordinum (WA 44,440,25).

[21] LW 37: 365.

[22] LW 37: 145.

earthly holiness. It is the sole mark by which "the Holy Spirit not only sanctifies his people, but also blesses them."[23] This is the cross we carry for being between the house and the street, risking exposure by speaking publicly and offering sanctuary as an expression of holy love. As Luther says, citing Rom 5:1-5, we are bound to face trouble, trial, and suffering, but that "produces hope."

[23] LW 41: 164.

SUBVERSIVE PRACTICES OF BEING CHURCH: SEEING, REMEMBERING, CONNECTING[1]

Karen L. Bloomquist

1. Subversive today?

"Subversive" is not how most of those associated with churches today would view themselves. In most countries of the North, and in many of the South, churches are viewed as upholders of the social order and its values and assumptions.

For example, about half of U.S. Americans when recently surveyed, think of theirs as being a "Christian" nation, and indeed such symbols are embedded in the political culture in countless ways. But this was not emphasized until the 1930s, when key business leaders "inspired a public relations offensive that cast capitalism as the handmaiden of Christianity." They also recruited key clergy to join their cause. For example, "the Rev. James W. Fifield – known as 'the 13th Apostle of Big Business' and 'Saint Paul of the Prosperous' – dismissed New Testament warnings about the corrupting nature of wealth, and... paired Christianity and capitalism against the New Deal's 'pagan statism'."[2]

Although this usually is more subtle today, there still is the expectation that churches and church leaders will support rather than critique the established order, with its assumptions, values and practices. That contributed to the upsurge in U.S. church growth in the 1950s; some today yearn to return to that time when churches were "growing and successful." Corporate business practices and ways of operating increasingly rule today. Pastors of congregations and leaders of church-related organizations who do not go along with

[1] This is developed much more fully in my book, *Seeing-Remembering-Connecting: Subversive Practices of Being Church* (Wipf and Stock, 2016).

[2] Kevin M. Kruse, "A Christian Nation? Since When?" *The New York Times,* March 15, 2015. A history professor at Princeton, Kruse is author of "*One Nation Under God: How Corporate America Invented Christian America*" (New York: Basic Books, 2015).

this continuing expectation for "success" and its associated values and practices are dismissed, silenced, or at least threatened with funding cutbacks. Of course, this is nothing new for many churches around the world, where being identified as a Christian has been long been considered subversive, leading to ostracism, persecution, and even death.

An increasing number of people today are disillusioned with, disaffiliate from, or refuse to join such established expressions of church, and the economic, political and cultural forces to which they have become captive. They wonder, why churches are not more forthrightly speaking out and acting to transform today's realities of domination – of the injustices, illusions, and empire – that fly in the face of the faith Christians confess. How then might churches become places where "subversions" of reality can be nurtured and alternative public visions held forth and pursued, for the sake of the world?

Walter Brueggemann refers to Scripture as a "sub-version" – a rendering of reality that lives under the dominant version,[3] a dominant imagination that screens out all other neighbors, who can be screened out if the God of all Neighborliness is fashioned instead as a God who celebrates individual achievement.

The typical practices of church are not usually considered as being "subversive." Yet when pursued more deeply in societies where neoliberal assumptions, practices, and expected outcomes prevail, the common ordinary practices intrinsic in being church are bound to lead in directions that go against the grain, challenge, and thus are seen as subversive of the status quo. We may not set out to "be subversive" but living out the heart of the faith we confess is likely to lead there. When it does, we are tempted to draw back, adapt so as to become more acceptable, so as not to upset the vested interest of the powers that rule. But in submitting to such fears, are we not denying the faith we claim to confess?

2. Domination in Luther's time and today

> In the sixteenth century, the crisis was over the gospel that frees people from the fear and bondage of sin, which became embedded in systems needing to be challenged. Today, people also are in fear and

[3] Walter Brueggemann, *The Word Militant: Preaching a Decentering Word* (Minneapolis: Fortress, 2010), 152.

> bondage – over the sin of greed, as embedded in the economic system. They fear what the future will hold, unless dramatic changes are made for the sake of global economic and environmental justice.... Systemic greed becomes like the domination or bondage of sin that is expressed through the theology of Paul (e.g., Romans 6) and Luther.[4]

New awareness of this state of bondage has continued to grow and become more obvious, but usually in ways that churches have not dealt with on explicitly theological grounds. People today are feeling acutely betrayed by the promises they have bought into, often with blind faith that now is increasingly feeling betrayed, e.g., by large corporate interests determined to keep the market as "free" as possible. Matters of basic meaning, hope and values were at stake at the time of the Reformation, as well as today. But there have been significant shifts in where that salvific hope is lodged.

In Luther's time, the Papacy had become the most powerful institution ruling over people's lives, with closely intertwined religious, social, cultural, and political aspects. Under this system, no one could do enough so as to be certain of his/her salvation. Luther came to view this institutional power of domination as a theological matter which threatened salvation itself.[5] His theological critique of this domination, which he raised out a pastoral concern for people's salvation, became the means through which Luther began to break through the whole Roman system of domination.

Luther seemed aware of the need to deal with both the objective and subjective realities of what was holding people in bondage. Rather than only mounting a frontal attack on the institution holding people captive then, he attacked the actual practices that played into and supported the reigning system of domination. And he did so on deeply theological grounds. Luther boldly declared that through the preaching of faith, centered especially in the doctrine of justification, practices such "indulgences, purgatory, vows, Masses, and similar abominations come tumbling down, taking with them the ruin of the entire papacy....solely by the Spirit."[6]

[4] Lutheran World Federation, "*Daily Bread Instead of Greed*," public statement of the 2010 Assembly, www.lwf-assembly.org/assembly-documents/

[5] Scott Hendrix, *Luther and the Papacy* (Minneapolis: Fortress, 1981), xii.

[6] Martin Luther, "Lectures on Galatians – 1535" in *Luther's Works,* ed. Jaroslav Pelikan and Walter A. Hansen (St. Louis: Concordia, 1963), vol. 26: 221, 223.

In other words, the subjective or personal dimension of God's justification/salvation has objective, external consequences. If justification remains confined to a personal dimension apart from the societal implications, or in distinction from the critical relational dimensions of communio that flow from it, then injustices will continue to have free reign, distorting our most basic relationship, to God, ourselves, and one another. This is not to imply that the world can be governed by the gospel. But what is unleashed is a power that cannot remain quiet or passive in the face of unjust systems – because of how they themselves distort theological anthropology and hold people in captivity both spiritually and materially. In this sense, justification and justice are intimately connected.[7] Exposing what is operating today is not simply a matter of denouncing and extricating ourselves from it. This must not lapse into an otherworldly escapism, and with it, an increasing privatization of the faith disengaged from the reigning material realities.

Yet we – especially those who benefit from "the way things are" – are too enmeshed in the complexities of this web for a straightforward denunciation of this idolatry to be authentic or persuasive. We are "in and of" that which we are called to critique. Typically people feel passive in the face of such, unable to exercise much moral agency that resists or transforms such captivity – especially when this agency is viewed individualistically. The indwelling Christ empowers such agency, but this is realized and practiced in community with others – i.e., as "church."

3. Toward a subversive *ecclesia crucis*

What is proposed is that church – or *ecclesia* – be re-envisioned as intentionally nurturing, over the long term, resistance practices, that are resonant with the Bible, and familiar in the history and practices of the church. This occurs within a horizon that continually draw us beyond what is, (i.e., that is eschatological) while at the same time being relevant to people and challenges today. Such practices are simultaneously transparent to those who have

[7] I recall how the Reformed churches (WARC) refrained from sign onto the Joint Declaration on the Doctrine of Justification until the connections between justification and justice were made more explicit. Although Lutherans had pursued that earlier, especially in relation to Latin American realities of injustice, this was not further pursued in theological work underlying the official Lutheran/Catholic dialogues on justification.

been formed by the church as well as inviting to those with no interest or involvement in the church (and whose numbers today are growing).

These are ongoing practices of what it means to be ecclesia in our day, a word intentionally used here in distinction from *Kirche* or "church," which has acquired so much institutional baggage and allegiance to the status quo for its survival, so that its possibilities for being subversive are limited. What is implied instead is the need for new forms of church, such as those in emerging church and similar movements, which draw deeply from distinctive practices of church yet are expressed in ways that connect with those who may be estranged from these traditional church practices.

Guillermo Hansen provocatively suggests how the "Lutheran theological code" might become transformative of the challenges we face in today's world. This code includes how the cross (dis)locates the sacred into the realm of the profane – into the world. The cross is a subversive code that challenges all cultural and religious notions of what is considering transcendent or successful in life.[8] It is where our current ways of knowing are questioned and destabilized, making room for what is truly new and different. It is a verdict that something is fundamentally wrong with how the world is structured.[9] The cross interrogates and destabilizes what is generally known, thus opening up space for what is truly new and different. The cross appears as the center of a new gospel, as a sociopolitical event. Furthermore, the God who transcends ("falls") into our world, justifies the victims of imperial power,[10] radically redrawing the boundaries of God's domain to include those considered outcasts. "God's twofold rule is for the sake of a public theology, to bring forth worlds in which people can live, through radical democracy as a living alternative through the networks spawned by empire."[11]

The church living by a theology of the cross is taken more fully and deeply into the world. This key emphasis in Luther's theology needs to be pursued further, for the sake of forming an *ecclesia* that becomes transformative, by

[8] Guillermo Hansen, "Resistance, Adaptation or Challenge: The Versatility of the Lutheran Code" in *Transformative Theological Perspective,* ed. Karen L Bloomquist , vol. 6 in the Theology in the Life of the Church series (Geneva: Lutheran World Federation/ Minneapolis: Lutheran University Press, 2009), 30.

[9] Hansen, 31.

[10] Hansen, 32.

[11] Hansen, 35.

first being subversive of the injustice, empire, and domination of many kinds that hold the world captive today.

The vantage point of the cross, along with a collective sense of the structural sin in which we are complicit, is a critique that should be undergone, rather than adopted and employed, thereby exposing vulnerability and fallibility. Thus, we must engage in practices to "see in truthful ways," so that the knowing might become compelling, so that we might "glimpse the presence of God and the holiness of the church in unlikely places."[12] In "privileging" sites of vulnerability, God and we ourselves can be seen more truly.

An epistemology of the cross becomes especially crucial when illusions fall apart, when they no longer hold. We begin to see what really is going on, understand our implications in it, and accept our accountability to act accordingly. The cross is the fulcrum for knowing – the hinge point of true reality and the gift to see it.[13] To know truly is to know from the margins…of life, sanity, dignity, power. Friends of the cross are those who "live in the world as it is, without illusions."[14] "The church of the cross becomes a visible alternative to the ways of the world in and through its immersion in it."[15]

4. An *ecclesia* that sees, remembers and connects

I suggest that the verbs "seeing, remembering, and connecting" are key practices through which *ecclesia crucis* for the sake of the world emerges. People regularly see, remember, and connect; there is nothing esoteric or "churchy" about these verbs. These are practices basic to what it means to be human, accessible to those who do not identify with the institutional church. But these practices also have theological underpinnings that can be formative over the long haul, forming inclusive communities that can resist ideological captivity, and open transcendent space for the redeeming, liberating, transforming power of God – in ways that cut across boundaries. In doing so, they

[12] Jason A. Mahn, "What are Churches *For?* Toward an Ecclesiology of the Cross after Christendom," *Dialog* 51:1 (Spring 2012), 18-19.

[13] Mary Solberg, *Compelling Knowledge: A Feminist Proposal for an Epistemology of the Cross* (Albany: State University of New York, 1997), 90.

[14] Solberg, 83.

[15] Mahn, 21.

are bound to be felt to be subversive by those whose interests are in keeping things as they are.

Most pivotally this occurs through two practices which for Lutherans have been central to what it means to be the church: practices of proclaiming the Word and celebrating the Sacraments. The Word provokes and unsettles, it is a foretaste of the subversive reality that God is bringing into our midst. In the Eucharist, "the Kingdom irrupts into time and 'confuses' the spiritual and the temporal. .....calls the church to be what eschatologically it is....living out a vision of what really is real....the reign of God disrupting dominating reigns of injustice."[16]

As the preacher stands up to preach among exiles, the primary task is to narrate and nurture a counter-identity, enact or incarnate a radical power of hope in a time of despair, to announce a deeper freedom from the pathologies, coercions, and seductions that govern our society, to impart the resolve, courage, energy and freedom of a counter-identity.[17]

We gather for Eucharist to remember and to tell the tale of why we gather. The anamnesis is where liturgical theology and political theology meet and enter into dialogue.[18] They meet against the background of world history and the ambiguity of human actions. In that context Eucharist is about narrative, memory and solidarity. It is a form of resistance. It offers a tectonic shift of paradigm; that provides a counter-narrative, an alternative version of history that prioritizes the poor and insignificant and takes them as its reference point....Eucharist is...a living memory of a living presence, a "dangerously liberating memory" that provides us with new perspectives....a "subversive memory" that denounces our own complicity in the injustice that holds our world "hostage."[19]

Another key practice is cited by Jason Mahn: "The holiness of the church is made visible – obscurely and compellingly – in its very repentance for

[16] William T. Cavanaugh, *Torture and Eucharist: Theology, Politics, and the Body of Christ* (Oxford: Blackwell, 2008), 206.

[17] Brueggemann, p. 144.

[18] Cf. Bruce T. Morrill, SJ., *Anamnesis as Dangerous Memory: Political and Liturgical Theology in Dialogue,* (Collegeville, University Press, 2000), passim.

[19] An excerpt from a paper by Sr. Margaret Scott, "Eucharist and Social Justice," for a course taught I taught in 2010 at Lutheran Theological Seminary in Philadelphia, "Bearing Public Witness in a World of Injustice."

sin."[20] The gathered worshipping community, through the opening liturgy of confession and forgiveness, "comes to see itself truly." This is a kind of re-locating, turning outside-in, and a re-envisioning. It is a sight check, both internally and externally. We "become aligned with God's knowing," seeing ourselves as *simul iustus et peccator*. Because of how deeply we are implicated in and complicit in the social nature of sin, we need one another to know truthfully. This beginning of the liturgy corresponds with the final sending, when again we are turned out to remember the poor, in other words, to be where a cross theology calls us to be.

In biblical prophetic confrontations, it is the issue of truth that is at stake.[21] Powerful interests are skillful in managing symbols and controlling information, in creating virtual realities apart from lived reality. (Jer 6: 14, 8:11, Eze. 13:10). They deliberately misrepresent what is occurring, and give false assurances or generate unfounded fears.

Truth telling emerges as we remember (a) who/whose we are in relation to God, (b) what has come before us, and (c) the realities of our neighbors globally as well as locally. Empowered through the Holy Spirit, this has the potential to transform what is occurring in light of God's in-breaking new reality. Subversive remembering is a theologically empowered social practice of expressing "when/who/what" has been forgotten or overlooked. It exposes our illusions, false gods and the domination (empire) and injustices they perpetuate, and impels truth-telling and organized action (resistance) for the sake of God's world.

The challenge is to be able to discern (to see) the places and times in which broken and damaging crises are "receiving a facelift from the high priests of the new global gospel"[22] that is based on neoliberal assumptions and practices. In short, we begin to actually see more deeply with new vision rather than captive to illusions that block our vision of what really is happening in our lives and world. This becomes possible as we remember a God who became radically incarnate and vulnerable in this world. This God frees and empowers us to engage with these realities today. We remember what has been forgotten in our past and we remember those who are forgotten around us and throughout the world today. We connect in ways that heighten the

[20] Mahn, 21, 22.

[21] Walter Brueggemann, 169.

[22] Vitor Westhelle, *The Scandalous God* (Minneapolis: Fortress, 2006), 59.

contradictions between the ideologies and the actual realities. We connect with those who are other from us, and we connect in collaborative actions with others for the sake of the world – connections made possible through the power of the Spirit, and that do make a difference in the world.

4.1 Seeing as subversive practice

Jesus heals those unable to see. He peels away what clouds vision. For example, in John 9,[23] an ordinary believer (poor, illiterate, excluded, not treated as fully human) becomes capable of judging and confounding what the learned "know;" he sees in ways they don't see or comprehend. The purpose of this story is to clear away the darkness of falsehood and illuminate us with the truth of God. Jesus identified with the popular culture even as he confronts the religious culture of his day. "Jesus told me to wash….and so I did, and then I could see." The man's transformation becomes a matter of judgment and crisis in their midst, their entire value system and basis for exercising control over the people is overturned or subverted.

To "see God" in Jesus' act of healing is to recognize the truth of the Word becoming flesh a dynamic truth that is challenging to assumptions, systems and structures of privilege. Jesus says, "I have come….so that the blind will see and those who see [or assume to] will become blind" (9:39). The blind one sees clearly what God is about, while those who believe they can see are those who are truly blind. Jesus subverts what can be seen; he shifts the interpretive framework or horizon.

Contrary to popular views, seeing is not what individuals do on their own. We see as part of and in relation to community. The assumptions, values and worldviews familiar in our context affect us and what we focus on, or ignore, in our seeing. Seeing has to do with what comes from outside of ourselves, what others provoke us to see what we would not on our own, as well as provoking us to see ourselves differently. We need those who are most other from us to see rightly.

Today, much of seeing is socially conditioned to become a distraction or diversion from what really matters – seeing that entertains rather than leading toward greater understanding, and allows the domination to continue. Thus, attention must be given to seeing that exposes "the big picture" of what is actually occurring – through wider social-economic-political analyses – in-

[23] Much of what follows is based on Gail O'Day's interpretation of John in *The New Interpreters Bible, vol. 9,* Leander E. Keck, ed., (Abingdon, 1996) , 575ff.

stead of what is assumed in customary, popularized or officially authorized interpretations that portend to be true or authoritative. This calls for seeing through the pretenses, honestly and authentically, seeing beneath the surface of what is assumed to be the case.

Helping people to see in such ways, especially by delving deeper into what is going on, is a crucial practice of what it means to be church that is at the same time both pastoral and prophetic. It is a practice that takes seriously what people are experiencing in their everyday lives but sets it within a wider framework of what needs to change.

4.2 Remembering as subversive practice

Writing from within a German context of the 1970s, amid the ongoing challenge of coming to grips with the horrors of the Holocaust, Johann Baptist Metz posits that remembering can be seen as the fundamental form of expressing the Christian faith.[24] The memory of Jesus Christ is a dangerous and liberating memory that continues to question what is reigning over the present and opens up our envisioning and moving into the future. Seen in this way, Christian faith becomes a dangerous, subversive memory, and is at the core of a critical consciousness, a dangerous and liberating memory over and against the controls and mechanisms of dominant consciousness and abstract ideals of freedom.[25]

Much of this became apparent in the testimonies of the many thousands who gathered in March 2015 in Selma, Alabama for the 50th anniversary of the "Bloody Sunday," an event that became such a turning point in the U.S. Civil Rights struggle. "I just had to be here," commented many. Seeing and remembering what occurred fifty years ago, and connecting with others across races, nationalities and ages are what made this pivotal event come alive again. In this sense, it became transcendent and transformative – not just as a past event but as one that empowers continuing action today for the sake of the future.

One of the key matters in Luther's protest against the reigning domination of his day, was how especially Holy Communion (the Eucharist) was being used by the Roman church for power and control over the people, and thus distorted as God's gift of grace and freedom. This was developed especially in his treatise, "The Babylonian Captivity of the Church." Although here he

[24] Johann Baptist Metz, *Faith in History and Society* (New York: Seabury, 1980), 90ff.

[25] Metz., 113.

did not explicitly address how this biblical allusion might apply to the dominating power of his day, it is significant that at that time, control over people's lives could be so powerfully exercised through sacraments.

In the 16th century, Holy Communion had become a locus where the church could exercise its control over the sacred. Yet there is a profound difference between a hierarchical institution appropriating the right to dispense the medicine of the Eucharist versus the belief that the Eucharist itself has the sacramental power to create a healthy social body. Mystery is the domain beyond human control but here sacramentality is no longer contrasted to instrumentality for the mystery itself has been instrumentalized."[26]

Instead, the Eucharist is located within the biblical context of remembering God's liberation and in-breaking justice. In this Meal, resurrection hope is practiced "by connecting the remembrance of God's saving works…with our lives." It is a praxis based on empathy, embodiment and reciprocity between God and human beings, of remembering painful memories and dealing with them in courageous and life-giving ways. At the center of this is the memory of Jesus death and resurrection, bringing to mind his ministry to the poor and sick, and God's saving work through the body of Christ in the world today.[27]

4.3 Connecting as subversive practice

What made Christ persuasive was his radical non-fearful love for others. He restores connections that have been cut off,[28] but without repeating the logic of possession by trying to control those he encounters. He empowers without dominating others. In turn, this makes him a threat to powers dependent on dominating people through fear. He systematically undercut the fear on which power depends by undoing the divisions that keep people suspicious and vulnerable.[29] By restoring connections, Christ radically subverts the order of fear. Subsequently, his crucifixion and resurrection inspire a new fearlessness in his followers, the early *ecclesia*.

[26] Regina M. Schwartz, *Sacramental Poetics at the Dawn of Secularism: When God Left the World* (Stanford University Press, 2008), 20.

[27] Andrea Bieler and Luise Schottroff, *The Eucharist: Bodies, Bread and Resurrection* (Minneapolis: Fortress, 2007), 163.

[28] Adam Kotsko, *The Politics of Redemption* (London: T&T Clark), 2010, 200.

[29] Kotsko, 201.

This connecting today is itself ecclesia, formed in ways that can challenge or at least go beyond the confines of the institutional church, or even the dominant societal assumptions. These practices come together in overlapping ways, leading us into alternative worldviews, interpretations, praxis, ways of being in this world, empowering us to engage with the realities out there. Indeed, when the forces of neoliberalism and empire have so thoroughly taken over the realities within which we live today, faith communities – of various kinds – may be among the last places around where a subversion of reality can be articulated and an alternative vision held forth. Through the power of the indwelling and connecting Spirit, active in and through our interconnections with those who are most different or "other" from "us," through their realities and perspectives, we are transformed. This transformative power becomes "subversive" of what we take for granted as inevitable certainties. This transforms what we are able to see, remember and connect.

Alan Lewis puts it together this way: Catholicity denotes the connectedness and universality of not only the church but also of the human race. The church catholic embodies "a subversion of and a proleptic deliverance from the pathological individualism, polarization, and sectionalism of our terminal society." Such connectedness and reciprocity contradicts prevailing cultural assumptions. Practicing such connectedness sets the church in conflict with our culture. We are unconditionally connected: God in Christ chooses our neighbors for us and connects them to us as brothers and sisters, in a way that transcends time and space and every identity boundary. The truth is revealed that we model the image of God's triune community as connected, related persons in community. Original sin is the self-deluding desire to deny this connectedness.[30]

Connecting is more than making visible and "feeling sorry" for those subjected to injustices. It goes beyond praying for those affected. Such expressions reflect appropriate compassionate solidarity, but they stop short of raising critical questions about the deeper more systemic causes, a questioning that cannot remain passive or quiet but because it is empowered from out of the promise at the heart of the faith, impels us toward action to change such in light of the in-breaking reign of God.

A common assumption is that such changes are led by individual heroic figures, such as Luther, and indeed individuals can make a difference. But it

[30] Alan Lewis, *Between Cross and Resurrection: a Theology of Holy Saturday* (Eerdmans, 2001), 348ff.

is through long-term collaborative, many-faceted efforts that such transformation comes about.[31] This is why the gathered community becomes so crucial, rather than relying only on solitary individuals. Not just any community, but one that is undergirded through solidarity over the long haul, and empowered through what the church has traditionally referred to as the "communion of saints."

5. So where does this occur?

In light of all the above, there need to be important shifts in where and how theological work inspired by the Reformation is pursued today. The main basis of accountability or conversation partner may no longer be primarily the university and/or seminary, and cast primarily in theoretical abstractions, but theological articulations in the midst of praxis in actual ministry situations, which themselves become a font for rich and creative theologizing – incarnate, dynamic, living theology that engages and readily resonates with people's deep yearnings. This is not theology that plays to a religious consumer market but that is deeply transformative of what holds people and creation captive.

This, in a much different era, was also the concern of Luther and other 16th century reformers. This is the ongoing challenge that preachers in the Reformation tradition need to grapple with every Sunday. Such theology is more akin to what is broadly referred to as "practical theology," that is, holistic, embodied theologies that are engaged with the real stuff going on in our lives and world today and must avoid the temptation to escape into theoretical discussions.

We need to shift decisively where our faith, desire and hope are lodged – from looking "upward" (to God on high identified with those who have succeeded) to looking "downward" – to those marginalized, left out, impoverished and despairing – around us and around the world. God becomes known through a theology of the cross. This calls for resisting desire as it has been constructed and being open to the emergence of alternative desires – desires that have to do with "my" good in relation to the good of others. This erupts

[31] A case in point today is that of the decades of struggle for gay, lesbian, transgendered. and bisexual persons to become more fully accepted in church and society. Where we are today in many (but not all) societies and churches is a far cry from only a few years ago.

not from above, but from below, from the underside, as we look outward and pursue solidarity with those who truly are left out, around us and around the world. There "God labors in solidarity with the people and resisting desire spreads from there."[32]

This also implies a more *communio*[33] understanding of *ecclesia*: that is deeply relational instead of focused on individuals; instead of aspiring to be self-sufficient churches, our interrelatedness; instead of our strength or know-how, our vulnerability, openness to listen and learn from others, and even be transformed by those different from ourselves rather than speaking and showing others, shifting from the arrogance of empire and theologies of success to attitudes of humility that are shaped by a theology of the cross.

Thus, *ecclesia* becomes a "place" of seeing, remembering and connecting, of putting together what is fragmentary, pointing to what is true, enabling us to see and act, including in organized actions with others. It implies the long-term challenge of nurturing and organizing communities of resistance against the dominant scripts and the injustices they entail – as was much of the New Testament church in its struggle in the midst of empire – communities today that are intentionally collaborative across boundaries of religion, geography and self-interest.

And so, "the church is the custodian of the events it attests to and chronicler of the events that keep happening"[34] It is "the space of grace, as the conduit of the Spirit that is at the *eschata*, the place of risk, of condemnation, but so also the place of healing and salvation,"[35] a place where liberation and transformation are not just announced but empowered through Word and Sacrament, and actually practiced.

[32] Joerg Rieger, *No Rising Tide* (Minneapolis: Fortress, 2009), 116.

[33] These multi-lateral relationships and understandings have been developed, for example, through various statements and publications of the Lutheran World Federation: A Communion of Churches.

[34] Vitor Westhelle, *The Church Event* (Minneapolis: Fortress, 2010) 74.

[35] *Ibid.*, 119.

AUTHORS

Charles AMJAD-ALI, originally from Pakistan, is the Martin Luther King, Jr. Professor of Justice and Christian Community (Emeritus) and Director of the Islamic Studies Program (Emeritus) at Luther Seminary, St. Paul, MN/USA, and the Desmond Tutu Prof. of Ecumenical Theology and Social Transformation in Africa, University of Western Cape, Cape Town/South Africa.

Karen BLOOMQUIST, has served as the Dean at Pacific Lutheran Theological Seminary in Berkeley (California) and directed the theological unit of the Lutheran World Federation and of church and society studies in the ELCA. She has been a parish pastor and on the faculty of three other ELCA seminaries.

Paul CHUNG, originally from South Korea, has been on the faculties at Luther Seminary and Wartburg Theological Seminary, and has taught at the Graduate Theological Union and Pacific Lutheran Theological Seminary. He is a pastor at Holy Shepherd Lutheran Church, California, an Asian-American ministry.

Wanda DEIFELT, originally from Brazil, is Professor of Religion at Luther College, Decorah, Iowa.

Peter Goodwin HELTZEL is Associate Professor of Theology, New York Theological Seminary.

Brigitte KAHL is Professor of New Testament at Union Theological Seminary in New York City; a native of East Germany, she formerly taught Ecumenical Bible Studies at Humboldt University in Berlin.

Karl KOOP is Professor of History and Theology and Director of the Graduate School of Theology and Ministry, Canadian Mennonite University, Winnipeg/Canada.

Cynthia MOE-LOBEDA is Professor of Theological and Social Ethics, Pacific Lutheran Theological Seminary of California Lutheran University.

Craig L. NESSAN serves as Academic Dean and Professor of Contextual Theology and Ethics at Wartburg Theological Seminary, Dubuque, Iowa.

Samuel TORVEND is University Chair in Lutheran Studies, Department of Religion, Pacific Lutheran University at Tacoma, Washington.

Hans G. ULRICH is Professor emeritus for Systematic Theology and Theological Ethics, Theological Faculty, University Erlangen-Nuremberg.

Vitor WESTHELLE, originally from Brazil, is Professor of Systematic Theology at the Lutheran School of Theology at Chicago and Chair for Luther Research at Faculdades EST, São Leopoldo, Brazil.

WEBSITE OF THE PROJECT

www.reformation-radical.com/www.radicalizing-reformation.com

Here you find information about the follow-up of the project, the abstracts of the chapters, and the translations of these, if available.